# Shorting Fraud

Jesper Sørensen

# Shorting Fraud

## How to Uncover and Profit from Fraudulent Companies

palgrave
macmillan

Jesper Sørensen
Copenhagen, Denmark

ISBN 978-3-031-81836-3 ISBN 978-3-031-81834-9 (eBook)
https://doi.org/10.1007/978-3-031-81834-9



This Palgrave Macmillan imprint is published by the registered company Springer Nature Switzerland AG
The registered company address is: Gewerbestrasse 11, 6330 Cham, Switzerland

*This book is dedicated to Janus, for giving me the opportunity to professionally explore investment & securities fraud; to Ketil, for his professional support when people tried to block my exploration.*
*It is also dedicated to Indre, Raimondas, Avani, and Tuukka for two joyful years working with investment & securities fraud; and to my sister and mother, for their moral support.*
*In loving memory of my father…*

# Preface

*"'Oh my, the Emperor's new clothes are wonderful! What a beautiful train on his robe! How well it fits!' No one wanted to admit they didn't see anything, because that would mean they were unwise and weren't fit for their jobs.*

*Suddenly, a child shouted, 'but he doesn't have anything on'! 'Good heavens, listen to the voice of innocence,' said the father uncomfortably. But in the crowd one person whispered to another, what the child had said. The whispers grew in strength and at the end the whole crowd shouted 'But he doesn't have anything on"*—**A translated excerpt from The Emperor's New Clothes from Fairy Tales, told for children, by Hans Christian Andersen (1837)**

While I have been working in a world of advanced crime, delusion, and deception for a decade, I noticed this old fairy tale captures the basic nature of the corporate fraud and its dynamics.

Almost two centuries after the fairy tale was written, we may use other semantics and concepts, but the core is the same.

One could say it is up to the responsible authorities and regulators to prevent corporate fraud, undermining the capital markets. That is true, but budgets are restricted, and resources limited. These limitations are known and actively abused by the corporate fraudsters.

Getting investors to focus on corporate fraud as part of an investment strategy, may help improve market integrity. The investors being rewarded for this contribution to society by the capital markets themselves. This is capitalism efficiently correcting its own fallacies.

Reading this book, investors may become the little obnoxious child from the fairy tale that sees things in a clear perspective that the rest of the world misses.

Copenhagen, Denmark Jesper Sørensen

# Disclaimer

# Contents

# About the Author

With a decade immersed in the world of cybercrime, corporate fraud, investment & securities fraud, Jesper Sørensen brings hands-on experience combating financial crimes across the spectrum.

From safeguarding Fortune 500 companies to collaboration with local and international law enforcement agencies on detecting, solving, and preventing multiple types of white-collar crime.

Jespers' expertise spans across asset management, investment banking, and corporate finance. Analyzing, detecting, and preventing advanced criminal activities at all levels—from small businesses to multinational corporations, financial institutions, and multiple types of investment funds.

# List of Figures

# List of Tables

# Part I

## Shorting Fraud—Profiting While Maintaining Market Integrity

# 1

# Introduction

## 1.1 Snow Avalanches and Proactive Investing in Fraudulent Companies

A way to understand the Fraud Investment Strategy at its core, is comparing it to snow avalanche science, and avalanche triggering, treated in Fraser (1978). Both Avalanche triggering and proactive fraud shorting address two highly poised complex systems, with underlying hidden interconnected relations, and a risk of a collapse of the system.

On the surface you might see nothing alarming; neither in the avalanche terrain, nor in the fraudulent company, at first sight.

However, deeper studies will reveal unstable conditions, and subsequent proactive actions will destabilize, and collapse the unsustainable system. This is true both for the situation of the fraudulent corporation and the imminent snow avalanche.

Understanding, finding, and analyzing these fraudulent hidden unstable conditions in publicly listed companies, subsequently investing with a short perspective, before then revealing the truth is the core of a proactive fraud investment strategy. To get an understanding, Table 1.1 outlines the similarities between avalanche triggering and a proactive fraud shorting investment strategy.

The corporate fraud, how it builds up and eventually collapses is treated in more detail from a complexity theory perspective in Sect. 7.2.


J. Sørensen, *Shorting Fraud*, https://doi.org/10.1007/978-3-031-81834-9_1

**Table 1.1** Similarities between avalanche triggering & fraud investment strategy

| Aspect | Avalanche triggering | Proactive fraud investment strategy |
|---|---|---|
| Objective | **Prevent larger avalanches**: Proactive risk reduction to protect lives and property | **Expose market distortion:** A profitable investment strategy that expose fraud, protects investors and market integrity in the long run |
| Assessment | **Snowpack analysis:** Evaluate terrain, snow conditions, etc. to find unstable areas | **Company analysis:** Assess financials, management, company, industry trends for red flags, to find fraudulent companies |
| Methods | **Explosives:** Calculated disruption to control the avalanche | **Public report:** Exposing Corporate fraud via research reports and media to disrupt valuation |
| Result | **Major Catastrophe avoided:** By not letting the conditions for major devastating avalanches build up over time | **Stock price decline or collapse:** That reflects the true intrinsic value of the fraudulent company, if any at all, helping markets discover the real share price |

## 1.2 Overview of a Proactive Fraud Investment Strategy

The main purpose of a proactive fraud investment strategy is searching for and finding fraudulent publicly listed companies, to target in a profitable activist short campaign. An overview of the proactive approach is illustrated in Fig. 1.1.

To successfully conduct a Fraud Short Investment Strategy, first, the investor must assess what opportunities and risks this investment strategy includes, as described in Chapters 2 and 3. Can a fraud investment capital gain be captured in a feasible way, at a cost and risk, which is acceptable to the individual investor?

Next the investor must understand the basic elements of corporate fraud described in Chapters 4–7.

Then the investor must screen the publicly listed companies to find the ones with the signs of corporate fraud as described in Chapters 8–16.

Subsequently the investor must conduct detailed deep-dive investigations of the potential target companies as described in Chapters 17–28.

Finally, the investor must execute a successful proactive fraud short investment campaign described in Chapters 29–33.

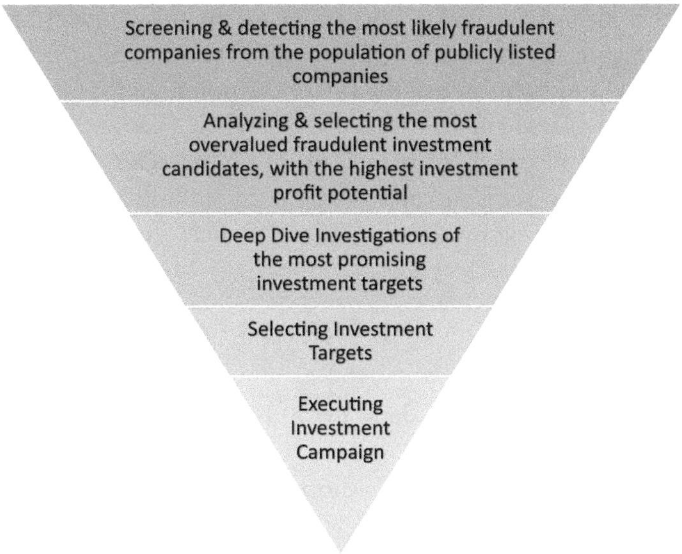


**Fig. 1.1** Overview of the proactive corporate fraud Investment Strategy

Searching for these fraudulent investment targets, finding them, and investing in them is a complex process. A process which should only be conducted after understanding the risks of every step of the process in detail. While the average retail investor may potentially learn from the book, the primary target is professional and institutional investors. Investors who can afford to set up this type of framework and dedicate the resources and time needed to conduct the investment strategy.

## 1.3 The Corporate Fraud Premium and The Corporate Fraud Exposure Capital Gains

A fraud short investment strategy is inverse in nature to a traditional long investment strategy. The perception might be counterintuitive to investors normally investing in long positions. Therefore, two simple illustrative core definitions are introduced for a straightforward introduction to help understand the fraud short strategy.

**The Corporate Fraud Premium (*CFP*)** is the difference between the share's inflated market price due to the corporate fraud $\left(P_{fraud}\right)$ and the corporation's real intrinsic value share price $(P_{real})$.

$$CFP = P_{fraud} - P_{real} \tag{1.1}$$

The worse the corporate fraud is, and the more the share price is inflated due to corporate fraud, the higher the Corporate Fraud Premium is. The higher the Corporate Fraud Premium is, the better the potential for Corporate Fraud Exposure Capital Gains are.

**The Corporate Fraud Exposure Capital Gains (CFCG)** are the capital gains that the fraud short investor realizes by taking a short position in fraudulent shares, betting on share price to fall after the investor exposes the corporate fraud in a research report.

$$CFCG = P_{fraud} - P_{exposedsale} \quad (1.2)$$

where the $\left(P_{exposedsale}\right)$ is the share price that the investor sells at after the corporate fraud has been exposed.

Generally, in a successful fraud short campaign $\left(P_{exposedsale}\right)$ should converge downwards on $(P_{real})$. As we will see in later sections, in some corporate fraud cases $(P_{real})$ might even be zero, when the corporation is a total fabrication, or the fraud collapse is all-encompassing.

## 1.4 The Proactive Fraud Investment Strategy Process

Figure 1.2 depicts a sequential overview of the process, where the investor is detecting, assessing, investigating, and eventually executing the investment campaign.

The individual steps of the proactive fraud investment process seldom move in a one-way direction as illustrated. They might jump back and forth, be paused, and continued, as new information enters the process over time, while working with potential investment candidates, and multiple types of data.

Working hands-on with the fraud investment process will require these feedback loops. For example, a feedback loop from the investigation step, back to the fraud assessment step. The potential might change significantly as the investor learns more about the company - either in a positive or negative direction.

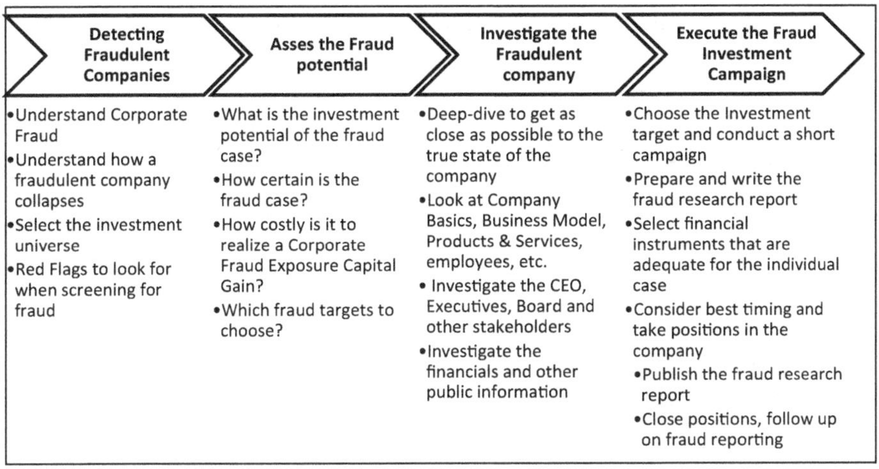


**Fig. 1.2** The end-to-end fraud investment process

## 1.5 The General Work With Methods, Models and Tools in Detecting Fraud

There are many methods, tools, and models publicly available to detect corporate fraud. These range from simple (but often potent) financial metrics and ratios at one end, to advanced Artificial Intelligence (AI) models at the other end. In addition to the publicly available models, financial institutions and financial software vendors have developed their own proprietary corporate fraud detection models and tools with varying success.

Some types of detection models and methods may complement each other, whereas other models have overlapping parts or are redundant in nature.

When the investor is carefully choosing models, methods and tools, the perspective of triangulation is important and discussed in Sect. 17.3. In Corporate Fraud cases, it is always encouraged to look at the same case from different angles with different methods, models, and tools, to understand the nature of the corporate fraud as best as possible. In sum, the collection of these methods, tools and models constitutes the Corporate Fraud Detection Frameworks, which the investor often will have to develop and tailor for the investor's specific situation.

These frameworks build on a variety of both quantitative and qualitative methods and models. Models utilizing quantitative data in the form of e.g., financial statements, public records on financial transactions or public records on import/exports, etc.

The frameworks also utilize models using qualitative data like text transcripts of earnings calls, management commentary in quarterly reports, news articles, or management's public statements in audio and video format. In addition to information from litigation- and court databases, patent, and other intellectual property databases, etc.

In addition to quantitative and qualitative models, a third category of models utilize network structures and the relationship between corporate entities, executives, corporate officers, and may expand relationships to a myriad of other structural entities.

### 1.5.1 Selection of Methods, Models, Tools and Constructing a Corporate Fraud Screening Framework

Depending on the resources and the scope of the investment universe that the investor has decided to embrace, the investor might want to build or buy tools to support their fraud detection framework. Some of the common building blocks, which should be considered when building the corporate fraud screening framework, are described in Chapters 8–16.

To get an overview of the various screening models and methods to detect corporate fraud, methods may be categorized in the three main categories of:

- Earnings Manipulation Metrics methods
- Traditional Statistical methods
- Advanced Machine Learning (ML) and AI methods

Much of the historic work and research have been done within financial statement fraud, but a growing body of research and work are being done outside financial statement fraud, in other areas like Natural Language Processing (NLP) of textual content, abnormal market activity analytics, corporate governance factors, etc.

As a practitioner one will experience that sometimes advanced AI/ML models will fail to find what a more rudimentary financial metric will catch.

Always have in the back of the mind that models that are more technically advanced may not necessarily perform better in a practical setting. Also bear in mind that models and methods may need to be adapted to the individual investor's situation and investment universe. Some models might have been constructed to fit a specific stock market or geographical setting. Things may then be "lost in translation" when the model is utilized on e.g., a different stock market, different time period, or different geographical setting without adaptation.

### 1.5.2 Finding Outliers, Anomalies and Suspicious Patterns

Common for all these models, methods and frameworks, no matter how advanced they are, is to find anomalies, outliers, or suspicious patterns that could indicate material corporate fraud.

However, finding anomalies, outliers and suspicious patterns indicating a potential material corporate fraud, is different from finding corporate fraud. They are only initial indicators of potential corporate fraud.

The investor cannot solely rely on these models alone. No matter how advanced these models and methods are, they will produce false positives in the form of companies that appear fraudulent at first glance but are not. Deep-dive investigations must follow screenings to sanity check and elaborate on the potential fraud case.

## 1.6 Deep-Dive Investigations and Due Diligence

After using models and methods to do the initial fraud screening, deep-dive investigations are necessary for two reasons.

The first reason is to sanity check what the models and methods found. Another reason is to collect more material to build the investment fraud case and have a solid body of evidence for the fraud research report. Evidence strong enough to support the case when the research report is published, and the fraud short strategy is executed.

Therefore, the investor needs to meticulously investigate the company in depth, before eventually deciding on executing the investment campaign.

## 1.7 Choosing Financial Instruments and Executing the Fraud Short Campaign

When the investor has chosen potential investment targets for a fraud short campaign and the fraud short report is ready, the investor must choose financial instruments for the investment campaign, before publication of the research report.

The best suited financial instruments for the individual investment case may vary based on the individual corporate fraud case, the jurisdiction and the investor's risk appetite.

When all the previous matters have been taken care of, the investor may execute the campaign and publicize the fraud short report, subsequently manage the risk, follow up, cut potential losses if the investment goes against the investor, or in the end realize the capital gains.

## Reference

Fraser, C. (1978). *Snow Avalanches*. Charles Scribner's Sons

# 2

# The Proactive Fraud Investment Strategy

## 2.1 Investment Strategies

Professional investors may utilize many different types of investment strategies when it comes to publicly listed companies. Table 2.1 shows an overview of some of them, along with the Proactive Fraud Investment Strategy.

## 2.2 Fraud Shorting

There are several motives for shorting stocks, many not related to fraud. An investor can base short selling on macroeconomic conditions, such as weakening economic conditions, leading to a decline in stock prices. The short selling motive could also be narrower in scope like industrial economics, where Creative Destruction as described in Schumpeter (1942) makes an entire industry, like DVD rentals obsolete, and short sellers target companies in the crumbling industry.

Short campaigns may also focus on an individual publicly listed company—e.g., suddenly lacking a demand for its products, a poor management wrecking the company, or the main focus of this book; the company may be involved in material fraudulent activity. Table 2.2 gives an overview of the different shorting strategies.


J. Sørensen, *Shorting Fraud*, https://doi.org/10.1007/978-3-031-81834-9_2

Table 2.1 Select equity investment strategies

| Investment strategy | Description of how to profit from the investment strategy |
|---|---|
| Long-short equity | Seeks to outperform the market by buying stocks that are expected to rise, and shorting stocks that are expected to fall |
| Value investing | Focuses on buying undervalued stocks, which are priced below their intrinsic value, and hold them long- term, until the market realizes their true value |
| Momentum investing | Identifies stocks that are trending, and trades them, hoping that the trend will continue, often based on technical analysis |
| High-frequency trading | Uses high-speed computers to trade in milli- or microseconds, to profit from small price discrepancies in prices |
| Event-driven investing | Takes advantage of specific events, such as mergers, acquisitions, spin-offs, or bankruptcies. |
| Fraud Shorting | Extensive research into potentially fraudulent companies. A short position is taken in companies thought to be fraudulent. Then the findings are exposed in a research report to the public. The short seller profits from a market integrity reward, correcting the manipulated share price down to its actual intrinsic value after the fraud exposure<br>Fraud Shorting is a subset of event-driven, activist investing, with the goal of realizing Corporate Fraud Exposure Capital Gains, related to the improvement of stock market integrity, with the publication of the short report (research report) |

## 2.3 The Impact of Activist Short Campaigns

Appel and Fos (2020) researched the impact of activist short campaigns with Cumulative Abnormal Returns (CAR), which measures the effect of an event on a company's share price over time. These are short campaigns with specific allegations against a company.

These specific allegations are related to accusations of e.g., fraud, insider trading, capital structure, industry, products, and business model. On average these activist short campaigns resulted in a share price drop of 8% within 20 days, and a 12.5% share price drop within 100 days. In addition to the share price drops, these campaigns may also lead to more negative media coverage, shareholder lawsuits and regulatory scrutiny affecting longer term impacts.

Broader specific research on short strategies specifically related to fraud shorting is currently sparse. However, an interesting observation by Bochman (2014), looking at 448 activist short campaigns, found that stock prices on fraud short campaigns fell 30% on an average. More interestingly, in valuation induced activist short campaigns, like the first three strategies in

**Table 2.2** Select short investment strategies

| Short strategy | Description | Examples | Factor |
|---|---|---|---|
| Boom-Bust Cycles | Speculative bubbles, periods of inflated asset prices, offer opportunities for short sellers | Overvalued assets during the dot-com bubble, Subprime Mortgages, and the Financial Crisis | Macroeconomics |
| Creative Destruction | Broken industries, those facing obsolescence or fundamental flaws, are susceptible to short selling. | Eastman Kodak during the decline of film photography. DVD Rental Industry. The rise of streaming services like Netflix disrupted the DVD rental industry, leading to the bankruptcy of Blockbuster and a decline of other DVD rental companies | Industrial Economics |
| Consumer Fads | Companies relying on fleeting consumer trends are vulnerable to short sellers | Hasbro's Cabbage Kids | Company Specific |
| Fraudulent Companies | Stocks of fraudulent entities often collapse upon exposure of their deception | Wirecard, Enron, Tyco, and Baldwin accounting frauds | Company Specific |

Table 2.2, the share price grew 3% on average. If these observations hold up in broader research, it makes fraud short campaigns more profitable than other types of company specific short campaigns, which have nothing to do with fraud.

The discovery of share price decline in fraud short campaigns is in line with the drops in share prices when fraudulent companies are exposed and they need to conduct financial restatements, as described in more detail in Sect. 3.2 .

Activist fraud short selling is predicting the risk and momentum of a collapsing corporation. A way to understand this is looking at complexity theory, working with the growth and collapse of complex systems like corporations already touched upon in Sect. 1.1. and described in further detail in Sect. 7.2

## 2.4 The Fraud Short Investor

Hunting for corporate fraud requires some skills and competencies. In addition, it also comes with some risks and costs. Detecting, shorting, and exposing white-collar crime may have a range of risks and potential personal costs for the investor.

### 2.4.1 Competencies and Personality traits of the Fraud Short Seller

The basic skills like financial analytics and investments may be taught and understood by a substantial portion of the population. Also, a sizable share of the population might be able to easily understand the concepts of fraud risks and red flags.

However, based on recruitment and training of financial employees this is not enough. While candidates may understand the theory and risks, they miss the obvious red flags, when it comes to actual live corporate fraud cases.

On top of the basic skills, there needs to be a layer of skepticism, curiosity, and broader understanding of how the world works, which financial industry employees often lack. Street smartness, situational awareness, and common sense are just as important as understanding the theoretical foundation of corporate fraud.

The investor needs to spot tiny cracks in the foundation of a corporate structure and see the bigger consequences and picture these tiny cracks eventually lead to. Finding the people with the right skill set to detect fraudulent activity is hard. Here are some things to look after. Few people master them all, but the more the investor has, the greater the chance of success.

**The personality traits and soft skills:**

- Skepticism—individuals who find the most fraud are contrarians; they are not yes-men or women
- Enjoy working with big complex real-world puzzles, constituting a myriad of different pieces
- Boundless curious and willing to learn strange types of subject matter and how the world works
- Be able to distinguish the right and wrong direction on a moral compass
- Does not cut corners or give up when things take much mental effort or time and are cryptic

- Be an outsider—be able to hold your ground when everybody else thinks you are wrong
- Pigheaded and willing to walk the plank for your idea
- Put the hard questions nobody else cares or dares to do and do not beat around the bush
- Not for sale, and immune to flatter
- See the worst in people, and never ignore it

**Hard skills:**

- Be able to analyze both quantitative data and qualitative data
- Fundamental understanding for the areas of finance, accounting, economics, stock markets and financial instruments, Law, and Law Enforcement
- Have business acumen and understand all types of business setups
- Understand complex patterns and systems
- Spot miniscule abnormalities in complex patterns—what is wrong with this picture?
- Basic understanding for human nature and behavior, including areas like psychology, sociology, criminology, ethics, and moral

### 2.4.2 Personal Risks and Costs

Anyone that works with crime, whether violent crime, organized crime, or financial crime faces risks from the criminals. While Law Enforcement Agents, Civil Servants and other similar roles enjoy some protection from the criminals, private persons like short sellers, share some of the same personal physical risks as investigative journalists. This includes physical threats that should always be taken into consideration.

On top of the risks of direct physical threats from the criminals, they may also attack legally. In the case the investor is wrong about the fraud case, the short seller might also face legal risk of damages and compensation, which might be an enormous cost that can financially ruin the investor, if not taken into consideration and proper safeguards are set up.

There are also some psychological risks and costs with short selling. This of course depends on the investor's setup and potential hedging strategy.

If the investor has a long position all she can lose is the money at stake, while the potential gain is in theory infinite. This puts the long investor in a psychological position where they know the worst-case outcome. However, in short strategies it is generally the opposite. In a traditional short position, the investor can maximum earn 100%, while the losses are in theory infinite. This poses a potential financial risk that might wipe out big parts of the investor's net worth in a brief time—the risk of ruin.

Therefore, short selling may be mentally taxing, especially during market rallies. The short seller faces pressure to close the position if prices rise, leading to potential losses. As seen in Sect. 29.1.3., a short seller might be right for years or decades before the fraud eventually is exposed. This could lead to a personal psychological frustration that the investor knows things are wrong with the company, but the world will not realize and accept that things are wrong with the company. An investor must have a special personality profile to be that kind of contrarian, just like the little kid in H.C. Andersen's fairy tale about the Emperor's new clothes.

## References

Appel, I., & Fos, V. (2020). *Short Campaigns by Hedge Funds* European Corporate Governance Institute (ECGI)—Finance Working Paper No. 609/2019. Retrieved September 14, 2024, from https://papers.ssrn.com/sol3/papers.cfm?abstract_id=3242516

Bochman, A. (2014). *Do Valuation Shorts Work?* Enterprising Investor—Practical Analysis for Investment Professionals. Retrieved September 14, 2024, from https://blogs.cfainstitute.org/investor/2014/09/29/do-valuation-shorts-work/

Schumpeter, J. (1942). *Capitalism, Socialism, and Democracy.* Harper & Brothers.

# 3

# Market Integrity Rewards and the Potential of Corporate Fraud Exposure Capital Gains

## 3.1 The Number of Listed Companies Ideal for a Fraud Investment Strategy

According to World Federation of Exchanges (WFE) in the period 2022–2024, the total global number of publicly listed companies registered on a stock exchange hovered between approx. 55,000 and 58,000, which can be seen in detail, broken down in regions, in ballpark numbers for Americas, Asia–Pacific (APAC) and Europe, Middle East, and Africa (EMEA) in Table 3.1.

However, these numbers do not include minor exchanges and venues that may also have companies of interest for some investors. For convenience, assume there are 60,000 listed companies in total, which is our investment universe.

During the initial assessment of fraudulent investment targets, a breakdown in regions is interesting. It tells where in the world listed companies and their market value is concentrated.

Imagine if 1‰ of listed companies are material fraudulent, there are only 60 potential companies to target in the investment strategy. If 1% are fraudulent, then there are 600 targets, and at 10%, 6000 target companies.

In the permille case, the proactive fraud investment strategy would be looking for platinum needles in a haystack. While in the 10% case, the investor would be looking for the gilded elephant in the room.

The basic nature of corporate fraudulent activity is to hide the true state of the company, hence there are uncertainties about the actual number of fraudulent companies. From working actively with fraudulent companies, it



J. Sørensen, *Shorting Fraud*, https://doi.org/10.1007/978-3-031-81834-9_3

**Table 3.1** Publicly listed companies in the world, based on data from WFE (2022) & WFE (2024)

| Region | ≈ Companies 2022/23 | % | Market Capitalization $ bn - 2023 | % |
|---|---|---|---|---|
| Americas | 12,000 | 20 | 5412 | 49 |
| Asia–Pacific | 33,000 | 55 | 3409 | 31 |
| EMEA | 15,000 | 25 | 2328 | 20 |
| Total | 60,000 | 100 | 11,159 | 100 |

is obvious what is disclosed to the public in statistics is only the tip of the iceberg. Official statistics are sparse, skewed and in some jurisdictions non-existent. Therefore, often proxies and extrapolations must be used, in lack of better data.

Looking at the numbers in the US, which is the biggest jurisdiction governed by one authority. According to SEC (2023), The Securities and Exchange Commission (SEC) had 784 enforcement actions in 2023. A part of these were not related to corporations but other parties like investment managers. Furthermore, if the enforcement falls under multiple areas only one is counted. Focusing on the enforcement actions related to fraud, in 2023, it is estimated the number of enforcement actions targeted between 100 and 300 individual companies—out of 5700 listed—or between 2 and 6% publicly listed companies facing enforcement.

Academic studies in the US by Dyck et al. (2023) estimate that accounting violations in the form of misrepresentation in financial reports take place in 41% of large public corporations every year. Even more serious, 10% of large public corporations allegedly commit securities fraud each year.Dyck et al. (2010)found that in the US, the probability of a large corporate engaging in misconduct in any given year to be about 14%. If we extrapolate the number to the total global listed companies, it means roughly 6000 to 8000 publicly listed companies (10–14%- of 58,200) each year commit securities fraud. For the average investor, these numbers might appear high. However, for a practitioner working with corporate fraud, discovering fraud cases daily, they are less surprising.

The 2022 Fraud Report by ACFE (2022) shows that the fraud problem is not only limited to big US companies. The report documents that fraud happened in 133 countries around the globe. This is in all types of industries and company sizes—private as well as public companies. Furthermore, the ACFE report states that on average 5% of companies' revenue is lost to fraud each year.

Doing some rough calculations—if we take 5% of the total World Gross Domestic Product (GDP) in 2022 stated by World Bank (2022), at around

$101 trillion, it means that about $5 trillion is lost to corporate fraud in 2022 on a global scale. The number is in line with other research by Gee and Button (2021) stating that 6.4% of annual global GDP is lost due to financial fraud, amounting to $5.38 trillion a year. These approx. $5 trillion encompasses all types of companies, legal entities and not limited to publicly listed companies.

In a proactive fraud short investment strategy, we are mainly interested in the subset of publicly listed companies. If one looks at the trailing twelve months revenue of the biggest 8,000 listed companies globally, on CompaniesMarketCap (2023, 30th Sep). These corporations' total revenue constituted a little more than $55 trillion. Five percent of $55 trillion is $2.75 trillion. If there is potential for close to $3 trillion on average, lost to fraud each year in the biggest 8000 publicly listed companies, it shows there is a great potential for discovering fraud in publicly listed companies. This supports a potential for a proactive fraud investment strategy.

The next question is, how much of the $3 trillion of corporate fraud may be converted into Corporate Fraud Exposure Capital Gains as was defined in Eq. 1–2. This of course depends on the total sum of Corporate Fraud Premiums as was defined in Eq. 1–1.

## 3.2 The Size of the Total Potential Corporate Fraud Premiums

While Sect. 3.1 revealed that there was a plentitude of corporate fraud going on in listed companies, for us to conduct a fraud shorting investment strategy, it must be possible to turn this potential Corporate Fraud Premium into capital gains, through investments. The question is if the corporate fraudulent activity is material enough to have an impact on the share prices, and how big the impact is. Is it even worth bothering with as a potential investment strategy?

Since the Fraud investment strategy is short in nature. We expect that when fraud is exposed in a publicly listed company, the company will lose market adjusted value—i.e., the share price will drop, after the corporate fraud exposure.

Therefore, to convert fraud losses into Corporate Fraud Exposure Capital Gains, we need to look at how much shareholder value is lost a year due to corporate fraud. Dyck et al. (2023) found that corporate fraud wipes out 1.6% of equity value on a yearly basis. This is equivalent to $830 billion in 2021 for the subgroup of US listed companies they researched.

If we once again look at the 8000 biggest global publicly listed companies, according to CompaniesMarketCap (2023, 7th December) their total market cap was approximately $93 trillion. This means about $1.5 trillion (1.6% of $93 tn) of equity value is destroyed due to fraud each year in the biggest 8,000 publicly listed companies on average. The $1.5 trillion once again cements that there is a potential to hunt for fraud in publicly listed companies.

Studies from GAO (2002) investigated Financial Statement Restatements of public companies. The research showed that the market adjusted company value dropped on average by 10% in the two-day trading windows around the publication of the restatement. Furthermore, the study found that the investigated companies lost $100 billion in market capitalization in the trading window. In the intermediate term, -60 days + 60 days trading window, the average was -18% market adjusted loss. The study included both accounting errors and fraud.

The short-term losses due to fraud restatements were also researched by Palmrose et al. (2004). They found in general, restatements resulted in a market adjusted loss of about -9% on average, including both error and fraud. However, focusing only on financial restatements related to fraud, the study found a market adjusted loss of an average -20% in the three-day trading window around the announcement. A similar -20% loss is also found by Dyck et al. (2010) in the two days around the fraud announcement.

Karpoff et al. (2008) found that a fraudulent company lost 38% of its market value on average after the fraud was made public. More interestingly, the study also found that for each dollar the company valuation was fraudulently inflated, it did not only lose that fraud inflated dollar after the fraud was revealed. However, when the fraud was exposed, it lost $4.08 for each dollar of fraud inflated overvaluation.

In addition to losing the fraud inflated dollar itself, $0.36 were lost because of likely legal penalties and $2.71 because of anticipated higher financing and contracting costs resulting in expected future lower cash flows, referred to as the reputational effect. Stakeholders engaging with the fraudulent company might stop working with the company, limit its engagement or enforce more strict controls on the fraudulent company, to avoid being defrauded themselves or related to a fraudulent entity.

This means on average for each dollar a company is fraudulently inflated, the fraud loss potential and hence fraud short potential is a factor four of the fraud inflated market value. This gives the fraud short investor a Factor 4 asymmetric advantage.

The potential for a fraud short investment strategy will vary with each case. Looking at cases like Enron or Wirecard, they lost 100% of the value going bankrupt. Looking at the VW fraud case, VW lost 30% of the market cap a week after the initial announcement according to La Monica (2015), but VW is still in operation and a major carmaker in 2025, a decade later.

Besides the obvious factor regarding how severe and material the fraud in the organization is, Carberry et al. (2018) found that several matters may determine the market reaction on corporate misconduct. One factor is media coverage and influence. Another factor is how pervasive and rooted the misconduct is in the organization—is it limited to a few persons or is it a fraud culture? Also, the restorative capacity of the company. How well can the company rectify the misconduct and take corrective actions?

Furthermore, it is not uncommon to see that fraudulent companies will counterattack, with aggressive rebuttals campaigns when the fraud is being exposed as described in Sect. 20.5.1. The fraudulent corporation might hire high profile Public Relations companies to counter facts, like when McCrum (2020, June 25) exposed the Wirecard fraud. In that case, even the German Financial Services Authority, (BaFin) used resources to support the fraudulent company and counterattack the journalist and sources, instead of investigating the fraudulent corporation.

All these factors are important when trying to profit from a fraud short investment strategy. Two similar corporate frauds that both eventually collapse to become worthless, will unlikely do it over the same timeframe, with the same momentum. The two similar cases might evolve completely differently over the short, medium, and long-time horizon from a share price and corporate valuation point of view. Section 29.1.3 looks at the extended timeline of the Wirecard fraud. As one of the biggest corporate frauds in history, it managed to roll the fraud forward for one and a half decade after the initial red flags of fraud were raised.

## 3.3 Detecting Companies With the Highest Potential Corporate Fraud Premiums

In the avalanche science metaphor from Sect. 1.1, the investor is interested in locating the places with the biggest potential for a hidden "avalanche" to be triggered, or in other words, a cataclysmic corporate collapse due to fraud. This could be factors like geography, industry, company size, company age, etc.

From a practical investment perspective, the investor must determine amongst the 60,000 publicly listed companies. Which companies have the highest available hidden Corporate Fraud Premium to be realized as capital gains by the investor? In the avalanche metaphor, where can the investor discover and trigger the biggest potential devastating avalanche?

## 3.4 Access to Realizing the Corporate Fraud Exposure Capital Gains

Knowledge of a Corporate Fraud Premium is not enough. In the avalanche metaphor, to trigger the avalanche, the investor needs to have access to the area, as well as access to the tools to trigger the avalanche. The most effective way to trigger an avalanche is explosives. However, it may also be triggered e.g., with ski cutting, snowmobile vibration, or the mythical (but highly unlikely method) of shouting.

- Institutional lock-in of Corporate Fraud Premium. The investor might find himself in a situation having spotted the biggest corporate fraud of the decade, with an enormous potential Corporate Fraud Premium. However, the circumstances of the local legislation, political system, or exchange, means that it is hard to realize the premium as Corporate Fraud Exposure Capital Gains. This is because the institutions that are made to protect the investors, instead protect the criminals, either willingly, due to corruption, or as useful idiots, fooled by the fraudsters. In avalanche terminology, a satellite imagery might show there is high avalanche hazard, but the investor is forbidden access to the area, to trigger it.
- Structural lock-in—the exchange or venue where the Corporate Fraud Premium is present might not allow or offer instruments to conduct the fraud short strategy. In avalanche terminology the investor has access to the area of the hidden avalanche but cannot use explosives.

## 3.5 Costs & Time Perspective to Monetize Corporate Fraud Exposure Capital Gains

In avalanche terms, the investor found the biggest potential avalanche in history. The problem is that it is on the most inaccessible part of Mount Everest. It takes a hundred-man and a three-year hazardous expedition to investigate and eventually trigger the avalanche. By that time, it might have collapsed on its own.

Similar in the fraud short strategy, there might be an analytical cost and time lock-in of the Corporate Fraud Exposure Capital Gains.

- The access to documents and evidence might be so cumbersome that the analytics will cost too much compared to the Corporate Fraud Exposure Capital Gains from the investment. In some jurisdictions the investor might have to physically sends staff to physically file and wait months for responses.
- Time is also a factor. Like avalanches collapse on their own, so do fraudulent companies. The risk of the company collapsing before the investor's investigations are done, means you were right, but missed the moment and potential Corporate Fraud Exposure Capital Gains, but not the costs of analyzing the case.

## 3.6 The Canadian Paradox—Geography, Culture, and Subculture

As a practitioner, having worked with financial criminals from more than 50 countries, on all continents except Antarctica, it has been observed that fraud and corruption is perceived highly differently in various geographical areas, cultures, and subcultures.

In some places, fraud and corruption are looked at as highly immoral and illegal, whereas in other parts of the world, they are seen as a natural way of life and how society works. It means culture impacts the underlying factors of Corporate Fraud Premiums.

The first intuitive thought that might come to mind is that the most corrupt countries in the world are where to find the highest Corporate Fraud Premiums. That can be a mental trap.

While it is true that these corrupt countries may have the highest number of fraudulent companies and high nominal value of corporate fraud, it is different from they necessarily have the publicly listed companies with the highest Corporate Fraud Premium on average. This is because fraud is expected and therefore may be factored into the stock prices.

Ng (2006) found that corruption leads to lower stock valuation. So, if fraud and corruption is expected amongst the publicly listed companies in a corrupt region, the market might already have factored in the risk of corporate fraud in the valuation of the publicly listed company. In other words, it is not that uncommon to find a corrupt or fraudulent company on a stock exchange in a region or country where corruption is common. This in return means that investors have factored in the general risk of fraud in the share price in a fraud-prone market.

In contrast, in low corruption and high trust countries with normally well-functioning stock markets, legal systems, transparent controls, auditing, etc. The investor is more inclined to accept what is being presented at face value. Hence, a higher undetected Corporate Fraud Premium might build up in publicly listed companies, in high trust countries.

Therefore, before engaging in trading at any venue, it is important to understand the perception of fraud and financial crime in general, since it may have an impact on profiting from fraud short investments.

A way to get an overview is analyzing the Corruption Perceptions Index (CPI) presented by Transparency International (2022) to get an idea where Corporate Fraud Premiums might be found or there is a high probability that corporate fraud is already factored into the share price and therefore less chance of finding high Corporate Fraud Premiums.

A main reason Corporate Fraud Premiums accumulate in high-trust countries could be what Davies (2021) refers to as the Canadian Paradox. A paradox, which also has been observed hands-on working with individual corporate fraud cases in the Scandinavian countries of Sweden, Denmark, Norway, and Finland. Along with Canada, these Scandinavian countries are according to research by e.g., Ortiz-Ospina and Roser (2016) the most trustful countries on the globe.

The Canadian Paradox is the conflict between the high level of trust and the surprisingly high frequency of fraud in the financial industry.

This indicates that corporate fraud is more profitable and easier to conduct in a society where the fraud is expected as an exception, and not the rule. With emphasis on expected, not actual underlying risk of corporate fraud.

In the low-trust countries it is more expected and harder to pull off corporate fraud, since the guards are up, and there might be a general expectancy of corporate fraud.

The Canadian paradox has been observed to have practical implications with regards to risk of fraud. Two of them which are touched upon in relation to corporate fraud risk. First and foremost, what we may refer to as a transplant risk. This happens when legal entities or natural persons move from operating in a low-trust cultural environment to operating in a high-trust cultural environment.

Most notable this may be seen in the Reverse Merger Wave of Chinese companies entering the US Stock Market in the 1990s, described in more detail in Sect. 18.10.2. Another recent possible ongoing case example described in Sect. 18.6 is Tingo. Over a few years, Tingo moved from Nigeria onto the US NASDAQ stock exchange, in an interesting way.

Nigeria figures in the low end of the Corruption Perceptions Index (CPI), and has been commonly known for its fraudulent activities, very innovative, sometimes on an industrial scale, with e.g., "fraud schools" training new fraudsterssee. e.g., Nwaubani (2019) for background history.

A history of fraud, starting with the criminal innovations of the Nigerian Prince Scam (419 scams). Later evolving into the biggest massive fraud schemes, the arrest by FBI and ten-year prison sentence for the CEO of the Invictus Group, Obinwanne Okeke as reported by DOJ (2021, February 16). Okeke, a Nigerian businessman, in 2016 hailed as Forbes Africa 30 under 30 entrepreneur, as reported by Dolan (2016).

The investor must be very careful, since not all natural persons and companies coming from Nigeria, or any other high-corruption country or region are fraudulent. However, the investor should not neglect the higher risk of fraud related to high-corruption countries either.

Working with corporate fraud, the investor must understand the cultural aspects and differences especially related to the corporate setting. This is research related to national cultural differences within the corporate environment. Some of these builds on the seminal work of Hofstede (1980) research of cultural differences, which is paramount to understand, working with corporate fraud in a global setting.

Differences in Earnings Management as well as other areas like budgeting, marketing and more general ethical differences between cultures have been found by researchers like Douglas and Wier (2005), Han et al. (2010), Lu et al. (1999), Scholtens and Dam (2007).

A more controversial risk is the risk associated with the natural person transplant; either CEOs or executive (see Sect. 20.7) or employees abused (touched upon in Sect. 18.8). If done incorrectly in an unbalanced manner, such profiling might be considered racial profiling, and in worst case outright racism. However, the investor should not shy away from the topic, since in some cultures fraud and corruption is more prevalent, as well as culturally acceptable than others. If not, there would not be a corruption index in the first place—all countries would be equally corrupt.

While fraud is committed by all races, genders, ages and sexualities, there is a risk of missing the obvious fraud, looking at fraud through stereotypical glasses and the stereotypical fraudster.

Like if the investor only looks for fraud with natural persons with a certain skin tone or sir-name, the investor will only find those as fraudsters, in a self-fulfilling prophecy. However, on the other side, the investor should not disregard the cultural background aspects of corporate fraud risk, whether we talk about national, regional, or corporate culture transplants.

A person moving from a cultural background with low trust to one with high trust might have experienced a high amount of fraud in the early part of her lifespan, and hence might know the basics on how to defraud effectively.

In addition, upbringing in the cultural setting will also mean that the natural person might have another moral compass. This fundamental moral compass would most likely not magically change on a 10-hour flight from a high-corrupt country to a low-corrupt country.

It has been observed that fraudsters abuse any popular and trending agenda, like e.g., diversity, racism, LGBTQ + , sexism or woke to their own advantage. This is done in two ways. The first way is to proactively craft a narrative being the poster child of the politically correct. This is seen in the Norwegian case treated in Sect. 8.5.

The second way is defensively abusing victimization and persecution as deflection, when there is a risk of exposure. Taking whatever popular and trending controversial subject, like Black Life Matters or the Pride issues, and slinging it in the face of the skeptics as a defense against exposure.

Both approaches might have the effect that skeptics might step back and ignore the underlying fraud risk problems, to avoid being ousted as being on the "wrong side of history." In both cases the fraudster hijacks a popular agenda for the benefit of the fraud and fraudster, and not for the benefit of the real cause.

## 3.7 High Corruption Societies and the Costs Related to the Fraud Short Investment Strategy

The investor might have detected a company with a high Corporate Fraud Premium. However, it is situated in a society where corruption is institutionalized. This means corruption is systemic, and embedded in institutions like the justice system, political system, media, other authorities and public institutions. So, despite the fraud, the corrupt system might protect the fraudulent company. Therefore, making it difficult and costly to realize the Corporate Fraud Exposure Capital Gains.

## 3.8 The Regulatory Landscape's Negative Perception of Short Selling & Fraud Shorting

According to WFE (2023) there are around 80 major stock exchanges globally, while Deloitte (2020) states there are more than 130 securities exchanges in total, spread across the globe.

The number of different venues in different countries poses another practical problem when conducting a Fraud Short investment strategy. The regulations of stock exchanges and venues may vary considerably depending on which jurisdiction they fall under.

Stock market rules and regulations differ between regions, countries and even between exchanges within the same country. Different exchanges have different rulebooks. It is out of the scope of this book to deal with the specific market rules and regulations on each stock exchange.

However, one should consider that some jurisdictions or venues might, temporarily or permanently, ban various financial instruments used in a Fraud Short investment strategy.

This sometimes, because of a faulty perception of short sellers and what they contribute with in a stock market. Short sellers are often associated with market decline and broader economic turndowns. Often falsely perceived as the cause of the underlying problem. Short sellers are the fever, not the underlying infection causing the disease. If short sellers are wrong, the short sellers' losses are potentially unlimited.

In several cases, short sellers are accused of manipulation or unethical wrongdoing, also referred to as short and distort. However, the higher scrutiny of FSAs into short sales compared to long positions and higher risk of litigation against short sellers, combined with the limited profits and unlimited loss potentials, make short selling a hard place to be in for the criminal. Are there criminal short sellers? Yes, but not as many as criminals that are long.

However, the view on short selling has had implications. For instance, short selling bans were imposed during the 2008 Financial Crisis in many countries according to Beber and Pagano (2013) and again in the 2020 Covid crash according to Fohlin et al. (2023). More recently South Korea, in November 2023, imposed new rules limiting short selling according to Lee (2023, November 5). Besides bans on a country level, the rule book of an individual stock exchange may also limit, or outright ban e.g. short selling. More interestingly, from a Fraud Shorting point of view, Financial Service Authorities might ban short selling of a single stock, like BaFin (2019) did in the German Wirecard Fraud case. Ironically, unbeknown to German Federal Financial Supervisory Authority Bundesanstalt für Finanzdienstleistungsaufsicht (BaFin) that they were protecting the fraudulent company and aiding it, to carry forward the corporate fraud.

Additionally, other financial instruments, such as options or derivatives, which could also be used to realize the Corporate Fraud Exposure Capital Gains, may not be easily accessible or even available in various geographical regions.

This means that in some geographical areas, even though the investor can locate a fraudulent target company, it might not be practically possible to realize the Corporate Fraud Exposure Capital Gain in the target company. This is because the local legal setting makes it cumbersome or even impossible.

## 3.9 The Short Selling Ban Paradox and the Corporate Fraud Premium

Research on Short selling and Corporate Fraud by Fang et al. (2016) and Karpoff and Lou (2010) indicates that financial instruments used for profiting from fraud shorting investments, like short selling, may help detect and prevent corporate fraud in publicly listed companies.

While many jurisdictions have corporate governance regulations and minority protections, some do not.

The concept of *tunneling* is where the controlling shareholder(s) are extracting value from the publicly listed company for personal gain, but at the same time harming minority shareholders. In some jurisdictions it might not be illegal, the use of self-dealing, favorable shareholder loans, etc. or transactions that in worst case borders on criminal breach of fiduciary trust or embezzlement in other jurisdictions. A study by Hou et al. (2017) on the Chinese stock market in the period 2005–2011, a period with multiple policy changes on short sales bans, found that short sales bans and tunneling had a reverse relationship. When short selling bans were lifted, tunneling activity fell, which indicates that unethical behavior is deterred to some extent by short selling.

It means in the stock markets with limitations on short selling, incidents of corporate fraud should be more prevalent. Ironically, in stock markets that allow short selling, relatively less incidents of corporate fraud should be found. This Short Selling disciplining effect induced by market participants should also be taken into consideration when searching for potential Corporate Fraud Premiums. There might be less fraudulent companies in areas with short selling allowed than in areas with short selling regulated or banned.

In contrast to the low-trust and high corruption cases, short selling bans also happen in high-trust and low corruption jurisdictions.

While the direct approach of short selling is one way to profit from investing in fraudulent companies, it is not the only way. Corporate Fraud Exposure Capital Gains may be realized by other means and financial instruments.

Of course, in any market it is always possible to conduct a fraud investment strategy by divesting detected fraudulent companies from an actively managed investment portfolio. Not having fraudulent companies in the investor's portfolio means when the corporate fraud is exposed, the investor's portfolio is not affected negatively.

If short selling is not a possibility, or the investor does not want to take the full risk of traditional short selling, but still wants to engage in a proactive Fraud Short strategy, there are alternative ways. Depending on venue and jurisdiction, the Fraud Short strategy could include other financial instruments (see Sect. 31 for details) like Stock Options, Stock Futures, Contracts for difference (CFDs), spread betting, selling equity swaps or synthetic stock shorts.

In a case where the fraudulent company is a component of an index, like Wirecard in the German Blue-Chip Deutscher Aktienindex (DAX), tools like Inverse Index Exchange-traded funds (ETFs) could be a viable instrument. In a case, where one expects, the corporate fraud is going to make the company default, Credit Default Swaps (CDS) on the company is a possibility.

In addition, to more traditional financial products, the investor might create other kinds of customized derivatives. Only the imagination and wallet of the investor set the limitations.

## References


ACFE. (2022). *Occupational Fraud 2022: A Report to the Nations*. Association of Certified Fraud Examiners. Retrieved September 14, 2024, from https://acfepublic.s3.us-west-2.amazonaws.com/2022+Report+to+the+Nations.pdf

BaFin. (2019, February 8). *General Administrative Act*. Retrieved September 14, 2024, from https://www.bafin.de/SharedDocs/Veroeffentlichungen/EN/Aufsichtsrecht/Verfuegung/vf_190218_leerverkaufsmassnahme_en.html

Beber, A., & Pagano, M. (2013). Short-Selling Bans Around the World: Evidence from the 2007–09 Crisis. *Journal of Finance, 68*(1), 343–381. Retrieved September 14, 2024, from https://ssrn.com/abstract=1502184

Carberry, E. J., Engelen, P.-J., & Van Essen, M. (2018). Which Firms get Punished for Unethical Behavior? Explaining Variation in Stock Market Reactions to Corporate Misconduct. *Business Ethics Quarterly*. Retrieved December 7th, 2023, from https://www.cambridge.org/core/journals/business-ethics-quarterly/article/which-firms-get-punished-for-unethical-behavior-explaining-variation-in-stock-market-reactions-to-corporate-misconduct/E98BB48190063F847C0FA12FDFF0136C2#ref76

CompaniesMarket Cap. (2023, 30th Sep). *Largest Companies by Revenue*. Retrieved December 7, 2023, from https://companiesmarketcap.com/largest-companies-by-revenue

Companies Market Cap. (2023, 7 December). Retrieved December 7th, 2023, from https://companiesmarketcap.com/

Davies, D. (2021). *Lying for Money: How Legendary Frauds Reveal the Workings of the World*. Simon and Schuster

Deloitte. (2020). *Bank of 2030: The Digital Future of Securities Exchange Operations*. Retrieved December 9, 2023, from https://www.deloitte.com/content/dam/assets-shared/legacy/docs/gx-digital-future-of-securities-exchange-operations.pdf

DOJ. (2021, February 16). Nigerian National Sentenced to Prison for $11 Million Global Fraud Scheme. *U.S. Department of Justice*. Retrieved December 7, 2023, from https://www.justice.gov/usao-edva/pr/nigerian-national-sentenced-prison-11-million-global-fraud-scheme

Dolan, K. A. (2016). Africa's Most Promising Entrepreneurs: Forbes Africa's 30 Under 30 for 2016. *Forbes*. Retrieved December 7, 2023, from https://www.forbes.com/sites/kerryadolan/2016/06/06/africas-most-promising-entrepreneurs-forbes-africas-30-under-30-for-2016/?sh=3b24a6261f43

Douglas, P. C., & Wier, B. (2005). Cultural and Ethical Effects in Budgeting Systems: A Comparison of U.S. and Chinese Managers. *Journal of Business Ethics, 60*, 159–174. Retrieved September 14, 2024, from https://doi.org/10.1007/s10551-004-6711-z

Dyck, A., Morse, A., & Zingales, L. (2010). Who Blows the Whistle on Corporate Fraud? *The Journal of Finance, 65*(6), 2213–2253. Retrieved December 7, 2023, from https://www.jstor.org/stable/23324409

Dyck, A., Morse, A., & Zingales, L. (2023). How Pervasive is Corporate Fraud? *Review of Accounting Studies*. Retrieved December 7th, 2023, from https://link.springer.com/article/https://doi.org/10.1007/s11142-022-09738-5

Fang, V. W., Huang, A. H., & Karpoff, J. M. (2016). Short Selling and Earnings Management: A Controlled Experiment. *The Journal of Finance, 71*(3), 1251–1294. https://doi.org/10.2469/dig.v46.n11.4

Fohlin, C., Lu, Z., & Zhou, N. (2023, March 26). *The Impact of Short Sale Bans During Crises: A Closer Look at the 2020 Covid Crash Response*. CEPR.

Retrieved September 14, 2024, from https://cepr.org/voxeu/columns/impact-short-sale-bans-during-crises-closer-look-2020-covid-crash-response

GAO. (2002). *Financial Statement Restatements: Trends, Market Impacts, Regulatory Responses, and Remaining Challenges* (Report No. 03–138). General Accounting Office, Government Printing Office. Retrieved September 14, 2024, from https://www.iasplus.com/en/publications/migrated/pub92

Gee, J., & Button, M. (2021). *The Financial Cost of Fraud 2021: The Latest Data from Around the World*. University of Portsmouth, The Centre for Counter Fraud Studies and Crowe UK. Retrieved September 14, 2024, from https://reputationup.com/wp-content/uploads/2022/04/Global-Financial-Cost-of-Fraud-2021.pdf

Han, S., Kang, T., Salter, S., & Yoo, Y. K. (2010). A Cross-Country Study on the Effects of National Culture on Earnings Management. *Journal of International Business Studies, 41*, 123–141. Retrieved September 14, 2024, from https://doi.org/10.1057/jibs.2008.78

Hofstede, G. (1980). *Culture's Consequences: International Differences in Work-Related Values*. Sage Publications.

Hou, Q., Jin, Q., Su, L., & Yu, X. (2017). Lifting of Short Sale Constraints and Tunneling of Controlling Shareholders (In Chinese). *China Economic Quarterly, 16*(03), 1143–1172. Retrieved September 14, 2024, from https://doi.org/10.13821/j.cnki.ceq.2017.02.14

Karpoff, J. M., & Lou, X. (2010). Short Sellers and Financial Misconduct. *The Journal of Finance, 65*(5), 1879–1913. Retrieved September 14, 2024, from https://doi.org/10.1111/j.1540-6261.2010.01597.x

Karpoff, J. M., Lee, D. S., & Martin, G. S. (2008). The Cost to Firms of Cooking the Books. *The Journal of Financial and Quantitative Analysis, 43*(3), 581–611. Retrieved December 7th, 2023, from https://www.jstor.org/stable/27647364

La Monica, P. R. (2015). Stockswatch Volkswagen has Plunged 50%. Will it Ever Recover? *CNN Money*. Retrieved December 7, 2023, from https://money.cnn.com/2015/09/24/investing/volkswagen-vw-emissions-scandal-stock/

Lee, J. (2023, November 5). S.Korea to Bring Retail Short-Selling Rules in Line with Institutions. *Reuters*. Retrieved September 14, 2024, from https://www.reuters.com/markets/south-korea-keep-stock-short-selling-ban-until-market-improves-regulator-2023-11-16/

Lu, L. C., Rose, G. M., & Blodgett, J. G. (1999). The Effects of Cultural Dimensions on Ethical Decision Making in Marketing: An Exploratory Study. *Journal of Business Ethics, 18*, 91–105. Retrieved September 14, 2024, from https://doi.org/10.1023/A:1006038012256

McCrum, D. (2020, June 25). Wirecard: The Timeline. *Financial Times*. Retrieved December 7, 2023, from https://www.ft.com/content/284fb1ad-ddc0-45df-a075-0709b36868db

Ng, D. (2006). The Impact of Corruption on Financial Markets. *Managerial Finance, 32*, 10, pp. 822–836. Retrieved December 7, 2023, from https://doi.org/10.1108/03074350710688314 - https://www.emerald.com/insight/content/doi/https://doi.org/10.1108/03074350710688314/full/html

Nwaubani, A. T. (2019, September 23). Letter from Africa: Why Nigeria's Internet Scammers are 'Role Models'. *BBC News.* Retrieved September 14, 2024, from https://www.bbc.com/news/world-africa-49759392

Ortiz-Ospina, E., & Roser, M. (2016). Trust. Our World in Data. Retrieved September 14, 2024, from https://ourworldindata.org/trust

Palmrose, Z.-V., Richardson, V. J., & Scholz, S. (2004). Determinants of Market Reactions to Restatement Announcements. *Journal of Accounting and Economics, 37*(1), 59–89. Retrieved December 7, 2023, from https://ssrn.com/abstract=474384

Scholtens, B., & Dam, L. (2007). Cultural Values and International Differences in Business Ethics. *Journal of Business Ethics, 75*, 273–284. Retrieved September 14, 2024, from https://doi.org/10.1007/s10551-006-9252-9

Transparency International. (2022). *Corruption Perceptions Index (CPI).* Retrieved September 14, 2024, from https://www.transparency.org/en/cpi/2022

U.S. Securities and Exchange Commission. (2023). *Fiscal Year 2023 Enforcement Statistics.* Retrieved September 14, 2024, from https://www.sec.gov/files/fy23-enforcement-statistics.pdf

WFE. (2022). Number of Listed Companies. By World Federation of Exchanges. Retrieved September 14, 2024, from https://focus.world-exchanges.org/articles/number-listed-companies

WFE. (2023). Market Statistics—March 2023. World Federation of Exchanges. Retrieved September 14, 2024, from https://focus.world-exchanges.org/issue/march-2023/market-statistics

WFE. (2024). *Extraction in March 2024 of Listed Companies and Market Cap.* Retrieved March 10, 2024, from https://statistics.world-exchanges.org/

World Bank. (2022). *Total GDP According to the World Bank.* Retrieved September 14, 2024, from https://databankfiles.worldbank.org/public/ddpext_download/GDP.pdf

# Part II

## The Corporate Fraud and The Corporate Fraudster

# 4

# The Corporate Fraud

## 4.1 Corporate Fraud and Financial Crime

Corporate Fraud is a subset of financial crime. Other distinct types of financial crime are Money Laundering, Sanctions Evasion, Terror Financing, bribery, corruption, tax fraud, other types of fraud, etc. In a real-world setting the lines between these financial crime types will often blur. A white-collar criminal might conduct several types of these financial crimes in combination.

Apart from some types of complex tax evasion and tax fraud schemes, corporate fraud is generally the most complex financial crime area. Have in mind that the corporate fraudster must swindle often very professional stakeholders like auditors, accountants, corporate lawyers, and professional investors, to pull off the corporate fraud.

At its core, the corporate fraud is about abusing the corporate entity to enrich the fraudster and/or third parties, at the expense of investors and often other stakeholders like lenders. Typical practical ways to conduct fraud are related to embezzlement, document forgery, financial statement manipulation, etc.


J. Sørensen, *Shorting Fraud*, https://doi.org/10.1007/978-3-031-81834-9_4

## 4.2 The Central Intelligence Agency's Basic Categories of Deception and Corporate Fraud

The corporate fraud often builds on highly crafted deception. Investors can learn a lot about deception, visiting Las Vegas and watching world-class magicians. If observant, one might even puzzle out how the magic tricks are done.

As with fraud, at the core of any magic trick is diversion of attention. Directing the audience's attention to where it least matters. Seldom, the trick is revealed looking directly at the magician. Instead, the focus should be on the rest of the darkened stage and audience. Maybe linger after the show and see who stays in the audience, to expose which of the "volunteers" are assistants and associates of the magician.

Before diving into the elaborate fraud schemes and types, it is important to understand two basic types of deception that fraud builds upon. The Central Intelligence Agency (CIA) outlined in CIA (1980) that deception may come in two main categories. The first is called A for Ambiguity and second M for Misdirection. The investor should always bear these two fundamental types of deception in mind when dealing with corporate fraud on a practical level.

### 4.2.1 Ambiguity Deception

This strategy aims to confuse the victim and decrease the likelihood of accurate understanding, by presenting the victim with a flood of conflicting information. In corporate fraud this have been observed by the fraudster conducting the following:

- Complex Financial Structures: A company might create complex financial structures that make it difficult for investors and regulators to understand the true financial position of the company. This could involve the use of off-balance-sheet entities, convoluted transactions, or unusual accounting practices. The goal is to dilute the perception of risk or poor performance.
- Vague Language: Management might use vague or non-committal language when discussing the company's prospects. This could involve statements that are open to multiple interpretations, or the use of jargon and buzzwords that obscure the true meaning.
- Future Projections: Management's projections about future performance can be inherently uncertain and may not always align with past or current financial results. For example, management might project future growth

based on new initiatives or market opportunities, even if current financial results are poor.

- Non-Generally Accepted Accounting Principles (non-GAAP) Measures: Management might use non-GAAP measures in their commentary, which can differ significantly from the Generally Accepted Accounting Principles (GAAP) measures presented in the financial reports. Non-GAAP measures can be useful for understanding certain aspects of a company's performance, but they can also create ambiguity if not clearly defined and reconciled to the most directly comparable GAAP measures.
- Complex Financial Transactions: Companies involved in complex financial transactions might have financial reports that are difficult to understand. Management commentary or footnotes might not fully clarify these transactions, leading to ambiguity.
- Strategic Decisions: Management might make strategic decisions that impact financial results, such as acquisitions, divestitures, or changes in business strategy. These decisions might be discussed in the commentary but might not be immediately apparent in the financial numbers.

The use of Ambiguity deception and potential red flags might be seen in the complexity of Management Discussion and Analysis (MD&A) section of the annual report. The MD&A section shows key information about a company's financial performance. The MD&A section addresses the company's performance and presents an analysis of the company's performance with qualitative and quantitative measures. It offers insights into a company's past financial performance, its present financial health, and management's outlook for future results.

A study by Lo et al. (2016) on the MD&A section found earnings management led to more complex language in the MD&A section. To assess readability, the researchers employed the Fog Index on the MD&A section within the annual report.

The study found that companies most likely to manipulate earnings to exceed the previous year's figures had less readable MD&As, suggesting increased complexity in language.

Ambiguity deception has also been observed in practical interaction with corporate fraudsters. When requesting specific information, they may try to drown stakeholders with tons of detailed information they never asked for and must sift to, for the stakeholder only to find what asked for is not there in the material. Sometimes the devil is not in the details, but the needless details the fraudster is carpet bombing the stakeholders with.

### 4.2.2 Misdirection Deception

In the other type of deception, the goal is to eliminate uncertainty in the victim's mind by leading them to accept a certain false narrative.

In corporate fraud, this could involve a company deliberately misleading investors about the company's prospects. For example, a company might release false or misleading statements about a new product's sales, leading investors to believe the company is more successful than it actually is. The goal is to direct attention away from negative aspects and towards fabricated positive aspects.

While the author has found no academic research on M-deception related to corporate fraud, from a practitioner's point of view some red flags examples have been observed. E.g., the outline of the financial report. How the financial report is designed and presented is important in misdirection deception. The management may want to present a story of a company that is in much better shape than it is.

It may be as simple as having a total revenue growth number of 250% making up most of the top part of the first page, and in a large, huge font, while the actual and more interesting organic -30% revenue decline is buried way down on page 23 of the company report.

Also, management might graphically emphasize financial results in a way that highlights positive aspects and downplays negative ones. This is sometimes done with graphs and charts. It could be cherry picking data or data ranges, like specific years to make it look better than it is, or manipulating the Y-Axis, omitting the baseline and similar. It could also be to selectively only show data and comment on the orderbook when orders are growing and drop the order book data and comments when the order situation is negative.

## 4.3 The Corporate Fraudsters

Fraudsters might work alone, they might work in small groups, or in worst case the problem is systemic and endemic, like in the financial crises where the entire system of banks and financial institutions were fraudulent in nature with regards to the subprime mortgages.

While insight into psychology, sociology and criminology is incredibly useful when working with fraudsters, this is not an exhaustive book on the criminal minds and how they work. However, some basics are discussed below, from a practical point of view combined with the relevant select theory.

Since Cressy (1953) more than 70 years ago, conducted his seminal study, and authored the book related to the psychology of fraud; thousands of scholars within psychology, sociology and criminology have studied the minds and behavior of fraudsters in thousands of studies and research papers.

Working hands-on, with hundreds of fraud cases, a few general observations stand out regarding motives in corporate fraud cases. These motives are good to bear in mind when hunting for fraudulent target companies. The motives might appear alone, but many times in combination.

- **Private Financial pressure**—steal the money or manipulate to cover for experienced or actual financial pressure, like being in debt or similar. Sometimes in the form of short term "loans," where the fraudster temporarily covers personal debt or financial problems, embezzling.
- **Pride**—Seen especially with entrepreneurs. Trying to do everything for the business not to go bankrupt.
- **Fear of failing**—especially amongst super competitive individuals, the fear of failing is a motive for fraud. High performers are used to winning, when they suddenly stop winning, they may abuse all tricks in the book to continue the appearance of winning and may eventually resort to fraud. They do not want to face investors, creditors, or the rest of the world, and admit failure.
- **Entitlement or revenge**—The fraudster might feel entitled to more than she is getting. Or getting back for being overlooked or feeling abused. The entitlement, perceived or actual abuse is then used as justification for the fraud.
- **Delusion— and psychiatric issues**—This is typical when the reality does not longer fit with the fraudster's self-perception or how the fraudster wants things to turn out. These are fraudsters that might suffer from severe mental problems. Alternatively, they might suffer from narcissism, sociopathy, or psychopathy. These can be the hardest fraudsters to detect and deal with.
- **Greed— and financial status**—some fraudsters are CEOs who are already well off. Their companies are doing well, but they simply cannot get enough, but want more and it does not matter how they get it. Also, if they had high financial status and the status implodes due to a failing business, they turn to fraud to prop up the company and keep up with the Joneses.
- **The Golden Opportunity**—This is the fraudster who never did anything wrong before, but sees a golden opportunity in front of her, where it is

highly unlikely that she is going to get caught in the act. Like finding a suitcase full of cash, abandoned in the middle of nowhere, with no witnesses seeing you found it.

- **Peer pressure— and group think**if we move up one level to sociology. The fraudster might be pressured or in other ways be incentivized into the corporate fraud from the social setting and surrounding. This can even be about helping a third party, and there is no immediate financial reward to the perpetrator, only social acceptance for helping the third party.

### 4.3.1 Corporate Fraud Motives in the 2020s

If we move from 1953 to 2025. Based on the general view of communications with actual white-collar criminals from fraud cases[1], the concepts of greed, vanity, fear, and delusion, appears to be overshadowing motives. If we look at it within the generational ranges as defined by Dimock (2019), there appears to be variations between generations.

Millennials (Generation Y) born 1981–1996 and Generation Z born 1997–2012 tend to be more motivated by vanity and appear more delusional. Fraudsters from those two generations want to look successful at almost any cost. While fraudsters from Generation X, born between 1965 and 1980 tend to be more motivated by greed, the fear of poverty and loss of obtained status.

From a practical standpoint, it has been observed that greed, vanity, fear, and delusion are emotions and behaviors that are often related to fraudulent behavior. This happens either on their own or in combination.

If you look at the greed factor. In corporate frauds, it is often people who are already extremely well off, making hundreds of times more than the average worker, and still wanting more regardless of what it costs, including deceiving everybody.

The fear of e.g., failure, poverty, or other significant personal loss in status, has been observed as another strong motive for fraud. The fear motive is related to the vanity motive. Here the fraudster might not fear failure or being poor, or other loss, but crave the admiration by one's surrounding, of one's achievements.

According to Colvin (2021), the fraudster Bernie Madoff in his own words was a people pleaser. This can be interpreted as a form of vanity. He wanted to look good, even better than he was - never losing money. If one looks at

[1] Disclaimer—these are general observations from + 60 fraud cases. Due to bank secrecy regulations, the specifics of the general observation experienced cannot be publicized. These observations compare to case studies or the more subjective Action Research field of the Social Sciences.

the case of Bernie Madoff. The guy was well-off, had a lifetime of success in the investment world. He could have done well without the money from the Ponzi Scheme, but to him it was not enough.

Consider Elizabeth Holmes, as described in more detail in Sect. 4.3.2, she came from an affluent setting. Had she finished her studies, she could probably have landed a more ordinary well-paid job. A degree and an ordinary job were not enough. She marketed herself as the female Steve Jobs, with an ambition to save the world. However, the gap between her self-perceived genius and reality might have driven her into corporate fraud.

Interestingly, from a practical viewpoint, skewed self-perception has been observed in other fraud cases. Vanity and self-delusion have been seen in female millennial entrepreneurs and businesswomen. Listening to recorded conversations, reading transcripts or e-mails. One can only speculate it has to do with the rise of social media. From an early age, the new generations of corporate fraudsters are accustomed to changing reality with filters, editing, or deleting Social Media posts in a way that everything comes out positive, instead of realistic—or "fake it till you make it!".

Delusional corporate fraudsters can be extremely hard to detect even when meeting in person. This is because in self-delusion, the fraudster has started believing and living their own lies.

Therefore, do not only listen to what a person of interest or the people around him say. Instead look at the evidence. As Lewis wt. MacDonell (1984) states: *"In the course of a trial, defense and prosecuting attorneys may lie, witnesses may lie, the defendant may certainly lie. Even the judge may lie. Only the evidence never lies!"*.

While knowing some of these basic human motives, when analyzing fraud, they may be useful to understand the fraudster. However, the investor does not need to know the actual fraud motives up front. In deep-dives they might come in handy sometimes, but analyzing or overanalyzing people's motives can cloud the investor's corporate fraud analysis. Instead focus on the evidence.

### 4.3.2 Philanthropists Grifters, Impact Investment Fraudsters and Greenwashers

An interesting observation in several corporate fraud cases has been the involvement of the elements of philanthropism, altruism and charity and the fraudsters' claim of wanting to make the world a better place. The fraudster cleverly uses these agendas as a deceptive tool. Just as mentioned in Sect. 3.6, where fraudsters used topics such as racism and diversity as leverage. The effectiveness of such brazen frauds is good, since the victims automatically lower their guards when faced with altruism.

The person conducting the corporate fraud portrays themselves as a Good Samaritan, wanting to help the world and the weak. Either in the business model, or in branding of the fraudster's general personal profile. Take The Abraaj Group. According to Financial Times (2019), Abraaj was a leading private equity firm, known for its impact investing in growth markets. They had charities investing with them. However, it collapsed by misusing these funds. Personas like Bill Gates and Barack Obama and their professional advisors were duped in these cases.

It shows that the mask of altruism is an effective method to lower the guards and kill skepticism of investors and other stakeholders.

Some fraudsters use it as a general tactic. Marketing that philanthropism is behind all they do, like in the Abraaj case. Other fraudsters turn to fake philanthropism when they are under pressure and risk getting caught. Both tactics are used for the sole purpose of countering fraud red flags with "good deeds."

It has been observed that it works on financial industry employees, who will waiver obvious fundamental information or turn a blind eye to red flags, because the fraudster is claiming to help refugees in Africa. The same tactic would never work if the fraudster was selling used cars.

Even more interesting. Signs of this counter-intuitive and twisted relationship between altruism and fraud have not only been observed in individual fraud cases, but also in general experiments conducted by psychologists.

In general, individuals are more likely to cheat and justify cheating when the spoils are split altruistically and shared with e.g. charity according to experiments conducted by Gino et al. (2013) and Chua et al. (2022). This with general random selected individuals in the experiments, which are not necessarily fraudsters.

Therefore, if one finds red flags and they are countered by an altruism campaign, or altruism is used as deflection, when asking tough questions, the red flags should count double.

Looking at Elizabeth Holmes TEDMED interviews, she tells a tale about her close uncle's death that inspired her to invent the Edison and make the world a better place. Later e.g. Carreyrou (2018) questions this Holmes anecdote, because of the timeline of the death doesn't fit with the startup of the company, and the family said they were not close. Interestingly, Holmes' fraud allegedly led to misdiagnosed cancer patients according to Carreyrou and Weaver (2016), Richards (2022) and SurvivorNet Staff (2023).

A combination of a good Samaritan and a sob story, often captures and convinces everybody, but the most coolheaded investors.

While Holmes' example is in the public domain, it is far from the only time this has been observed amongst other fraudsters in cases. Therefore, altruism, charity and philanthropy in a corporate setting should always be analyzed with a great deal of skepticism. Legitimate philanthropists do not talk about it, or do not connect their altruism directly towards their business. The motive is not to gain sympathy from investors or other stakeholders, but to do good in the world.

The Rise of ESG (Environmental, Socially Responsible and Good Governance) has also resulted in the exploitation of the ESG-agenda by corporate fraudsters. Having the corporations appear to look much better and in line with ESG than they really are.

The observations made in practice on ESG is supported by research from Kjær and Kirchmaier (2023) on ESG and Corporate Scandals. The study includes many of the biggest corporate fraud cases. About 50% of the S score cases are related to financial corporate crimes like bribery, corruption, accounting fraud and other types of fraud.

The study finds that one year prior to a corporate scandal the Social Responsibility score (the S in ESG) is significantly higher for scandal corporations than non-scandal corporations. This is counterintuitive and controversial, but not surprising to practitioners working with corporate fraud, used to see the window dressing made by corporate fraudsters. Nothing is off limits for the corporate fraudster.

Greenwashing and other types of purpose "washing" will be described in more detail in Sect.5.2.2 .

### 4.3.3 The Executive Fraudster

The white-collar criminals are executives, often highly respected individuals, heading publicly listed companies. Since we deal with Corporate Fraud, the fraud happens on a legal entity level but is done by one or more executives at the helm of the company. Like the CEO, CFO, and other C-level executives with control of the entire corporate entity. Often knowingly or unknowingly with assistance from internal stakeholders like lower-level employees and external stakeholders like lawyers, auditors, external partners, etc.

We look at Corporate Fraud as an act of deception conducted by white-collar criminals against shareholders, by abusing the corporation that the shareholders own, but the white-collar criminal controls.

## 4.4 The Victims

The victims of the corporate fraud are the investors (owner) and other stakeholders like the financiers losing the credit facilities and loans provided to the corporation, customers, or vendors, losing money. Other victims are employees who might lose their pension and salary and be discredited working for a fraudulent corporation. Finally, society at large. The society may be missing out on taxes, wrongfully subsidizing the corporation, suffer from additional pollution or externalities and costs from the company.

Victimology is a vast area in general fraud research. It is of course interesting to know why victims are conned and what effect it has on them. However, this is not covered in this book. Instead, we focus on the perpetrator and the anatomy of the corporate fraud. How can we uncover the corporate fraud.

However, early, or former victims, might be a source of information to uncover the fraud. Like employees and customers, whistleblowing on job boards as discussed in Sect. 19.5 and 19.7 or litigation by stakeholders as described in Sect. 16.3.1

## References

Carreyrou, J. (2018). *Bad Blood: Secrets and Lies in a Silicon Valley Startup*. Knopf Publishing Group.

Carreyrou, J., & Weaver, C. (2016). Agony, Alarm and Anger for People Hurt by Theranos's Botched Blood Tests. *The Wall Street Journal.*

Central Intelligence Agency. (1980). *Deception Maxims: Fact and Folklore*. Office of Research and Development.

Chua, S. L., Chang, J., & Riambau, G. (2022). Lying Behavior When the Payoffs are Shared with Charity: Experimental Evidence. *Journal of Economic Psychology, 90*(102512). Retrieved September 14, 2024, from https://doi.org/10.1016/j.joep.2022.102512

Colvin, G. (2021). Bernie Madoff and the Disorienting Mix of Motives that Led to History's Largest Ponzi Scheme. *Yahoo Finance*. Retrieved September 14, 2024, from https://finance.yahoo.com/news/bernie-madoff-disorienting-mix-motives-190304863.html?guccounter=1

Cressy, D. R. (1953). *Other People's Money; A Study of the Social Psychology of Embezzlement*. Free Press.

Dimock, M. (2019). Defining Generations: Where Millennials End and Generation Z Begins. *Pew Research Center*. Retrieved September 14, 2024, from https://www.pewresearch.org/short-reads/2019/01/17/where-millennials-end-and-generation-z-begins/

Financial Times. (2019). *Abraaj Scandal a 'Wake-Up Call' for Advisory Industry.* Retrieved September 14, 2024, from https://www.ft.com/content/c31e6040-78b0-11e9-b0ec-7dff87b9a4a2

Gino, F., Ayal, S., & Ariely, D. (2013). Self-Serving Altruism? The Lure of Unethical Actions that Benefit Others. *Journal of Economic Behavior & Organization, 93*, 285–292. Retrieved September 14, 2024, from https://doi.org/10.1016/j.jebo.2013.04.005

Kjær, C., & Kirchmaier, T. (2023). Deceived by 'S': Corporate Scandals and ESG. *SSRN Electronic Journal*. Retrieved September 14, 2024, from https://doi.org/10.2139/ssrn.4428468

Lewis, A. A., with MacDonell, H. L. (1984). *The Evidence Never Lies: The Casebook of a Modern Sherlock Holmes.* Holt Rinehart & Winston.

Lo, K., Ramos, F., & Rogo, R. (2016). Earnings Management and Annual Report Readability. *Journal of Accounting & Economics (JAE).* Retrieved September 14, 2024, from https://ssrn.com/abstract=2848537

Richards, T. (2022). False Dawns: Implications for Patients of the Theranos debacle. *The BMJ*, 376(o178).

SurvivorNet Staff. (2023). Theranos Blood Test Failed to Identify and Misdiagnosed Cancer. *SurvivorNet2*

# 5

# The Main Types of Corporate Fraud

## 5.1 Overview of the Main Types of Corporate Fraud

While there are hundreds of ways and variations conducting a corporate fraud, to get an overview, the corporate fraud may be categorized in broader types as illustrated in Fig. 5.1, which is showing a breakdown of the main categories of corporate fraud.

As we will see in later sections, the risk characteristics, and the likelihood of certain types of corporate fraud might vary across e.g., the life cycle stage of the corporation, the industry, the jurisdiction, and stock exchange that the corporation is part of.

## 5.2 Material Misrepresentation

While there are multiple ways that Material Misrepresentation may happen from a practical point of view, two are of particular interest. These are Financial Statement Misrepresentation and Greenwashing.

### 5.2.1 Financial Statement Misrepresentation

Financial Statement misrepresentation or financial statement fraud is the deliberate misrepresentation of the corporation's financial statements. Financial statement fraud happens by omission or exaggeration, with the intent to


J. Sørensen, *Shorting Fraud*, https://doi.org/10.1007/978-3-031-81834-9_5

| | |
|---|---|
| Material Misrepresentation | Financial Statement misrepresentation |
| | Greenwashing (Social Washing, Bluewashing, Fairwashing and Purposewashing) |
| | Overstatement of Assets under Management (Financial Institutions) |
| | Tampering with Investment performance (Financial Institutions) |
| Material Abuse of corporate Assets or funds | Direct Material theft, embezzlement or abuse of corporate assets or funds for personal benefit |
| | Material misdirection of corporate funds or assets from shareholders to stakeholders or Third-parties |
| | Misappropriation clients' assets or funds under management. (Financial Institutions) |
| Other Material Corporate Fraudulent Activities | Material misappropriation of funds, assets or infrastructure outside the corporate mandate |
| | Material misappropriation of corporate funds, assets or infrastructure for fraudulent activity |
| | Misc. Material Fraud Condut for Financial Instiutions. Self-dealing, frontrunning clients, market manipulation, insider trading and Ponzi Schemes (Financial Institutions) |

**Fig. 5.1** A corporate fraud taxonomy

create a false impression of the corporation's financial position, performance, and cash flow. The motive of the corporate executive white-collar criminal is to make the company look different from its actual fundamental state. Most often (but not always), the motive is to make the corporation look better than it really is.

### 5.2.1.1 Examples of Financial Statement Misrepresentation

There are many examples of Financial Statement Misrepresentation each year, both amongst listed and unlisted companies. A few of the most prominent Financial Statement Fraud cases are listed in Table 5.1.

### 5.2.1.2 Detecting Financial Statement Misrepresentation

Detecting Financial Statement Fraud may be done by meticulously, manually analyzing the numbers in financial statements and the financial ratios to find signs of potential financial statement fraud like described in Chapter 23. Investors and analysts deep-diving into financial statements analyzing them

**Table 5.1** Notable Financial Statement Misrepresentations, sources Bondarenko (2024), Young (2004, March 12), NBC News (2004, January 21), BBC News (2011, April 6)

| Company | Years | Description | Executives | Fraud |
|---|---|---|---|---|
| Enron | 1996–2001 | Enron manipulated financial statements using several methods. E.g. mark-to-market accounting to record potential future profits on the date of signing. They also created Special Purpose Entities (SPEs) to hide debt & toxic assets. Additionally, they inflated revenue by recording trading own securities as revenue | Kenneth Lay (CEO & Chairman), Jeffrey Skilling (CEO & COO), Andrew Fastow (CFO) | +$60 bn |
| WorldCom | 1999–2002 | WorldCom used multiple fraudulent accounting techniques to inflate profits. A method was shifting certain costs from operating expenses to capital expenses. Also misclassified costs in the books to artificially boost bottom line. Another method was manipulating reserves. Setting aside to cover estimated losses | Bernard Ebbers (CEO) | +$11 bn |

(continued)

**Table 5.1** (continued)

| Company | Years | Description | Executives | Fraud |
|---|---|---|---|---|
| HealthSouth | 1996–2002 | HealthSouth overstated earnings. Used various accounting tricks to inflate earnings, overstate assets & hide expenses. CEO acquitted on fraud, convicted of other FinCrime | Richard Scrushy (CEO), William Owens (CFO) | +$4 bn |
| Satyam Computer Services | 2005–2009 | The founder and director falsified accounts, boosted stock prices while embezzling significant amounts of money. The company's chairman Ramalinga Raju admitted that the firm had falsified revenues, margins and cash balances | B. Ramalinga Raju (Chairman and CEO) | +$1 bn |

by hand is time consuming, while it can be very fruitful to get a deeper understanding of the corporation.

Prior to manually diving into and analyzing financial statements, screening with advanced or statistical metrics specifically designed to detect Financial Statement fraud described in Chapter 11 may be a beneficial way to detect potential fraud targets. For the most advanced analyst, Machine Learning models that detect Financial Statement Fraud is a potent option. Training these models to detect financial statement fraud and then having it analyze thousands of corporations to find potential fraud candidates is described in Chapter 12.

### 5.2.2 Greenwashing

Material misrepresentation extends beyond the financial statements. It could also pertain to areas in the ESG reporting, where executives are trying to make the company look much better than it is. This is supported amongst others by Keeble (2022) that reported 58% of executives admit overstating sustainability efforts.

Greenwashing is the new kid on the block and of specific interest because of its omnipresence to all corporations, with the focus on sustainability and ESG.

Similar overlapping washing terms are being used to capture other aspects and disconnects between ESG claims and reality. Bluewashing is used to describe disconnects within responsible economic and community factors. Fairwashing disconnects between fair trade or ethical trade and reality. Purposewashing describes companies' tendency to boast of social commitments, like inclusion, fairness, and respect but with the sole purpose of improving their image. Social washing is when companies mislead the investors with overstated or baseless claims about their social responsibility efforts.

With the focus on climate change, sustainability, social responsibility, etc. any type of "washing" is a significant and growing risk of material misrepresentation, which has a direct effect on the shareholders and the share price. There are multiple examples that corporations claiming they are green or follow some ethical standards within the ESG space, but then it is found they are not. This can be misstatements of the corporation's carbon footprints, net-zero products, employee diversity, employee safety or any of the UN 17 Sustainable Development Goals in annual reports and legal documents.

If one looks at the general growth in climate change litigations Setzer and Higham (2021) found that more than 800 cases were filed between 1986 and 2014. However, since 2015, there has been a substantial number of cases globally, with over 1000 cases filed 2015–2021. These are the total numbers for all entities like governments, state-owned enterprises etc. A growing number of these cases are against corporations and more involving investors as plaintiffs.

In 2021 there were 38 cases against corporations according to Setzer and Higham (2022). In 2023 Setzer and Higham (2023) found 40% of the cases filed in the past 12 months (2022/2023) outside the US, targeted corporations, or trade bodies as defendants. These cases often challenge greenwashing.

Amongst Financial Corporations, in ESG investments and financing, the greenwashing cases were growing with 70% from 2022 to 2023 according to Reprisk (2023).

Also, ESG can be another way to hide the lack of financial performance in a company. A general tactic observed used by fraudsters is to have investors and stakeholders focus on other things than the fundamental problems or red flags that will indicate the fraud—to fabricate or spin a positive story. Besides observing ESG deflection tactics in actual cases, this is supported by

Flugum and Souther (2023) that found companies missing projected earnings are more likely to turn to stakeholder language like ESG, in their communication. CEOs may try to switch from being judged by objective financial results to more subjective criteria like ESG.

This sudden usage of stakeholder language is unrelated to the actual underlying commitments by the company to these stakeholder issues. This deflection with sudden switch from objective performance to subjective stakeholder language appears to work, making CEOs less likely to lose their jobs despite missing performance goals.

Therefore, it is important to assess if stakeholder objectives are an actual part of the company or just convenient rhetorical manipulation, to cover for other shortcomings, including corporate fraud.

#### 5.2.2.1 Examples of Greenwashing and Securities Fraud

SEC (2022, April 28) shows an example of the Brumadinho dam collapse case. In January 2019, the Brumadinho dam in Brazil collapsed, which resulted in the death of 270 people and significant environmental damage. The dam was owned by Vale S.A., which lost more than $4 billion in market capitalization.

Subsequently, the SEC initiated a case against Vale S.A., accusing the company of false and misleading claims regarding the safety of its dams. The SEC stated that: "*Vale manipulated multiple dam safety audits; obtained numerous fraudulent stability certificates; and regularly misled local governments, communities, and investors about the safety of the Brumadinho dam through its environmental, social, and governance (ESG) disclosures.*"

Vale S.A. settled the case with the SEC (2023, March 28), paying a $55.9 Million settlement regarding material misrepresentations in their ESG-related disclosures.

Another case in the Financial Industry is the Global Asset Manager, DWS case. DWS Group, a subsidiary of Deutsche Bank, was raided by German Police in 2022 and subsequently faced allegations of greenwashing, according to SEC (2023, September 25) and Storbeck (2023). The SEC charged DWS with disseminating significantly inaccurate information regarding its procedures for integrating environmental, social, and governance considerations into its investment decisions.

DWS promoted itself as an innovator in ESG, following policies for incorporating ESG factors into its investment strategy. Despite the ESG policies, from August 2018 to ultimo 2021, DWS failed to fully implement certain aspects of its global ESG approach, contrary to what it communicated to investors. The SEC discovered that DWS did not establish and execute policies and processes that were suitably planned to verify the correctness of its public declarations regarding the ESG integrated products.

ACCR (2023, June 26) shows another (at time of this writing still ongoing) example case. The Australasian Centre for Corporate Responsibility (ACCR) vs. Santos Ltd. ACCR claims that Santos Ltd is misleading the investors. The ACCR vs. Santos case revolves around alleged greenwashing. ACCR claims that Santos' portrayal of its natural gas as "clean energy" and its net zero emissions plan as "clear and credible" were misleading. ACCR argues these statements were material misrepresentations, potentially influencing investment decisions. Santos' undisclosed contingencies and dependencies for achieving net zero emissions were key points of the dispute.

#### 5.2.2.2 Detecting Greenwashing

While the Financial Statement Misrepresentation is more straightforward, Greenwashing, ESG and Sustainability Fraud are trickier to detect. How do we know if what is disclosed about ESG in the annual report is actually true. From a manual due diligence point of view sanity checking is the way forward. Like in the Brumadinho dam collapse case are the certificates etc. actually there. Often public records are available to anyone who bothers to look for them and go through the due diligence processes, obtaining them, as described in Sect. 18.6. More advanced ML tools, like e.g. NLP explained in Sect. 34.3 may also be constructed. These may help detect when text is just fabricated to disclose positive ESG disclosures and when they are real disclosures.

### 5.2.3 Overstatement of Assets Under Management (Financial Institutions)

Publicly Listed financial institutions, which have Assets under Management (AUM) might overstate the value of these AUM. The motive might be for the financial institution to appear bigger than they are and show a growth rate on the return of AUM, which outperforms the market or peers. This means they will attract more new capital and continue to extract fees based on the inflated AUM.

#### 5.2.3.1 Examples of Potential Risk of Overstatement of Assets Under Management

The overstatement of assets under management is a tricky area. A gray zone, since valuation of some assets under management is not an exact science and often open for interpretation and subjectivity.

The Department of Justice (DOJ) in DOJ (2016, December 19) indicted multiple executives of the Privately held hedge fund Platinum Partners L.P. In 2016 Platinum were indicted on several different counts of securities fraud, wire fraud, etc. Amongst one of the charges were overvaluation of assets under management. The DOJ claimed that assets had been overvalued to extract fees and create an image of a stellar performance record for Platinum. Reading the prosecutor's statement from the court document is interesting:

> ....deceived the investors by vastly over-valuing Platinum's interest in a small oil company named Golden Gate Oil LLC, and it eventually purchased the remaining interest in that company (52%) for a mere $3.2 million, and yet still touting an enterprise valuation of at least $170 million" (id., ¶ 2″ MDK Hijos Tr. v. Nordlicht, Index No.: 159029/2018, 3 (N.Y. Sup. Ct. 2020).

If one base the valuation on the prosecutor's statement, the valuation of the Oil Company should be:

$$V = \frac{3.2\,million}{0.52} \approx 6.15\,million \tag{5.1}$$

$6.15 million is far from $170 million. More of the executives were convicted on multiple of the other counts of fraud, according to e.g. DOJ (2019, July 9). However, they were acquitted on the valuation count, despite the significant discrepancy of valuations.

The publicly listed company Ichan Enterprises (IEP) gained media attention in 2023, when Hindenburg Research (2023) amongst other things questioned the valuation of the assets held[1] by IEP.

In the Hindenburg report, it was mentioned that IEP e.g. held a 90% stake in Viskase, a meat packaging company that was publicly traded. At that time, the total market value of Viskase was $88.7 million. IEP marked the value of their 90% stake in the company at $243 million, applying about a 200% premium, even though the market price did not show any significant changes.

[1] While not technically AUM it illustrates what investors should look for.

Furthermore, the Hindenburg report stated that IEP assessed the value of its "Automotive Parts" division at $381 million in December 2022, but a critical subsidiary declared bankruptcy in January 2023. Also, IEP reported $455 million in "real estate holdings," a figure that had remained constant over time despite a decrease in net income. Among these holdings were assets such as the former Trump Plaza in Atlantic City, which was demolished in 2021.

In sum, investors should always be skeptical about valuation of assets under management. Especially in financial industry entities and funds with unlisted assets under management, where "fair" valuation practices have been observed abused.

#### 5.2.3.2 Detecting Overstatement of Assets Under Management

Detection of overstatement of assets under management may be a cumbersome process. However, more financial institutions like Private Equity Managers and Hedge Fund Managers are publicly listed entities. The level two assets and portfolio companies of these entities are of interest, since artificially inflating valuations will help inflate both fees and valuations of the listed entities. Hence, the investor needs to sanity check the valuations of level two assets and compare them to the results on the publicly listed entity level.

### 5.2.4 Tampering with Investment performance (Financial Institution)

Publicly listed investment companies or managers might Tamper with their investment performance. This to keep up the appearance that they are doing well, even in times when they are not.

#### 5.2.4.1 Example of Tampering with Investment Performance

With a primary listing on the Frankfurt Stock Exchange, Allianz is one of the largest multinational financial companies in the world, providing a variety of financial services.

Part of Allianz was the Allianz Structured Alpha Funds, a collection of investment funds, which were under the management of Allianz Global Investors U.S. LLC (AGI US), these funds were promoted to around 114 institutional investors according to SEC (2022).

The SEC found that Allianz's Asset Management in the US was involved in an investment performance tampering fraud, which basically was simple and to some extent "poorly" executed document forgery.

The fund managers claimed they made money on a sophisticated options strategy, but in reality, they tampered with the numbers in sometimes mathematically impossible ways.

In 2020, the Alpha funds suffered significant losses during the Corona market crash. Subsequently, the SEC & DOJ began an investigation of the Alpha Funds. Allianz Global Investors US and three previous senior portfolio managers were charged with a massive fraudulent scheme that led to billion-dollar losses.

The portfolio managers hid the massive downside risks of the complex "Structured Alpha" options trading strategy. Furthermore, the managers manipulated financial reports and other investor information.

In one instance, the defendants minimized the projected losses in a risk report for a market crash scenario. They altered the figure from a loss of 42.1505489755747% to just 4.1505489755747% by just omitting the digit '2'. In another instance, they manipulated the performance data that was shared with investors. They halved the loss value for a particular day from 18.2607085709004% to 9.2607085709004%, effectively "smoothing" the data.

According to DOJ (2023), AGI US resolved its legal issues with the DOJ, SEC and investors with financial penalties consisting of more than $463 million in seized assets, over $3.23 billion in investor compensation, and fines exceeding $2.33 billion. Around $6 billion in total.

While the direct fraud victims were only limited to the 114 institutional investors in the Alpha Fund, the fraud was so material that it affected the shareholders of the publicly listed controlling company, Allianz SE.

According to the data from the Frankfurter Börse, the share price of Allianz SE dropped about 8% after the first announcement from Allianz SE on the investigation on Sunday August 1, 2021, which can be seen in Fig. 5.2.

According to Allianz. (2021) there was about 408 million shares outstanding on the date, which constitutes a loss in Allianz SE Market Capitalization of $6.83 billion.

$$\text{Market Cap}_{\text{30-Jul}} = 210.45 \times 408\,mn = 85.86\,bn \tag{5.2}$$

$$\text{Market Cap}_{\text{2-aug}} = 193.7 \times 408\,mn = 79.03\,bn \tag{5.3}$$

$$\text{Drop in Market Capitalization} = 85.86\text{ bn} - 79.03\text{ bn} = 6.83\text{ bn} \tag{5.4}$$

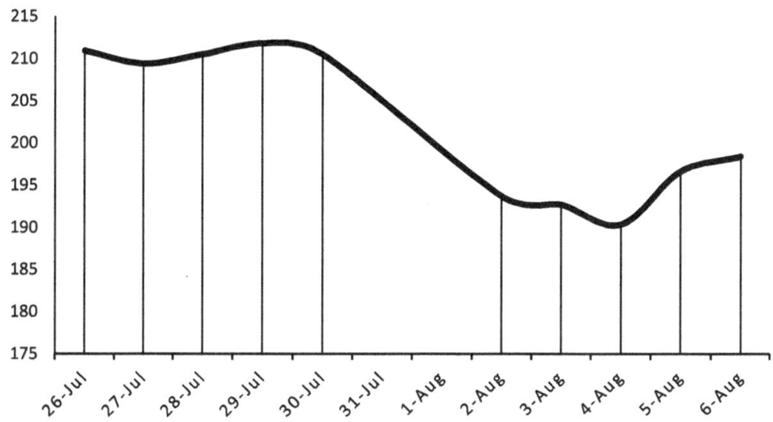


**Fig. 5.2** Closing Price—Allianz SE—Summer 2021, based on share prices from Frankfurter Börse

#### 5.2.4.2 Detecting Tampering with Investment Performance

To detect tampering with investment performance, the investor can deep-dive into the investment material, manually analyze and sanity check them. This entails manually analyzing potentially thousands of pages in documents for inconsistencies, which is time consuming. In addition, if the underlying assets are complicated structured products, other cross-referencing and recalculation are necessary, which is time consuming.

However, in this type of performance tampering, analytic models like Benford's Law described in Sect. 11.8 or more advanced ML models may be developed to effectively detect these types of document forgery. Replacing or complementing manual work with these automatic or semi-automatic solutions may cut analytics from days to hours or less.

## 5.3 Material Abuse of Corporate Assets or Funds

The material abuse of corporate assets or funds happens when executives pillage the corporation they are controlling. It may fall in two categories depending on who benefits from the corporate looting. One is direct personal benefits from executives at the expense of the shareholders. The other is benefiting other stakeholders or other external parties at the expense of the shareholders.

### 5.3.1 Direct Personal Benefits of the Abuse of Corporate Assets and Funds

This benefits the executive and his nearest family and relations. It can either be direct embezzlement of corporate money, or it can be more hidden practices. It may be hidden bonus payments, or financing assets with corporate funds, whose main purpose is personal usage at the expense of the shareholder. Like a fleet of corporate private jets, corporate property in strange places, corporate yachts, lavish private parties and similar activity paid for with corporate funds, but with no relation to the operations of the company.

#### 5.3.1.1 Examples of Direct Personal Benefits

The Tyco International scandal of 2002 treated in SEC (2002, September 12) and related documents is an example of corporate fraud involving a publicly traded company, where the top executives exploited corporate assets and funds for personal gain.

The key person to the scandal was Dennis Kozlowski, the then CEO of Tyco. Kozlowski was involved in questionable financial transactions in the hundreds of millions of dollars that were not disclosed in Tyco's financial reports.

To conceal illegal financial transactions, Kozlowski had help from other Tyco officers and lower-ranking employees. The problem escalated when Kozlowski's second wife began getting money diverted from Tyco International.

The court process revealed that Kozlowski had stolen millions of dollars from Tyco International. Kozlowski's illegal financial dealings were vast. In 2005, CFO Mark Swartz and CEO Kozlowski, were sentenced to prison.

Their convictions were based on several charges, including the receipt of millions in unauthorized bonuses. Furthermore, corporate funds were borrowed and used for personal expenditures, encompassing items like luxury yachts, art, jewelry, upscale apartments, and holiday properties. These funds were also used for personal entrepreneurial projects and investments, none of which had any relation to Tyco business areas. These loans were kept hidden from shareholders. This Despite that federal securities law mandates disclosure of such loans.

This case underscores how the blending of personal and corporate assets facilitated Kozlowski's misuse of the company's assets for personal needs.

#### 5.3.1.2 Detecting Direct Personal Benefit

Often the co-mingling of executives' private funds and corporate funds can be hard to detect unless the investor has access to the books and bank account statements. Discrepancies between executives' net worth and public display and lifestyle is an obvious red flag.

When the abuse becomes material, one may start to observe the signs of red flags, when combing through the financial statements as described in Chapter 23. Another way is when scrutinizing public records and adverse media screening described in Sect. 16.4. Also, purpose-built ML models based on text analysis and NLP explained in Sect. 34.3, may be used to detect lifestyle anomalies related to potential fraudulent behavior of the executives in a more systematic way.

### 5.3.2 Third-Party or Stakeholder Benefit of the Abuse of Corporate Assets and Funds

In this case the executive might abuse the power to direct funds to other stakeholders or third-parties. While this is beneficial for the third-party, the executive might not profit directly from it.

The more obvious transactions are huge donations of corporate money to charities or political organizations, where there is no benefit to the corporation and shareholders. It may also be sponsorships to sports or arts, where the corporation has no marketing benefit from the sponsorship.

A final category, which is hard to detect, is vanity deals and contracts to show off as part of the elite. Here executives want to engage with tier one financial institutions or top-notch management consultancies and pay excessive fees and costs. It can also be making excessive deals with first-rate vendors, despite the vendor's services being overkill compared to the size of the corporations and what is needed.

#### 5.3.2.1 Examples of Third-Party Benefits

In the Tyco International case a "finder's fee" to an independent director and chairman of the compensation committee/corporate governance committee is an illustrative example of third-party benefits.

According to The New York Times (2004, January 8) and SEC (2002, December 17), Frank E. Walsh Jr., was a retired investment banker, co-founder and former Principal of the Private Equity Firm, Wesray Capital

Corporation,[2] who got a finder's fee of $20 million for connecting Tyco International Ltd. with The CIT Group Inc. Meanwhile, Walsh had a relationship with Albert R. Gamper Jr., who was the CEO of CIT.

On Tyco's board, Walsh voted in favor of the corporate acquisition of CIT Group but failed to disclose his $20 million finder's fee to the board. According to The Washington Post (2002, December 18), $10 million went into Walsh's own pocket and $10 million went to the charity, the Community Foundation of New Jersey. CBS News (2002, December 18) reported that Walsh pleaded guilty on criminal charges of Securities Fraud. In this case, the third-party charity unwittingly gained from the corporate fraud.

Another example was the privately held crypto exchange company FTX and crypto Hedge fund Alameda Research. According to Popli (2022). The CEO Sam Bankman-Fried donated company money to national and local political parties, both Democratic and Republicans.

#### 5.3.2.2 Detecting Third-Party Benefit from the Corporation

One can scrutinize the financial statements of corporations to try and detect the outflow of funds to third parties. However, scrutinizing financial statements might expose little of the outflow. Instead, one may flip it around and look for the third-party beneficiaries of the fraud. Often these beneficiaries, like charities, political parties and universities must disclose where contributions and donations came from, or the beneficiaries do it voluntarily for ethical reasons. Many times, this often happens in public announcements that should be exposed when doing media screening as explained in Sect. 16.4. Depending on the jurisdictions there might be public record databases or Non-Government Organization databases tracking donations and contributions to various types of entities, like charities, political parties, or universities. For more detail see Sect. 16.3

### 5.3.3 Misappropriation of Clients' Assets or Funds Under Management (Financial Institutions)

In financial institutions, funds and assets might also illegally move from being the clients' property onto the company's balance sheet, by theft of client's

[2] https://www.bloomberg.com/profile/company/0728779D:US.

funds or co-mingling of funds. On the surface, the balance sheet of the company still looks fine. However, it is only because it is propped up with funds belonging to clients.

#### 5.3.3.1 Examples of Misappropriation of Clients' Assets or Funds Under Management

According to legal and public documents referenced below, MF Global Inc. was a brokerage firm listed on the Over-the-counter (OTC) market and OTC Pink market. MF Global made some risky investments in European bonds and engaged in numerous repurchase agreements.

These investment strategies failed and MF Global faced liquidity problems. In an attempt to cover the cash crunch, MF Global improperly transferred customer funds. The co-mingling of customer and corporate funds led to more than a billion-dollar shortfall in customer funds, when the company was declared bankrupt.

Subsequently the MF Global Ltd. holding company were convicted and fined in NY Federal Court for co-mingling according to CFTC (2013, 2014). According to CFTC (2017) Jon S. Corzine was instructed by a New York federal court to pay a fine of $5 million due to his participation in the illicit usage of close to $1 billion of client funds by MF Global. The court has further barred Corzine from any form of registration with the CFTC. The court order also includes a penalty of $500,000 and constraints on employment for Edith O'Brien, a former assistant treasurer of MF Global, for her role assisting illegal utilization of client funds by MF Global.

While there were reports of co-mingling in the days prior to the bankruptcy of MF Global, according to Ahmed et al. (2011) there were speculations amongst investigators that MF Global's co-mingling of customer and corporate funds had happened even months before the bankruptcy.

A more recent case of co-mingling is the 2022 high-profile fraud case against Sam Bankman-Fried in DOJ (2022). The case involves FTX Trading Ltd. and Alameda Research. FTX Trading Ltd. was a cryptocurrency exchange and Alameda Research was a quantitative cryptocurrency trading firm providing liquidity in cryptocurrency and digital assets markets. Both FTX and Alameda were controlled by Sam Bankman-Fried. In addition, Alameda was a market maker for FTX. While these legal entities were not publicly listed companies, they involved illustrative co-mingling of customer funds in an unprecedented way.

As stated in the case by the Department of Justice, funds from customer accounts were misdirected and co-mingled with Alameda Research funds.

$8 billion of customers' funds were used for risky investments by Alameda, other ventures, and personal loans to the executives. Sam Bankman-Fried was found guilty on all seven counts in Manhattan federal court on Nov 2nd, 2023, according to CourtListener (2024, February 27).

#### 5.3.3.2 Detection of Misappropriation of Clients' Assets or Funds Under Management

It can be extremely hard for an outside investor to detect misappropriation of clients' funds directly. A red flag could be when there appears to be lags, halts or extended repayment periods for withdrawing funds.

There might also be other subtle signs. If the financial company suddenly changes bank connection, custody service or auditor, especially all at once, it can be a red flag.

If investment clients start to complain on customer review sites like Trustpilot, or employees voice concerns on places like Glassdoor as mentioned in Sects. 19.5 and 19.7. These might be the first red flags that something is wrong.

An alternative way to sanity check and look for red flags. If the investor is both a shareholder in the financial company, and a client of the financial company. The investor may test sell assets/funds or make free of payment transactions to other financial institutions. If the services take longer than normal, it is a red flag and an indication the financial company might be shuffling things around.

## 5.4 Other Material Corporate Fraudulent Activities

Instead of directly stealing or abusing funds and assets for their own or third-parties' benefit, the corporate executives might abuse their position and control to conduct, facilitate, or condone material fraudulent activities with the help of the company. While both the company and the shareholder may benefit in the short run from this type of corporate fraud, in the long run they will suffer when the fraud is exposed.

This type of fraud may be done in multiple ways. We will look at the two main categories observed. The first is Material misappropriation of corporate funds or assets outside the corporate mandate. The second is Material misappropriation of corporate assets for fraudulent activity.

### 5.4.1 Material Misappropriation of Funds, Assets, or Infrastructure Outside the Corporate Mandate

In the case of misappropriation outside the corporate mandate, the executives use funds or assets outside the boundaries that might be outlined by articles of association, the strategic purpose, or the guidance by the board of directors.

The executives violate their fiduciary responsibility to the shareholder. Think of a CEO of a furniture production company suddenly and covertly engaging in something absolutely unrelated (but not necessarily illegal or loss-making) like real estate investment, without any mandate to do so. This pattern might be seen when the core business is not doing well, and the CEO is trying to make up for it. A furniture production company turned real estate investor is a more clear-cut case. Often these cases are gray zones and borderlines.

#### 5.4.1.1 Examples of Material Misappropriation of Funds, Assets, or Infrastructure Outside the Corporate Mandate

The Japanese Olympus Scandal of 2011 included more types of fraud. One was misappropriation of funds outside the corporate mandate. In the Olympus acquisitions strategy, Olympus bought several questionable entities outside its core business of optical manufacturing. According to Duncan (2011) and Carozza (2012). Especially three specific acquisitions where highly questionable:

- The company *Altis* was primarily engaged in the recycling business for medical waste. This raised questions about its relevance to Olympus's core operations. The field of medical waste recycling is a highly specialized one that necessitates specific expertise and regulatory compliance. With no apparent relation to Olympus's core business of manufacturing optical equipment.
- Two other companies also lacked apparent relations to the optical manufacturing business. *Humalabo*, a company specializing in facial cream production, and *News Chef*, a manufacturer of plastic plates and containers for microwaves.

#### 5.4.1.2 Detection of Material Misappropriation of Funds, Assets, or Infrastructure Outside the Corporate Mandate

One way to detect this type of Corporate Fraud is through monitoring and analyzing Mergers & Acquisitions, direct or indirect investments, Joint Ventures, and Strategic Alliances. Finding unrelated activity outside the mandate is a red flag.

### 5.4.2 Material Misappropriation of Corporate Funds, Assets, or Infrastructure for Fraudulent Activity

Another category are cases where corporate assets, funds or infrastructure are misappropriated for outright fraudulent activities. This could be development projects, or product developments that are material fraudulent in nature.

#### 5.4.2.1 Examples of Material Misappropriation of Corporate Funds, Assets, or Infrastructure for Fraudulent Activity

An example of this is Volkswagen's "Dieselgate." The case is not only mere marketing greenwashing, but more elaborate usage of material misappropriation of assets, funds, and infrastructure for fraudulent activity.

According to FTC (2016, March 29), the "Dieselgate" scandal began when Volkswagen Group of America, Inc. was discovered to have misled consumers with a marketing campaign that touted the environmental friendliness of its "clean diesel" VWs and Audis. Reported by Hotten (2015),VW had installed a "defeat device" in its diesel engines. The software could sense when the vehicles were in the process of emissions testing, and then would adjust the engine's performance to pass the test.

The fallout from this deception was substantial. DOJ (2017, January 11), stated that in the US alone, around 590,000 diesel vehicles were affected. Globally, Volkswagen confessed that approximately 11 million cars, including eight million in Europe, were equipped with the "defeat device."

In the aftermath of the scandal, Volkswagen AG admitted guilt to three felony charges and was fined $2.8 billion. Additionally, the company faced SEC charges for defrauding U.S. investors stated by SEC (2019, March 14).

In response to the scandal, Volkswagen initiated an internal investigation and allocated €6.7bn to cover the associated costs. The company's CEO at the time, Martin Winterkorn, resigned due to the scandal.

#### 5.4.2.2 Detecting Material Misappropriation of Corporate Funds, Assets, or Infrastructure for Fraudulent Activity

This type of material misappropriation may be very hard to detect from an outside point of view by the investors hunting for fraud. E.g. in Dieselgate the investor had to have access to very sophisticated test equipment to sanity check. Alternatively, crack the code of the "defeat device" in the car, and understand the cheat lines.

However, the way the investor might encounter this is through tips from whistleblowers and disgruntled employees. Either directly or indirectly by monitoring or screening online forums like Reddit, Glassdoor, 4chan or darknet sites. In publicly listed companies with hundreds or thousands of employees, these secrets on fraudulent activity are hard to keep a secret forever. They may surface at any time, when disgruntled employees leave or have second thoughts on the fraud they are participating in.

### 5.4.3 Misc. Material Fraud Conduct for Financial Institutions

Especially for Financial Institutions there is a range of possibilities to conduct fraudulent activity that the infrastructure of a financial institution is particularly good suited for.

These types of fraud include self-dealing, front running, insider trading, market manipulation and Ponzi Schemes. This book does not go into detail in these sometimes-sophisticated areas of fraud which may be conducted in the financial industry. Both the company and the employees might benefit from these fraudulent schemes.

#### 5.4.3.1 Example Cases of Material Fraud Conduct for Financial Institutions

- The Frontrunning case of HSBC where Global Head of HSBC's Foreign Exchange Cash-Trading, Mark Johnson was sentenced 24-month in prison according to DOJ (2017, 2018). While HSBC was fined $100 million in 2018, for front running its clients.
- More than 5300 Wells Fargo employees were fired due to systemic fraudulent practices according to BBC (2020) and WSJ (2023). This fraud case of Wells Fargo was running from 2002 till 2016 and may be looked at as a material systematic self-dealing case.

- In an aggressive attempt to create profit growth, bank advisors created new accounts and products that their bank clients did not need. In many cases the clients had not asked for or were even aware they had the specific accounts or products. This was done in a systemic way with knowledge of multiple layers of management. Wells Fargo made a $3 billion settlement, the CEO, several executives, were personally fined, and one got a probationary sentence.

#### 5.4.3.2 Detecting Material Fraud Conduct for Financial Institutions

To detect frontrunning, insider trading and market manipulation, the investor needs to monitor the markets, order books and insider disclosures very intensely. While monitoring media reports for certain keywords of suspicious activity, using tools like described in Sect. 16.4. Also monitoring Open-Source Intelligence (OSINT) sources, like internet forums regarding whistleblowing etc. Or customer complaint sites like Trustpilot for evidence of clients being ripped off in a systematic way.

## References

ACCR. (2023, June 26). *Australasian Centre for Corporate Responsibility Updates Case Against Santos in Federal Court*. Australasian Centre for Corporate Responsibility. Retrieved September 14, 2024, from https://www.accr.org.au/news/australasian-centre-for-corporate-responsibility-updates-case-against-santos-in-federal-court

Ahmed, A., Protess, B., & Craig, S. (2011, December 11). A Romance with Risk That Brought on a Panic. *The New York Times*. Retrieved September 14, 2024, from https://archive.nytimes.com/dealbook.nytimes.com/2011/12/11/a-romance-with-risk-that-brought-on-a-panic/

Allianz. (2021). *Group Financial Results 2021*. Retrieved September 14, 2024, from https://www.allianz.com/content/dam/onemarketing/azcom/Allianz_com/investor-relations/en/results/2021-fy/en-allianz-analyst-presentation-fy-2021.pdf

BBC. (2020, February 21). Wells Fargo Reaches $3bn Fake Accounts Settlement. *BBC News*. Retrieved September 14, 2024, from https://www.bbc.com/news/business-51594117

BBC News. (2011, April 6). Satyam and PwC are Fined in US for Accounting Fraud. Retrieved September 14, 2024, from https://www.bbc.com/news/business-12981738

Bondarenko, P. (2024). Enron Scandal | Summary, Explained, History, & Facts | Britannica. Encyclopedia Britannica. Retrieved September 14, 2024, from https://www.britannica.com/event/Enron-scandal

Carozza, D. (2012, March/April). The Real Cost of 'Choosing Truth Over Self'. *Fraud Magazine*.

CBS News. (2002, December 18). Tyco Dealmaker Admits Fraud. Retrieved September 14, 2024, from https://www.cbsnews.com/news/tyco-dealmaker-admits-fraud/

CFTC. (2013). Press Release Number 6776-13. Retrieved September 14, 2024, from https://www.cftc.gov/PressRoom/PressReleases/6776-13

CFTC. (2014). Press Release Number 7095-14. Retrieved September 14, 2024, from https://www.cftc.gov/PressRoom/PressReleases/7095-14

CFTC. (2017). Press Release Number 7508-17. Retrieved September 14, 2024, from https://www.cftc.gov/PressRoom/PressReleases/7508-17

CourtListener. (2024, February 27). United States v. BANKMAN-FRIED, 1:22-cr-00673. Retrieved September 14, 2024, from https://www.courtlistener.com/docket/66631291/united-states-v-bankman-fried/?page=2

DOJ. (2016, December 19). Platinum Partners' Founder and Chief Investment Officer Among Five Indicted In A $1 Billion Investment Fraud. U.S. Department of Justice. Retrieved September 14, 2024, from https://www.justice.gov/usao-edny/pr/platinum-partners-founder-and-chief-investment-officer-among-five-indicted-1-billion

DOJ. (2017). *Former Global Head of HSBC's Foreign Exchange Cash-Trading Found Guilty of Orchestrating Multimillion-Dollar Front-Running Scheme*. United States Department of Justice. Retrieved September 14, 2024, from https://www.justice.gov/opa/pr/former-global-head-hsbcs-foreign-exchange-cash-trading-found-guilty-orchestrating

DOJ. (2017, January 11). *Volkswagen AG Agrees to Plead Guilty and Pay $4.3 Billion in Criminal and Civil Penalties; Six Volkswagen Executives and Employees Are Indicted in Connection with Conspiracy to Cheat U.S. Emissions Tests*. U.S. Department of Justice. Retrieved September 14, 2024, from https://www.justice.gov/opa/pr/volkswagen-ag-agrees-plead-guilty-and-pay-43-billion-criminal-and-civil-penalties-six

DOJ. (2018). HSBC Holdings Plc Agrees to Pay More Than $100 Million to Resolve Fraud Charges. United States Department of Justice. Retrieved September 14, 2024, from https://www.justice.gov/opa/pr/hsbc-holdings-plc-agrees-pay-more-100-million-resolve-fraud-charges

DOJ. (2019, July 9). Platinum Partners' Founder and CIO Mark Nordlicht and Co-CIO David Levy Convicted of Defrauding Bondholders in a Multi-Million Dollar Scheme. U.S. Department of Justice Retrieved September 14, 2024, from https://www.justice.gov/usao-edny/pr/platinum-partners-founder-and-cio-mark-nordlicht-and-co-cio-david-levy-convicted

DOJ. (2022). U.S. v. Bankman-Fried Indictment. Retrieved September 14, 2024, from https://www.justice.gov/d9/press-releases/attachments/2022/12/13/u.s._v._bankman-fried_indictment_0.pdf

DOJ. (2023). Allianz Global Investors U.S. sentenced in connection with multibillion-dollar fraud scheme. United States Department of Justice. Press Release, July 12, 2023. Retrieved on September 14, 2024, from https://www.justice.gov/usao-sdny/pr/allianz-global-investors-us-sentenced-connection-multibillion-dollar-fraud-scheme

Duncan, G. (2011, October 29). Zooming in on the Olympus scandal. *Digital Trends*. Retrieved September 14, 2024, from https://www.digitaltrends.com/photography/zooming-in-on-the-olympus-scandal/

Flugum, R., & Souther, M. (2023). Stakeholder Value: A Convenient Excuse for Underperforming Managers? *Journal of Financial and Quantitative Analysis (JFQA)*. Retrieved September 14, 2024, from https://ssrn.com/abstract=3725828 or https://doi.org/10.2139/ssrn.3725828

FTC. (2016, March 29). *FTC Charges Volkswagen Deceived Consumers with Its "Clean Diesel" Campaign*. Federal Trade Commission. Retrieved September 14, 2024, from https://www.ftc.gov/news-events/news/press-releases/2016/03/ftc-charges-volkswagen-deceived-consumers-its-clean-diesel-campaign

Hindenburg Research. (2023, May 2). *Icahn Enterprises: The Corporate Raider Throwing Stones from His Own Glass House*. Hindenburg Research. Retrieved September 14, 2024, from https://hindenburgresearch.com/icahn/

Hotten, R. (2015, December 10). Volkswagen: The Scandal Explained. *BBC News*. Retrieved September 14, 2024, from https://www.bbc.com/news/business-34324772

Keeble, J. (2022). What It Will Take for CEOs to Fund a Sustainable Transformation. *Global Sustainability*. Retrieved September 14, 2024, from https://cloud.google.com/blog/topics/sustainability/new-survey-reveals-executives-views-about-sustainability?hl=en

NBC News. (2004, January 21). HealthSouth Fraud Larger Than Estimated. *NBC News*. Retrieved September 14, 2024, from https://www.nbcnews.com/id/wbna4016152

Popli, N. (2022). Here's What We Know About Sam Bankman-Fried's Political Donations. *Time*. Retrieved September 14, 2024, from https://time.com/6241262/sam-bankman-fried-political-donations/

Reprisk. (2023, October). *On the Rise: Navigating the Wave of Greenwashing and Social Washing*. Retrieved September 14, 2024, from https://www.reprisk.com/news-research/reports/on-the-rise-navigating-the-wave-of-greenwashing-and-social-washing

SEC. (2002, December 17). Tyco Former Lead Director and Chairman of Compensation Committee Frank E. Walsh, Jr. Charged with Materially Misleading CIT's and Tyco's Shareholders by Collecting Secret $20 Million "Finder's Fee" in

Connection with Tyco's 2001 Acquisition of The CIT Group, Inc. U.S. Securities and Exchange Commission Retrieved September 14, 2024, from https://www.sec.gov/litigation/litreleases/lr-17896

SEC. (2019, March 14). SEC Charges Volkswagen, Former CEO With Defrauding Bond Investors During "Clean Diesel" Emissions Fraud. U.S. Securities and Exchange Commission. Retrieved September 14, 2024, from https://www.sec.gov/news/press-release/2019-34

SEC. (2022). SEC Charges Allianz Global Investors and Three Former Senior Portfolio Managers with Multibillion Dollar Securities Fraud. Retrieved September 14, 2024, from https://www.sec.gov/news/press-release/2022-84

SEC. (2022, April 28). SEC Charges Brazilian Mining Company with Misleading Investors about Safety Prior to Deadly Dam Collapse. Retrieved September 14, 2024, from https://www.sec.gov/news/press-release/2022-72

SEC. (2023, March 28). Brazilian Mining Company to Pay $55.9 Million to Settle Charges Related to Misleading Disclosures Prior to Deadly Dam Collapse. Retrieved September 14, 2024, from https://www.sec.gov/news/press-release/2023-63

SEC. (2023, September 25). Deutsche Bank Subsidiary DWS to Pay $25 Million for Anti-money Laundering Violations and Misstatements Regarding ESG Investments. Retrieved September 14, 2024, from https://www.sec.gov/news/press-release/2023-194

Setzer, J., & Higham, C. (2021). *Global Trends in Climate Change Litigation: 2021 Snapshot*. Grantham Research Institute on Climate Change and the Environment and Centre for Climate Change Economics and Policy, London School of Economics and Political Science.

Setzer, J., & Higham, C. (2022). *Global Trends in Climate Change Litigation: 2022 Snapshot*. Grantham Research Institute on Climate Change and the Environment and Centre for Climate Change Economics and Policy, London School of Economics and Political Science.

Setzer, J., & Higham, C. (2023). *Global Trends in Climate Change Litigation: 2023 Snapshot*. Grantham Research Institute on Climate Change and the Environment and Centre for Climate Change Economics and Policy, London School of Economics and Political Science.

Storbeck, O. (2023, July). DWS Closes in on Settlement over Greenwashing Scandal. *Financial Times*.

The New York Times. (2004, January 8). Ex-director Explains Fee From Tyco. Retrieved September 14, 2024, from https://www.nytimes.com/2004/01/08/business/exdirector-explains-fee-from-tyco.html

The Washington Post. (2002, December 18). Ex-Director of Tyco Arrested. Retrieved September 14, 2024, from https://www.washingtonpost.com/archive/business/2002/12/18/ex-director-of-tyco-arrested/c2c2a10d-11e8-4129-8d73-c69df36b885a/

U.S. Attorney's Office, Southern District of New York. (2023). Allianz Global Investors U.S. Sentenced In Connection With Multibillion-Dollar Fraud

Scheme. United States Department of Justice. Press Release, July 12, 2023. Retrieved September 14, 2024, from https://www.justice.gov/usao-sdny/pr/allianz-global-investors-us-sentenced-connection-multibillion-dollar-fraud-scheme

U.S. Securities and Exchange Commission. (2002, September 12). SEC v. L. Dennis Kozlowski, Mark H. Swartz and Mark A. Belnick, Civil Action No. 02-CV-7312 (JSR) (S.D.N.Y.). Retrieved September 14, 2024, from https://www.sec.gov/enforcement-litigation/litigation-releases/lr-17722

WSJ. (2023). Why Wells Fargo Is Still Trying to Fix Itself—The Journal. *WSJ Podcasts*. September 19, 2023. Retrieved September 14, 2024, from https://www.wsj.com/podcasts/the-journal/why-wells-fargo-is-still-trying-to-fix-itself/6ff227e9-ef0e-4273-9015-f6fa8347400c

Young, S. (2004, March 12). MCI to State Fraud Was $11 Billion: Final Restatement to Grow. *The Wall Street Journal*. Retrieved September 14, 2024, from https://www.wsj.com/articles/SB107904677290353181

# 6

# The Risk of Corporate Fraud

## 6.1 A Practical Model to Detect Corporate Fraud Risk

Many models trying to determine the risk of fraud exist. However, when it comes to the practical setting of corporate fraud, new inspiration has been found in an old model in the academic field of Institutional Economics, studying inter-firm relationships, trust, and opportunism.

The model was outlined in the 1990s. While the model is not directly built to detect corporate fraud, some of the thoughts behind it have been useful in the practical work and understanding of the risk related to corporate fraud.

The model, developed by Nooteboom (1996) was originally developed to explain opportunistic behavior and trust between entities in inter-firm relationships and risk determinants of opportunistic behavior. Dealing with the general study of whether markets or institutions is the better choice conducting a task.

However, some of the core concepts and thoughts in the Nooteboom model have been observed working with fraud and may be repurposed and applied in the field of corporate fraud risk and detection. The model is extensive and complex and may serve as inspiration and foundation for e.g. ML models to detect fraud. Here the focus is on three core elements of the model, namely Propensity to Opportunism, Incentives to Opportunism, and Opportunities for Opportunism from the original model.

These three core determinants are interesting from the perspective of corporate fraud, and should be kept in mind when screening for, or analyzing


J. Sørensen, *Shorting Fraud*, https://doi.org/10.1007/978-3-031-81834-9_6

potential corporate fraud. The first two are related to the fraudster and the last related to the environment that the fraudster is working in.

## 6.2 The Habit and Tendency of Corporate Fraud

The Propensity to Opportunism is the likelihood or predisposition of an individual to act opportunistically. This is influenced by personal characteristics and traits, such as ethics, morality, and risk tolerance. For instance, an individual with low ethical standards and high-risk tolerance might be more likely to commit fraud, such as embezzling funds or cooking the books.

One of the first things to look for is the existence of a history of fraud, or other dubious activity, related to the CEO or other executives. While it may happen, it is seldom that a CEO one day wakes up 45 years old, and suddenly decides that next quarter she will become a fraudster. Often there have been smaller or bigger signs historically about the CEO, which were problematic, and often successfully hidden. The fraudster might have been so good at manipulating herself to the top and never get caught in the act of lying, or managed to bury the misconduct, through manipulation.

## 6.3 The Temptation and Incentive of Corporate Fraud

Incentives to Opportunism refers to the potential rewards or benefits that might motivate an individual to engage in opportunistic behavior. In the context of corporate fraud, this could be financial gain, career advancement, self-promotion or avoiding negative consequences such as dismissal. The CEO might manipulate a company's financial statements to attract more investors or avoid the investors dumping the shares.

Another determinant is the temptation of fraud. This is harder to detect, since these are the individual circumstances, which the CEO is currently facing which might tempt her to commit the fraud.

On the general level, it could be that the company does not meet earnings expectations from e.g. equity analysts. It may also be historic forward-looking statements or announcements from the company that failed to deliver. It could be on e.g., Mergers & Acquisitions, major development projects, turnarounds and restructuring that failed to deliver on the bottom-line. To-good-to-be-true and lofty expectations that never materialized.

It could also be that the financial performance of the company is interlinked with personal gains like executive remuneration. Alternatively, it could be the financial performance is related directly to the financing needed for expansion, or even just bare cash flow needed for continuation of a going concern.

## 6.4 The Possibility of Corporate Fraud

Opportunities for Opportunism are related to the circumstances or situations that allow opportunistic behavior to occur. In terms of fraud, this risk is related to e.g., weak internal or external controls, lack of oversight, or complex transactions or set-ups that are difficult to understand and monitor.

### 6.4.1 Preventive Mechanisms, Fraud Controls and Mitigation

To close the loopholes and prevent corporate fraud, there are several types of prevention mechanisms in play, like laws and regulation, cultural prevention, corporate controls, mitigating actions and compliance. Enforcement and penalties for violations. These prevention mechanisms involve institutions like Financial Service Authorities, Law Enforcement agencies and stakeholders, like banks, institutional investors, stock exchanges, auditors, and accountants. This third risk determinant is related to the loopholes in the corporate systems and setups allowing the person(s) conduct their fraud.

While there are many rules and regulations across different jurisdictions, set up to prevent and mitigate corporate fraud, fraudsters systematically look for loopholes to be exploited and get away with it.

### 6.4.2 Corporate Complexity and Loopholes

It has been observed that complex corporate systems are a problem with regards to risk, preventing and mitigating corporate fraud.

There are two fundamental ways complexity may be abused by the corporate fraudster. One is to abuse a legitimate complex existing corporate setup. In this case few people internally and externally have a true oversight and understanding of the complex corporate setup. The executives sitting at the top will know this and have the possibility of abusing it.

For instance, a big bank with tens of thousands of employees, and thousands of financial products, thousands of IT-systems and thousands of departments is hard to get an actual oversight of. This lack of oversight, by internal and external auditors or the Financial Services Authorities, may be abused by corporate fraudsters.

A second way to abuse complexity in corporate fraud has also been observed. The fraudster might intentionally build an overly complex system, which is extremely hard to understand, for anyone other than the fraudster(s). A corporate setup which is built with the purpose to commit fraud. A deeper discussion of corporate fraud and complexity theory is conducted in Sect. 7.2.

## 6.5 A Rudimentary Corporate Fraud Risk Calculation

For simplicity and as a starting point, taking parts of the Nooteboom model and repurposing it to work with the risk of corporate fraud. Say that the core risk of corporate fraud could be based on three, (assumed) independent probabilities, together representing a corporate fraud risk, using the joint probability of independent factors with the multiplication rule.

$$P(T \cap I \cap P) = P(T) \cdot P(I) \cdot P(P) \tag{6.1}$$

P(T), P(I), and P(P) represent the probabilities of three independent factors: (T), (I), and (P).

Where:

T: is the tendency to conduct corporate fraud

I: is the incentive to conduct corporate fraud

P: is the possibility to conduct corporate fraud

A corporate fraud risk example:

Let us assume we find that a CEO has committed fraud in all companies she has worked for in her career, then the P(T) = 1. Her current corporation is not doing too well with no feasible way out, so her incentive is high to commit fraud—P(I) = 0.9. At the same time, the board of directors is weak, with little external oversight and controls stopping the CEO conducting a fraud, so P(P) = 0.8

$$P(T \cap I \cap P) = P(T) \cdot P(I) \cdot P(P) = 1 \cdot 0.9 \cdot 0.8 = 0.72 \tag{6.2}$$

In this example there is a 72% chance that the CEO will commit corporate fraud once again. This probability equation is always good to be mindful of when working with corporate fraud. You may use it with subjective probabilities or develop more elaborate models based on diverse types of data supporting the individual probability of each of the three factors. Of course, more elaborate models with dependence between the independent factors could be discussed. Like will the possibility of fraud affect the tendency and similar.

## Reference

Nooteboom, B. (1996). Trust, Opportunism and Governance: A Process and Control Model. *Organization Studies, 17*(6), 985–1010. Retrieved September 14, 2024, from https://pure.uvt.nl/ws/portalfiles/portal/955820/TRUST___.PDF

# 7

# The Time Dimension of Corporate Fraud

## 7.1 Compounding Interest of Fraud—Growth and Collapse of Corporate Fraud

Time is an interesting factor in a Corporate Fraud sense. From the time the crime is committed, first signs emerge, till the fraud is eventually exposed and the company collapses have some similarities. Some patterns might be similar, but the timeframe and timing will vary.

Look at the corporate fraud as removing something from a system and pretending it is still there. Or adding something to a system that was never there in the first place. No matter which way you look at it, something is off. Often the fraudster is of the opinion that what is missing can be put back again, or the fraudster can make up for what was never there in the first place by somehow adding it in the future.

The problem is that when the fraudster removed something from the system, she dug a special hole. The hole is not a normal one-to-one relationship hole. The fraudster thinks she can dig the hole and fill it with the same amount of stuff she dug out. Take some cash from the register and put it back later. However, corporate fraud holes often grow bigger on their own. Most obvious in Ponzi like setups, which are mathematically unsustainable, which means a constant inflow of new investors to cover the hole, until it is not feasible anymore and the scheme collapses. Artzrouni (2009) explains how this works in detail.

However, even frauds that do not constitute a pyramid structure or are exponential in nature might also dig their own holes deeper due to compounding interest.



J. Sørensen, *Shorting Fraud*, https://doi.org/10.1007/978-3-031-81834-9_7

Even a one-time embezzlement case might grow bigger over time due to the original "hole" of misappropriation growing. Hence time is not only an enemy to the fraudster because of the risk that she will be exposed by auditors, regulators, etc. Holes must be covered, and it is often only possible to do so by fraudsters digging new, and often deeper holes, covering the old holes.

In a simplified view. This is like the future value of a series of cash flows, which can be calculated using the formula for the future value of an annuity.

The annuity is the amount embezzled each year, and the future value represents the total amount missing from the firm, including the returns that would have been earned on the embezzled funds, using the return on equity. The future value (FV) of the embezzled funds can be calculated as follows:

The formula for the future value of an annuity is:

$$FV = \mathcal{P} \times \left( \frac{(1+r)^n - 1}{r} \right) \tag{7.1}$$

where:

**P** is the amount embezzled each year,

**r** is the Return on Equity (ROE), and

**n** is the number of years.

This can be illustrated in two simplified illustrative scenarios running over 15 years. Scenario 1, the fraudster takes $100 in year one. Scenario 2, the fraudster takes $10 each year over the period.

**Scenario 1: $100 is embezzled in year one only.**

In this case, the future value of the embezzled funds is calculated as the future value of a single sum, not an annuity, because the embezzlement occurs only once. The formula for the future value of a single sum is:

$$FV = P \times (1+r)^n \tag{7.2}$$

So, the future value of the $100 embezzled after 5, 10, and 15 years with and r = 12% would be:

After 5 years:

$$FV_5 = 100 \times (1+0.12)^5 \approx 176.2 \tag{7.3}$$

After 10 years:

$$FV_{10} = 100 \times (1+0.12)^{10} \approx 310.5 \tag{7.4}$$

After 15 years:

$$FV_{15} = 100 \times (1 + 0.12)^{15} \approx 547.3 \tag{7.5}$$

**Scenario 2: $10 is embezzled each year.**

In this case, we use the formula for the future value of an annuity because the embezzlement occurs each year. So, the future value of the $10 embezzled each year after 5, 10, and 15 years would be:

After 5 years:

$$FV_5 = 10 \times \left( \frac{(1 + 0.12)^5 - 1}{0.12} \right) \approx 68.64 \tag{7.6}$$

After 10 years:

$$FV_{10} = 10 \times \left( \frac{(1 + 0.12)^{10} - 1}{0.12} \right) \approx 235.30 \tag{7.7}$$

After 15 years:

$$FV_{15} = 10 \times \left( \frac{(1 + 0.12)^{15} - 1}{0.12} \right) \approx 658.4 \tag{7.8}$$

As one can see from the two scenarios. It is not only the original funds misappropriated, but what they would have incurred of interest. This is one of the reasons that fraudsters must make elaborate schemes to cover the holes by moving internal funds around, cooking the books or similar tactics.

While these examples are simplistic in nature it illustrates the fundamental problem, that time always works against the fraudster.

### 7.1.1 The Corporate Fraud Collapse and Bankruptcies

To relate this to the real world of corporations. In 2020, the Swedish credit reference agency, UC (2021) found that amongst all bankruptcies in Swedish corporations (listed/unlisted) about 33% were related to fraudulent activities.

This means in Sweden, which is considered one of the least corrupt countries in the world according to Transparency International (2022), there is a high degree of association between bankruptcies and Corporate Fraud. This is consistent with a similar study by the Swedish Enforcement Agency, Kronofogden (KFM). KFM (2010) found that in 2009, of 5572 general bankruptcy cases, 1962 (35%) resulted in a criminal action.

In Norway, another low corruption country, bankruptcies studies by Langli (1994) and Langli (1995) show up to two thirds of bankruptcies may be related to crime. In Germany, also a low corruption country, research conducted by Liebl (1988) and Weyand (1998) shows numbers even higher. Up to 90% of bankruptcies may be related to crime.

It has two implications for chasing corporate fraud. First, at some points the holes dug by fraud cannot be covered anymore and the corporation collapses into bankruptcies.

Second, with a significant portion of bankruptcies related to crime or fraud. OSINT on historic bankruptcies and natural persons and legal entities relations to historic bankruptcies is a major risk red flag when uncovering corporate fraud.

It means bankruptcies are a crucial factor to bear in mind for the investor, when analyzing legal entities and natural persons relations. Regardless if it is e.g. adverse media screening in Sect. 16.4, screening public record activity of corporate officers in Sect. 16.3, the deep-dive due diligence in Chapter 17 or network analysis in Chapter 28.

## 7.2 Complexity Theory and the Corporate Collapse

Complexity theory explains how complex systems and events emerge, grow and collapse. Besides avalanches, upon which we already have touched. These complex systems may be naturally occurring phenomena like living organisms, Earth's crust, the tectonic plates, their movements, earthquakes, and volcano activity (lithosphere), the earth's climate and weather systems, deep sea ecosystems, etc.

In parallel to complex natural systems, mankind has also created complex systems. Examples are agricultural systems, infrastructure, and transportation systems. Our entity of interest in relation to corporate fraud is the corporation, which may also be studied as a complex system, consisting of many interrelated parts. The collapse of a complex corporate system due to fraud is our main interest related to fraud shorting.

Explaining the entire scientific field of complexity theory is outside the scope of this book. For a general digestive introduction, Lewin (1992) is suggested. Furthermore, background on unstable and collapsing complex systems may be found in many works including e.g. Capra and Luisi (2014) and Gimzewski et al. (2016) From these major works a general overview of the key concepts from Complexity theory, and their relevance and specific relation to the collapse of the company, and fraud shorting are outlined in Table 7.1.

## 7.3 Corporate Fraud and Survivorship Bias

During World War II, statisticians studied the damage patterns on returning bomber planes. They did so with the aim of reinforcing the areas on the planes most frequently hit.

Wald (1943) realized they only saw the planes that made it back. The airplanes hit in the least damaged areas were the ones that did not return but were shot down. These areas on the downed planes were the areas that needed actual strengthening.

This survivorship bias insight is particularly important with regards to corporate fraud, since only the tip of the corporate fraud iceberg is actually revealed to the public. Looking at the tip of the iceberg, the main focus is on those fraudsters who got caught, ignoring the large number of enterprises and fraudsters going undetected.

There are many learnings from the big corporate scandal cases that make it to the public eye. However, they are only part of the picture.

While these high-profile cases are subsequently studied by academia, some corporate frauds do not surface at all. These fraud phantom companies are not being studied by academia but are quietly handled outside the public eye. Like the warplanes shut down, these corporate frauds are never studied, and may skew the research, be a dark number in the statistics, and lead to wrong conclusions. Therefore, the investor should know about this.

- Many fraudulent companies are shut down in the early stages by external stakeholders, without the involvement of authorities. Long before they grow and become a public company. This means that the repetitive fraudster will try again, with a new setup, new stakeholders, learning from her previous failure, coming back even stronger.
- Many fraud cases are quietly wound down, masked as bankruptcies as described in Sect. 7.1.1.
- The Corporate Fraud is hidden in Mergers & Acquisitions (M&A) activity. A prominent example is "Project Panther". Wirecard's desperate and failed

**Table 7.1** The key concepts of complexity theory and their relations to fraud induced corporate collapse

| Key concept | General complexity theory | Corporate collapse due to fraud example |
|---|---|---|
| Networks | Complex systems involve networks of interconnected elements. The structure of these networks influences how the system behaves | A fraudulent corporation often fosters a complex network of individuals and legal entities (executives, employees, shell companies, etc.) engaged in dubious activities. These networks allow for the concealment of wrongdoing and make fraud detection cumbersome |
| Observability | In complex systems, complete observability is often impossible. Many internal interactions remain hidden | The legitimate complex corporate system can be hard to observe and understand even for insiders. In the case of the fraudulent complex corporate system, it is even harder. With Fictitious transactions, manipulated accounts, and concealed risk exposure that tie various parts of the corporate system together in ways that are obscure, the true state of the complex system is intentionally hidden from the investors |
| Growth patterns | Complex systems often exhibit non-linear growth patterns, marked by sudden bursts, plateaus, or even chaotic fluctuations that defy simple prediction | A genuine complex corporate system, a gradual growth. That could be logarithmic (slowing growth), S-curve starting with slow growth, then enters a period of rapid expansion, followed by a leveling off as the market matures. Corporate Frauds often see suspicious linear growth or unbelievable exponential growth |

(continued)

**Table 7.1** (continued)

| Key concept | General complexity theory | Corporate collapse due to fraud example |
|---|---|---|
| Nonlinearity | Complex systems often do not respond in a proportional way to changes. Major changes might have negligible effect, while seemingly minor ones can trigger massive shifts | The escalating deception: It might start with small deceptions and fraudulent practices being tolerated initially. This leads to an illusion of stability in the complex corporate system. However, the fraudulent acts gradually escalate out of control as the consequences are not immediately severe or visible |
| Feedback Loops | Feedback loops occur when outputs of a system loop back as inputs. This either amplifies changes (positive feedback loops) or dampens them down (negative feedback loops) | Fraud Reinforcement: Early successes in covering up fraud can breed a false sense of invincibility, leading to more bold and risky behavior (positive feedback). At the same time, attempts to manage the complexity of the fraudulent complex corporate system might introduce more errors and complications, further destabilizing the system (negative feedback) |
| Resilience | This is the ability of a complex system to survive disturbances and maintain its core functions | Phantom Resilience: A fraudulent complex corporate system lacks true resilience. While it might endure some challenges, its foundation is fundamentally compromised, making it fragile under pressure |
| Phase transitions | Complex systems may shift abruptly between different states or phases. Like water boiling or water freezing | Fraud Scandal Trigger: A sudden regulatory investigation, a whistleblower report, short seller report or a market swing can trigger a rapid change in the complex corporate system's state—going from perceived stability to scandal and collapse. |

(continued)

**Table 7.1** (continued)

| Key concept | General complexity theory | Corporate collapse due to fraud example |
|---|---|---|
| Brittleness | Complex systems that appear stable might be remarkably fragile to specific types of shocks or changes | Deceptive Vulnerability: The complex structure of lies and deceit makes the system very vulnerable to certain triggers. Something as insignificant event like misfiling a single document could unravel the entire facade |
| Tipping points | Tipping points are thresholds and points of no return within a system where an insignificant change triggers an irreversible and drastic shift | Fraud Threshold: There is often a point at which the weight of fraudulent activity and the pressure to keep it hidden reach a breaking point. Regulatory action, the discovery of evidence, or the confession of a participant can create that final nudge into a cascade of failure |
| Adaptation potential | Complex systems possess the potential to adapt and reconfigure themselves in response to changing environments or internal disruptions | Little of no Adaptation potential in the fraudulent complex corporate system. There is often little or no room for adaptation. The fraudster is often locked into the original scheme, and cannot pivot, without revealing the true nature of the fraud. The fraudster is captured by her own fraudulent success |
| Cascading failures/Domino effect | The collapse of one element in a highly interconnected system can trigger a domino effect throughout the whole network. | The Corporate Implosion: As the fraud unravels, panic sets in. Key players and stakeholders attempt to shift blame or flee. Investors rush to withdraw funds, and the corporation implodes in a devastating chain reaction |

takeover of Deutsche Bank, with the assistance of McKinsey & Co., reported by Storbeck (2020)

- Some get away with transitory fraud, continue normal operations and have success subsequently. If the fraud is eventually revealed, the statute of limitations is expired, nobody but historians and investigative journalists will have an interest in the case.

As a practitioner, several corporate fraud cases have been observed that never made it to the public or were picked up by the authorities. Sometimes they were shut down in their initial stages because of the elevated risk of fraud. Also observed a corporation rejected, because of substantial risk of fraud, then the corporation moved on to the next financial institution, and two years later, were exposed as a major fraud scandal.

Therefore, it is important that the investor has survivorship bias on the radar when investigating and analyzing corporate fraud.

Furthermore, when the investor builds statistical tools and ML models. If the investor trains models with publicly known fraud case data sets, they may in some cases only be looking at the tip of the iceberg.

The investor must bear in mind that some of the false positives an ML model detects, might not be false positives, but false negatives. They are actual undetected fraud cases that no human mind could detect. A situation that has been experienced working hands-on with ML models.

## References


Artzrouni, M. (2009). The Mathematics of Ponzi Schemes. *Mathematical Social Sciences, 58*(2), 190–201.

Capra, F., & Luisi, P. L. (2014). *The Systems View of Life: A Unifying Vision.* Cambridge University Press.

Gimzewski, J. K., Stieg, A. Z., & Vesna, V. (2016). Self-Organization and Emergence of Dynamic Systems. In W. Bainbridge & M. Roco (Eds.), *Handbook of Science and Technology Convergence*. Springer.

KFM. (2010). *Temagranskning brottsanmälningar i konkurs 2010.* Kronofogden. Retrieved September 14, 2024, from https://web.archive.org/web/20180422205205/http://kronofogden.se/download/18.6f6dad1813c5c1430f6800020352/1371144398605/Temagranskning_brottsanm%C3%A4lningar_i_konkurs_2010.pdf

Langli, J. C. (1994). *Konkurskriminalitet: en empirisk analyse av aksjeselskaper som har gått konkurs* (Vol. 71). Handelshøyskolen BI.

Langli, J. C. (1995). *Illegal regnskapsmanipulasjon: årsaker og konsekvenser ved konkurser* (Vol. 11). Handelshøyskolen BI.

Lewin, R. (1992). *Complexity: Life at the Edge of Chaos.* Macmillan Publishing Company.

Liebl, K. (1988). Geplante Konkurse?: Prüfung d. Vorhersehbarkeit e. Konkurses u. Konkursanalysen anhand einschlägiger Bankrottverfahren in d. Bundesrepublik Deutschland (2nd ed.). Pfaffenweiler: Centaurus-Verl.-Ges. ISBN: 978-3-89085-183-9

Storbeck, O. (2020). Wirecard: The Frantic Final Months of a Fraudulent Operation. *Financial Times*. Retrieved September 14, 2024, from https://www.ft.com/content/6a660a5f-4e8c-41d5-b129-ad5bf9782256

Transparency International. (2022). *2022 Corruption Perceptions Index*. Retrieved September 14, 2024, from https://www.transparency.org/en/cpi/2022

UC. (2021). Bygg-, bemannings- och fastighetsservicebranschen överrepresenterade bland företagsbedrägerier [Press release] 15 February, 2012. Retrieved September 14, 2024, from https://web.archive.org/web/20240107093214/https://www.uc.se/pressartiklar/pressrelease/3073539---Bygg--bemannings--och-fastighetsservicebranschen-%C3%B6verrepresenterade-bland-f%C3%B6retagsbedr%C3%A4gerier/?c=UC%20or

Wald, A. (1943). A Method of Estimating Plane Vulnerability Based on Damage of Survivors. Statistical Research Group, Columbia University. CRC 432—Reprint from July 1980. Center for Naval Analyses. Retrieved September 14, 2024, from https://web.archive.org/web/20190713234912/https://apps.dtic.mil/dtic/tr/fulltext/u2/a091073.pdf

Weyand, R. (1998). *Insolvenzdelikte: Unternehmenszusammenbruch und Strafrecht* (4th ed.). Erich Schmidt.

# Part III

## Screening Markets and Companies for Corporate Fraud

# 8

# Screening and Detecting the Fraudulent Publicly Listed Company

## 8.1 The Proactive Approach to Corporate Fraud Detection

Finding fraudulent companies starts by proactively looking for them. It is a change of mindset. The interaction the investor has with the surroundings on investments is about spotting the often-tiny clues, the negligence of facts hidden in plain sight, anomalies and things that simply do not logically add up. This mindset will eventually lead to fraudulent companies.

Though an investor or shareholder does not have direct access to look inside a corporation and what happens on a day-to-day basis, publicly listed companies are by law required to publicize certain information about the state of the company. The details of information vary with jurisdiction and listing exchange, but normally include quarterly and yearly results and significant events as a minimum.

Depending on the jurisdiction, other required interactions between the corporation and its surroundings, like import/export documents, legal documents, tax/vat documents, patent applications, etc. are publicly available for the outsider to scrutinize.

All these publicly available quantitative and qualitative data points might be used to screen, detect, and later examine in depth for signs of fraudulent activity.

With potentially 8000 of 60,000 listed companies conducting material fraud there is a need for systematic methods and models of screening. Also, the individual investor cannot target each company proactively at once. There needs to be a prioritization of target companies.


J. Sørensen, *Shorting Fraud*, https://doi.org/10.1007/978-3-031-81834-9_8

## 8.2 Fraud Investment Target Case Assessment and Selection

From the fraud short investment perspective, we are interested in realizing the highest possible Corporate Fraud Exposure Capital Gains at the lowest possible costs. This means we are interested in companies with the highest probability and amount of material fraud tied to their market capitalization.

At the same time, we are interested in the companies that cost the least to investigate. In addition, we are interested in the listed companies where it is easiest to open a short campaign and execute that campaign successfully and profitably. For this we can create an illustrative simplified ***Corporate Fraud Risk Index (CFRI).***

$$CFRI = \frac{P \times F \times N}{C} \times I \tag{8.1}$$

where:

- **P**: Probability of material fraud. This assesses the likelihood of significant fraudulent activity based on historical data, red flags in financial reports, management behavior, and industry risks.
- **F**: Fraction of the market capitalization related to fraud. This estimates the portion of the company's valuation potentially compromised by fraud, indicating the relative severity of the issue.
- **N**: Total nominal value of the company's market cap. This factor provides context for the potential magnitude of the fraud impact based on the overall company size. The nominal value has an impact on how the corporate fraud is perceived from the market and general society.
- **C**: Expected cost to analyze the company. This includes the expenses involved in a potential fraud investigation, such as hiring experts, conducting data analysis, acquiring, cleaning, aggregating, and analyzing data, etc.
- **I**: Instrument factor. This factor represents the cost, accessibility, and efficiency associated with the specific financial instruments or strategies required to realize a Corporate Fraud Exposure Capital Gain. Not all fraud targets are created equal, from a stock market perspective. Depending on jurisdiction, exchange, liquidity of the individual company or margin requirements, the costs to conduct the fraud short might vary across potential targets. This should also be taken into consideration when choosing targets. Considerations for the instrument factor include:

- **Market and Instrument accessibility:** The ease of acquiring or utilizing the necessary financial instruments.
- **Liquidity:** The ability to buy or sell the instruments quickly and at a fair price.
- **Costs/Fees:** Transaction fees, borrowing costs, margin requirements, or other expenses associated with using the instruments.

**How the CFRI Works:**

1. **Core Fraud Assessment:** The numerator in Eq. 8–1 including P, F, N is related to the benefit from the direct fraud short investment. While the denominator C is the direct fraud analytic costs related to the fraud short investment. The higher the numerator (benefits) are relative to the denominator (analytical costs), the higher the Corporate Fraud Index is, and the more attractive the company is with regards to fraud shorting.
2. **Instrument Adjustment:** The instrument factor (I) modifies the core CFRI to reflect the realities of the investment strategy:
   - **I < 1:** High instrument costs, limited accessibility, or low liquidity decrease the CFRI. These are cases where it will be hard to make the campaign. Legal boundaries, smaller companies without an efficient traded derivatives market
   - **I = 1:** Neutral scenario, no impact on the CFRI.
   - **I > 1:** Cases where the financial instruments offer exceptional advantages or leverage increase the CFRI. These are cases where there are plentitudes of financial instruments suitable for the campaign available off the shelf. Think major listed companies on major exchanges that might have a plentitude of liquid financial instruments attached to them.

The simplifications by such an index of course have some implications, which might be questioned. The CFRI's heavy weighting of market capitalization (N) might cause it to overlook smaller companies engaged in substantial fraudulent activities, even though these could offer significant Corporate Fraud Exposure Capital Gains. However, it appears that the bigger the company the bigger the scandal and media exposure. Media exposure is relevant with regards to the fraud exposure part of the investment strategy.

While the instrument factor (I) attempts to address the complexities of executing a short campaign, it might oversimplify the nuances associated with different financial instruments, market regulations, and some potential risks of short selling.

To illustrate CFRI let us look at two practical example scenarios:

**Scenario 1: High CFRI, Favorable Short Opportunity**

Company X, a well-known technology firm, exhibits several red flags:

- **P (Probability of Fraud):** High. Whistleblower allegations and inconsistencies in financial reporting suggest a strong likelihood of fraudulent activities.
- **F (Fraction of Market Cap):** Moderate. The suspected fraudulent activities seem to be concentrated in a specific business unit, representing about 30% of the company's market capitalization.
- **N (Market Cap):** High. Company X is a large-cap stock with significant market value.
- **C (Cost to Analyze):** Moderate. While some investigation is needed, publicly available information and media coverage provide a good starting point.
- **I (Instrument Factor):** High. Company X is listed on a major exchange with ample liquidity and a variety of financial instruments available for short selling.

In this scenario, the CFRI would be relatively high due to the combination of a high probability of fraud, a significant portion of market cap affected, and favorable analytical costs and instrument conditions. This suggests that Company X could be an attractive target for a fraud-focused short seller.

**Scenario 2: Low CFRI, Less Attractive Opportunity**

Company Y, a small pharmaceutical company, shows some signs of suspicious activity:

- **P (Probability of Fraud)**: Moderate. There are rumors of data manipulation in clinical trials, but concrete evidence is limited.
- **F (Fraction of Market Cap)**: High. The potential fraud appears to be widespread, affecting the company's core drug development platform, which represents a significant portion (e.g., 60–70%) of its market capitalization.
- **N (Market Cap)**: Low. Company Y is a relatively small company with limited market capitalization.
- **C (Cost to Analyze)**: High. Investigating the allegations would require significant resources and expertise in pharmaceutical research.
- **I (Instrument Factor)**: Low. Company Y has a low trading volume and limited options for short selling.

In this case, the CFRI would be relatively low. The moderate probability of fraud, lower nominal market cap, high investigation costs, and unfavorable instrument conditions make Company Y a less attractive target for fraud-focused short selling, despite the presence of some red flags and a high fraction of market cap affected.

## 8.3 Corporate Fraud Detection Frameworks from Simple to Advanced

Like everything else in life, the Keep It Simple Stupid or KISS-concept applies to building Corporate Fraud Detection Frameworks. How advanced the framework will be will depend on the investor's:

- Financial resources
- Investment scope
- Risk appetite
- Current competence level

The investor might start out with a simple detection framework with some basic financial metrics and ratios related to corporate fraud, and gradually evolve into using highly advanced ML models and AI.

When designing the framework, the investor must choose between which tasks should be conducted by humans and which tasks should be conducted by machines. With the two extremes of an all-human strategy at one end, and an (almost) all machine strategy at the other end.

## 8.4 Tips, Rumors and Crowdsourcing—A Simple and Cheap Way to Detect Fraud Targets

Sometimes the simple solution is the cheapest. The investor does not find the fraud targets but let the fraud targets find the investor.

*Three may keep a secret, if two of them are dead.* (Franklin, 1733–1758)

It is human nature that people may have a hard time keeping secrets. Especially if they have inner conflicts about the secret, which would be natural with a corporate fraud case. In bigger corporate fraud cases insider employees, as well as all types of external stakeholders might have suspicions that something is wrong, long before any investor.

These people might then tip or blow the whistle to authorities. If the authorities for some reason fail to listen or act, these people might vent their frustrations on social media platforms, tip ordinary media or activist short sellers directly. These whistleblowers might be disgruntled employees out for revenge, or they feel a moral obligation to expose the fraud, but do not dare to expose it themselves in public.

It has been observed that many activist short sellers have set up tipping forms on their websites and this way harvest tips on potential targets.

In a more advanced setup, the investor may either manually, or with automatic scraping and analytical tools to monitor social media for discussions and tips of suspicious companies and potential corporate frauds.

Here is of course the legal and ethical problem with regards to insider trading the investor must be aware of. Is the investor acting on material inside information, obtained from an insider? The legal implications will vary across jurisdictions, so the investor should always consult local legal representation before using and acting on such information or setting up such scraping or tipping tools.

## 8.5 Too-Good-to-Be-True Business Fairy Tales

Another simple and relatively cheap way to detect fraud targets is following business news stories. Like many ordinary investors do anyway. The difference is reading the news stories as the devil's advocate, from a fraudulent point of view. Instead of skimming for the next big thing, the investor looks for the next big collapse.

The author has found several corporate fraud cases by simply reading news stories and watching features on specific companies. Stories that everybody can find in mainstream or niche business media.

When an investor has read thousands of business stories, some stories just stand out from the rest as suspicious. It is not like the business feature says this is a fraudulent corporation, often on the contrary. It is more that things do not add up. At first it might be a very tiny detail, which does not make logical business sense. Like a fast-growing phone app business model, targeting an African country where there is no possibility to download the app, and an extremely low diffusion of smartphones.

Such a strange, small detail encourages the fraud short investor to dig deeper into the business, research, dismantle and take the business apart piece by piece to scrutinize each of the pieces.

Besides the narrative itself is too good to be true, it often is centered around a product or service, which is often claimed to revolutionize the world. It might also be centered around the story of the founder or CEO of the company, for example depicted as a David vs. Goliat story, or the CEO as the savior of mankind, on a hero's journey of redemption.

Priming is a phenomenon in psychology, originating from Lashley (1951) when encountering one stimulus affects an individual's reaction to a later, related stimulus. The informational setup may have created a bias in our understanding of subsequent situations.

In many cultures, fairy tales, folktales, bedtime stories, novels and films are part of a deeply rooted cultural fabric. These narratives often follow some specific basic structures, which may be abused as priming in corporate frauds. Many corporate frauds may follow fairy-tale or folktale narratives that have been embedded in us as children and are wired into our brain. This means we may easily accept them with no questions asked.

One example is the rags to riches, where the ugly duckling turns into a swan, where we root for the underdog who succeeds against all odds. While times have changed, the underlying narrative is the same, but it might be woven into politically correct recent major themes that the public immediately resonates with—like the diversity agenda or the sustainability agenda.

Modern day investments even adopted the fairy-tale animal the Unicorn. Everybody in investments knows that a Unicorn is a startup that is valued at $1 billion.

Forbes crowned Elizabeth Holmes in 2014 the world's youngest self-made woman billionaire.[1] Holmes, a young female dropout. Her story was seen as a classic "rags to riches" tale, as she dropped out of Stanford to start Theranos, a company that promised to revolutionize healthcare. However, it was later revealed that the technology she touted did not work, leading to her downfall and conviction of corporate fraud.

Similarly, the Forbes 30 under 30 candidate in 2019, Charlie Javice, founder of the company *Frank*, was promoted as a successful entrepreneur.[2] She started a company that aimed to make college more affordable for students. Her story could be seen as an "ugly duckling" tale, as she was a

[1] http://web.archive.org/web/20141002032854/https://www.forbes.com/profile/elizabeth-holmes/.

[2] http://web.archive.org/web/20201124045448/https://www.forbes.com/profile/charlie-javice/.

young female entrepreneur in a field dominated by established companies, where she succeeded against all odds by selling her company to JP Morgan.

However, subsequently JP Morgan sued Charlie Javice accusing her of inflating number of users before the sale, as reported by Franklin (2023). Later, Ms. Javice was also indicted by the DOJ on multiple counts of fraud according to DOJ (2023, April 4). Ms. Javice has pled not guilty, released on bail, awaiting trial, at the time of writing.

Another interesting case is the Wirecard Fraud case described in more detail in Sect. 29.1.3. Here Markus Braun, the CEO of the Wirecard Fraud case was known as the German Steve Jobs. Markus Braun was the person that Germany desired. The German business success stories were mostly decades old at the time. A new fintech growth company like Wirecard was exactly what Germany needed. They needed it so much that most investors and financial authorities turned a blind eye to the red flags of the fraud for decades.

Another example from Norway is the fraud case of Waleed Ahmed, a 19-year-old juvenile, referred to as Norway's Zuckerberg by the national TV-station and featured in NRK (2023) where Ahmed appeared as a rising star on the startup scene.

Ahmed first hoodwinked the Minister of Trade, Trond Giske. Giske gave Ahmed a six-digit startup grant for a solar-powered mobile phone cover, which would charge itself by light. Something that Ahmed claimed to have invented. In addition, Giske promoted Ahmed publicly, so Ahmed became a media darling. This despite the phone cover Giske got from Ahmed did not work and was not Ahmed's invention. Later in an interview with the Minister of Trade for a TV Documentary by Zentropa (2021), the Minister of Trade acknowledged that the story was so well suited they were uncritical. It was the success story they "needed"—a young, ethnic minority entrepreneur with a green invention. This is another example of people wanting to believe in a politically correct narrative without fact checking anything, which is commonly abused by corporate fraudsters.

## 8.6 Creating a Systematic Detection Framework to Spot Potential Fraud Targets

While the two previous methods might get potential fraud targets on the investor's radar in a cheap and simple way, covering all the 60,000 publicly listed companies in a systematic way is another undertaking. Naturally, it will take more effort and insight to build up such a framework.

The next chapters will focus on some of the potential building blocks of such a corporate fraud screening framework. These building blocks will look at and screen e.g. abnormal:

- Stock market activity related to the corporations.
- Financial statements and reports from the corporations.
- Official public statements and disclosures from corporations.
- Other activity related to the corporations.
- Corporate Governance factors of the corporations.
- Network relationships and structures of the corporations.
- Adverse media related fraud signals of the corporations.

The above building blocks of the screening process and following chapters are not necessarily to be conducted in the order presented.

While having as many areas covered when screening for potentially fraudulent activity should be a goal, there are often practical limitations with each investor.

Depending on the jurisdictions and market venues that the investor works in, some of the screening areas and chapters might not be widely accessible or possible. Another limitation that the investor might face is limited skilled specialist staff to help build the framework. So, an individual situational approach is needed to design and develop the framework, to suit the individual investor.

## References

DOJ. (2023, April 4). Former Start-Up CEO Charged In $175 Million Fraud. U.S. Department of Justice. Retrieved September 14, 2024, from https://www.justice.gov/usao-sdny/pr/former-start-ceo-charged-175-million-fraud

Franklin, B. (1733–1758). Poor Richard's Almanack.

Franklin, J. (2023). JPMorgan Claims Frank Founder Told Staff to Overstate User Numbers. *Financial Times*. Retrieved September 23, 2024, from https://www.ft.com/content/3191f614-8fd6-478b-b9ab-00db3f838b7c

Lashley, K. S. (1951). The Problem of Serial Order in Behavior. In L. A. Jeffress (Ed.), *Cerebral Mechanisms in Behavior; the Hixon Symposium* (pp. 112–146). Wiley.

NRK. (2023). *Waleed Ahmed*. Retrieved September 14, 2024, from https://web.archive.org/web/20240000000000*/https://www.nrk.no/emne/waleed-ahmed-1.11046697

Zentropa. (2021). Trust Me—The Story of Waleed Ahmed [TV Documentary] (timestamp 19 minutes:32 seconds). Retrieved September 14, 2024, from https://www.imdb.com/title/tt13238680/

# 9

# Screening Abnormal Market Activity for Potential Fraud Indicators

## 9.1 Market Indicators of Potential Corporate Fraud

Multiple market indicators might show before the collapse of a fraudulent company. Ranging from up to a few years before, down to months, weeks, or days.

Indicators that may come months or years before the collapse could be insiders or related parties selling shares, knowing that the company is unsustainable, and the fraud will eventually be exposed. So, they cash out early and funnel personal funds away, well in time before a share price collapses or authorities can freeze funds.

However, some market indicators might only be seen in later stages, as the company is approaching the fraud exposure and potential corporate collapse. This happens in parallel, with the problem becoming obvious for the investors.

The signals may include development in short seller interest and activity by blockholders. Also trading activity patterns of retail investors, professional and institutional investors. In addition to abnormal and unexplainable share price developments.


J. Sørensen, *Shorting Fraud*, https://doi.org/10.1007/978-3-031-81834-9_9

## 9.2 Short Seller Activity and Interest in Companies

The investor might not be the first person to suspect something is wrong in a company. One straightforward way to see if others think something could be wrong, is to monitor short selling activity.

While the motive for a short position could be something benign as a broader hedge, it could also be an indication of something is perceived wrong in the company by the investor taking it. Therefore, look at who is taking the short position. Is it a large financial institution like Blackrock, or a known activist or specialist short seller.

It is beneficial to follow e.g. built up of short interest in a specific company. Especially in cases where the fundamentals look good for the company. Official websites like Financial Industry Regulatory Authority (FINRA)[1] offer the public short seller data on stock exchanges like NYSE and NASDAQ, which can be used for simple monitoring, or building more advanced models. Also, there are private websites and vendors offering consolidated data gathering and analysis, across multiple exchanges and jurisdictions.

Have in mind that the short seller interest might not be fraud driven. If you do not see the logic, it may also be event-driven, like cyber-attacks, that have not been disclosed by the company, but revealed by the hackers in a darknet underground forum. It might even be short sellers engaging in illegal insider trading.

## 9.3 Insiders and Their Trades

How executives, the board, insiders, and related parties in general trade the stock is interesting to screen. Following the insider trade patterns might reveal something is wrong.

While many jurisdictions have strict regulations on insider trading, others still have some room of maneuver for the cunning fraudster. In some fraud cases, it has been observed that insider trade activity was a prelude to the fraud. These individual observations are supported by research from He et al. (2021) that found on a general level, abnormal insider sales may be related to future stock price crashes. More specifically related to corporate fraud, Agrawal and Cooper (2015) studied 500 U.S. firms, which publicized earnings-decreasing restatements between 1997 and 2002. The researchers found

[1] https://www.finra.org/finra-data/browse-catalog/short-sale-volume-data.

that top managements' sale of shares in companies associated with accounting scandals were abnormal. The CEOs were selling more shares when earnings were manipulated.

While this gives an idea of how the top management may behave in corporate fraud cases, it must be stated that the study pre-dates Sarbanes–Oxley Act in 2002 (SOX), which in the U.S. imposed stricter regulations on auditing, financial disclosures, better internal controls, and greater personal liability on corporate executives. However, other jurisdictions do not necessarily have the same SOX regulations, and the CEO insider trading may be used for screening here.

In the US, insider trades might be found in places like the Electronic Data Gathering, Analysis, and Retrieval (EDGAR) database https://www.sec.gov/edgar/search/ or at websites like openinsider.com.

The reader is encouraged to use the above to analyze historic cases of e.g. Lehman Brothers. This is to see how insiders and related parties like family members traded in the period up to the collapse.

## 9.4 Blockholders and Block Trades

Another interesting area of trade to monitor is blockholder activity. Investors that own a significant stake in the company, e.g. over 5%, will have a specific interest in the company and are expected to track the company more closely. This also includes partnerships and joint ventures with equity stakes and their activity. Especially look for reversals or contradictions. Like major public support from blockholders or partners, followed by subsequent sell-off. Any unusual activity in block trades is interesting from a fraud perspective.

## 9.5 Institutional Ownership and Corporate Fraud

Another area to screen is the type of investors who own shares in the listed company. Logically one would expect that the more professional and institutional investors that own shares in a company the less likelihood there would be fraud. After all they are professional investors with the right tools and competencies to own shares.

However, research suggests that this relationship is not as simple and straightforward. Burns et al. (2010) found a relationship between institutional ownership and financial misreporting is a multifaceted relationship.

Though a higher institutional ownership concentration might result in less financial misreporting, the specific type of institutional ownership is also important.

The research suggests that transient institutions, those with short investment horizons, are less incentivized to monitor fundamentals, compared to dedicated institutions with longer horizons. This makes sense. A transient hedge fund might be less interested in the fundamentals of the corporation than a long-term holder, like a pension fund or endowment.

It also means that if there is a high amount of transient ownership, the top management may be more incentivized to manipulate earnings, since the transient owner may drop the share in the blink of an eye, while the long-term holder will stick with the company for bad quarters.

With regards to fraud screening this has the following implications. The type of institutional investors, and their concentration and their trading patterns becomes significant.

An example of a red flag, which should be looked for and has been seen in fraud cases, is when a long-term holder like an insurance company starts trading like a hedge fund. Like aggressively taking a 12% stake in a corporation, only to drop everything over the next 60 days with a loss.

## 9.6 Shareholder Concentrations and Corporate Fraud

Another factor observed when hunting fraud is that shareholder concentration can influence the risk of corporate fraud. This is supported by Zhao et al. (2021) that found that there is a tendency of lower risk of corporate fraud in the form of disclosure fraud with multiple large shareholders, holding 10% or more. The study found lower risk of fictional profits, fictional assets, falsified records, late and falsified disclosures, omission of material information, and improper general accounting.

## 9.7 Retail Investors vs. Professional and Institutional Investors

Another thing to screen is professional investor trading activity compared to retail investor trading activity.

An example of this was seen in the fraud induced collapse of the Danish company OW Bunker e.g. reported by Holmstad (2024). In this case, the final month up to the collapse, professional investors dumped shares on a net basis, while retail investors were buying the share on a net basis, according to Bindslev (2014). A partial analysis of trend trading platforms showed retail investors net bought 2 million shares, while institutional investors net sold 3 million in the period 1st October until collapse 3rd of November.

Hence, a potential fraud red flag to look for is a conflict between the trade patterns of retail investors and professional investors in a listed company.

## 9.8 Stakeholders and Related Parties

Also, stakeholders and related parties with stakes in the company are interesting to monitor and observe. In the financial industry, regulatory compliance is in place in most jurisdictions. This should theoretically place "walls" between e.g. sell-side and buy-side parts of financial institutions. However, there are sometimes "holes" in these walls, being abused.

If suddenly, the Asset Management arm of the company's house bank begins offloading the company shares out of the blue, that could be an indication that something is wrong in the corporation, there may have been illegit "wall crossing" and insider trading by the asset management arm of the financial institution.

## 9.9 Comparative Monitoring of Stock Market Metrics

Outliers in stock price development. The investor may analyze how stock prices perform according to the general market and peer companies in the industry. Outlier patterns may initiate further investigation into why the stock behaves this way. Of course, outliers in stock price performance may be induced by fundamentals or market psychology. However, in some cases it has been observed they are related to fraudulent activities. Advanced ML models could be built to monitor and analyze these complex patterns.

## References

Agrawal, A., & Cooper, T. (2015). Insider Trading Before Accounting Scandals. *Journal of Corporate Finance, 34*, 169–190. Retrieved September 14, 2024, from https://doi.org/10.1016/j.jcorpfin.2015.07.005

Bindslev, J. C. (2014, November 28). *Store investorer flygtede længe inden OW-krakket*. Børsen. Retrieved September 14, 2024, from https://borsen.dk/nyheder/penge/store-investorer-flygtede-laenge-inden-ow-krakket

Burns, N., Kedia, S., & Lipson, M. (2010). Institutional Ownership and Monitoring: Evidence from Financial Misreporting. *Journal of Corporate Finance, 16*(4), 443–455.

He, G., Ren, H. M., & Taffler, R. (2021). Do Corporate Insiders Trade on Future Stock Price Crash Risk? *Review of Quantitative Finance and Accounting, 56*, 1561–1591. Retrieved September 14, 2024, from https://doi.org/10.1007/s11156-020-00936-3

Holmstad, D. (2024). Private Investors Agree to Settle Almost 10 Years After OW Bunker Collapse. *Shipping Watch*. Retrieved September 14, 2024, from https://web.archive.org/web/20240518113719/https://shippingwatch.com/suppliers/article17103104.ece

Zhao, X., Yang, D., Li, Z., & Song, L. (2021). Multiple Large Shareholders and Corporate Fraud: Evidence from China. *Frontiers of Business Research in China, 15*(9). Retrieved September 14, 2024, from https://doi.org/10.1186/s11782-021-00106-9

# 10

# Screening the Official Statements, Material and Disclosures from Publicly Listed Companies

## 10.1 Screening Public Disclosures of Listed Companies for Corporate Fraud

Publicly listed companies have strict requirements regarding public disclosure related to the company. Often involving the exchange that they are listed on and potentially the authorities that have oversight of the markets in the jurisdiction where the company is listed.

Though these requirements may differ in detail depending on jurisdiction and the venue the company is listed on, they often include at minimum the Quarterly and Annual Reports with Financial Statements, Earnings Announcements, Publication of Material events, issuance of equity and other relevant material events.

The official and most comprehensive statements are the quarterly and annual reports including financial statements. The earnings announcements (often in press release format) are the condensed view of these reports in a public statement from the company.

Subsequently to the financial reports and earnings announcements the management (CEO & CFO) often conduct earnings calls where they present the results, discuss the financial results, and may take questions from investors and equity analysts. How companies conduct earnings calls may depend on the jurisdiction and company size. NIRI (2016) found more than 90% of their members conducted earnings calls. National Investor Relations Institute (NIRI) represents around 1500 members, mainly in the US, but also Canada, UK, and a few other countries.



J. Sørensen, *Shorting Fraud*, https://doi.org/10.1007/978-3-031-81834-9_10

The most important and detailed data is in the actual financial reports. However, also how the earnings announcements are presented, and how the potential subsequent earnings call is played out is important, when looking at corporate fraud.

With tens of thousands of listed companies, it is of course impossible to read all company reports, company announcements, and participate in all earnings calls, assessing the viability of what is written and spoken by the management, on a continuous basis.

However, as presented in subsequent sections, machine learning models can be used to help analyze the vast amount of quantitative and qualitative data points. Natural language processing (NLP) might scrutinize the reports and earnings call transcriptions for clues of fraud. This combined with e.g. special ML models focusing on lie detection in audio and video recordings of management earnings calls. These ML screening methods may screen thousands of companies and CEOs on a continuous basis.

## 10.2 Financial Reports—Quarterly and Annual reports

At the current time, financial data analytics is the field that has progressed the most with regards to analytical methods screening for fraud.

While countries sometimes may adopt different local accounting standards and reporting practices, two major standards are dominant on the global scale, especially amongst publicly listed companies.

- International Financial Reporting Standards) (IFRS): Used in over 140 countries, creating greater global compatibility as found in IFRS Foundation (2024)
- US Generally Accepted Accounting Principles (US GAAP): The standard for companies operating in the United States as found in Financial Accounting Foundation (2024)

Since the focus is publicly listed companies, the standard is that these listed companies on a general level are required to publish their financial reports on a regular basis. The frequency of publication can vary by jurisdiction, but typically includes:

- Quarterly reports are normally published within 45 days of each quarter-end. These reports provide an update on the company's financial performance during the past three months.
- Annual reports are usually published within 90 days of each financial year-end. The reports are supposed to provide a comprehensive overview of the company's financial performance over the past twelve months.

The quarterly and annual reports of listed companies follow a certain format with variations depending on jurisdiction. They are the official state of the company as presented by management.

Published every quarter, the quarterly reports are an ongoing view of the company's financial position throughout the year. Depending on factors like jurisdiction, size of the company, exchange, etc. these quarterly reports are usually unaudited, but reviewed by auditors.

Annual reports are the official state of the company, released by the management of the company and are normally audited. These reports should include a full overview of a company's business and financial condition for the entire year and include:

- **Audited financial statements** — income statement, balance sheet, cash flow statement and footnotes.
- **MD&A**— Management's commentary on areas like performance, corporate strategy, and the future outlook. They might also choose to offer earnings guidance, which is future projections or estimates of future financial performance.
- **Sustainability reports** are becoming a norm in a growing number of jurisdictions. This type of report outlines the company's environmental and social impact.
- **Auditor's Report & Opinion** is the independent auditor's opinion on whether the financial statements accurately reflect the company's financial health and adhere to accounting regulations and standards. In the hunt for fraud this is normally the section to read first for finding red flags.

### 10.2.1 Auditor's Report and Opinion

The most interesting part of the company report from a fraud perspective is the Auditor's Report & Opinion. Hence systematically screening listed company reports for problematic auditor opinions and comments for red flags is a way to discover potentially fraudulent companies.

From a fraud perspective this is always the first section to read in the annual report. This should (at least in theory) be the independent view on the financial statement of the company. These auditor's comments and especially the auditor's opinions are important to corporate fraud detection. The main conclusions or auditor's opinion come in several categories.

- **Unqualified Opinion**—A clean opinion, nothing found by the auditor—green flag from the auditor.
- **Qualified Opinion**—something is wrong, check the fine print of what it is—yellow/ red flag from the auditor.
- **Adverse Opinion**—materially misstatements not complying with accounting standards, which is a major red flag from auditor.
- **Disclaimer of Opinion**—auditor has been hindered to do audit. It could be missing data and/or lack of cooperation from management, which is a major red flag from the auditor.

In addition, there are two special cases, especially relevant with regards to fraud, since they have been observed in actual fraud cases.

- **Modified Opinion**—The auditor's opinion has been changed from the standard unqualified opinion.
- **Withdrawal of Opinion**—While rare, the auditor initially issued an opinion. However, subsequently discovered information that prompted the auditor to withdraw the initial judgment on the financial statements. In this case something is very wrong.

In addition to the opinions a few other concepts in the report are important from a fraud perspective.

- **Emphasis of Matter Paragraph**—In the case of unqualified or qualified opinion this is the auditor highlighting a significant matter requiring closer scrutiny by financial statement users. The auditor circles a specific area that might be interesting in relations to fraud.
- **Going-concern Considerations**—Here the auditor express doubt whether the company is able to continue operating as a going concern and remain in business.
- **Shared Audit Responsibility**—In big and complex organizations there might be multiple auditors working on distinct parts of the financial statements. This means comments and opinions are limited to only the part that the auditor is responsible for. This means that no single auditor has

the full overview. It may also be used as a deliberate "divide and defraud" strategy by management. E.g. shady legal entities done by a shady auditor, and the holding company done by a respected auditor.

- **Key Audit Matters**—A requirement for auditors of listed companies. Key Audit Matters are places where the auditor focuses on specific areas of the audit that were particularly complex or involved significant judgment. From the fraud perspective it might be interesting for the investor to look at these hard parts and scrutinize them further.

### 10.2.2 Financial Statements

Another key element to analyze is the financial statement. It is an official record of the financial activities of the company. It provides insight into the company's financial condition in both the short and long term. The financial statement consists of the Income Statement, Balance Sheet, Cash Flow statements and Footnotes to be scrutinized.

The **Income Statement** shows the company's revenues and expenses during the period. Revenues stating the income from normal business activities, and the expenses representing the cost of conducting the business. Net Income is the amount by which revenues exceed expenses.

The **Balance Sheet** is a summary of a company's assets, liabilities, and equity at a particular point in time. It details Assets (resources owned by a company), Liabilities (the company's debts or obligations), and Shareholders' Equity, which is the net assets of a company (total assets minus total liabilities).

The **Cash Flow Statement** illustrates the impact of changes in the balance sheet and income statement on a company's cash and cash equivalents. These are broken into analysis of cash flow related to operating, investing, and financing activities.

**Footnotes** are often overlooked by investors. However, they are immensely important in corporate fraud screening, since they are the small print where it is clarified how a company calculated the financial statement. From a fraud perspective, they are important since they might tell a lot about how conditions or fundamental assumptions in calculations were changed.

There are several publicly available quantitative and qualitative ways to analyze the content of the annual and quarterly reports from a fraud perspective. Especially methods and models targeting the Financial Statement parts from a quantitative perspective are widespread.

The common goal of these methods is to see if the numbers add up or if there is manipulation of the earnings of the company. In addition, there is a growing number of public and private proprietary models looking at the qualitative areas of the annual and quarterly reports with regards to fraud detection.

Lastly, there are also research looking at the context that the reports and other company announcements are conducted within, like e.g. timing, as described in Sections 15.1 to 15.3.

### 10.2.3 Accrual Accounting and Earnings Manipulation

Accruals in accounting are revenues earned or expenses incurred before the cash changes hands. It also involves non-cash assets and liabilities. Properly done, accrual accounting should ensure financial statements reflect a company's true financial position.

However, accruals can easily be manipulated, affecting net income and profitability shown in the financial statement. This is because accruals rely on estimates (at the discretion of corporate executives) until the actual transactions occur. Examples of this misuse include recording revenue too early, falsely reporting liabilities, or capitalizing ordinary expenses on the balance sheet. The following fraud metrics try to detect earnings manipulation.

This book will not visit all statistical methods available to detect fraud but show a few, with a theoretical foundation, most of which have been utilized successfully to detect Corporate Fraud in a practical setting.

## References

Financial Accounting Foundation. (2024). GAAP and Public Companies. Retrieved September 14, 2024, from https://accountingfoundation.org/Page/PageContent?PageId=/overview-accounting-and-standards/gaap/gaappubliccompanies.html#section_1

IFRS Foundation. (2024). IFRS—Home. Retrieved September 14, 2024, from https://www.ifrs.org/

NIRI. (2016). NIRI Earnings Process Practices Research Report, National Investor Relations Institute. Retrieved September 14, 2024, from https://www.niri.org/NIRI/media/Protected-Documents_ExcludeGlobalSubs/Analytics%20Reports/Analytics_Guidance/NIRI-Earnings-Process-Practices-Report-2016.pdf

# 11

# Using Statistical Methods to Screen for Earnings Manipulation and Corporate Fraud

## 11.1 Analysis Techniques: Time Series, Cross-Sectional, and TSCS Approaches

There is a plentitude of statistical methods and models, which can be used to detect potential corporate fraud in a practical setting.

The general types of models include e.g. regression analyses. The treatment of general statistical models is outside the scope of this book. However, the main purposes of these statistical methods in relation to fraud detection are:

- **Time series analysis** is a useful tool detecting fraud within a corporation. By examining a company's financial data and other data points over time, time series models can reveal trends, cycles, and anomalies in accruals, earnings quality, or other key metrics. These changes may indicate fraudulent activity or signal a developing pattern of fraudulent behavior.
- **Cross-sectional analysis** is valuable to detect fraud by comparing multiple companies at the same point in time. Using this method, one may benchmark against industry averages or peer companies. Searching for and highlighting anomalies, unusual patterns, and outliers, which could potentially indicate fraudulent activity that warrants further investigation.
- **Time-series + cross-sectional (TSCS) Analysis:** Is the final and most advanced approach that combines the cross-section dimension and the time series dimension. Analyzing multiple data points for multiple companies over time to detect fraud.


J. Sørensen, *Shorting Fraud*, https://doi.org/10.1007/978-3-031-81834-9_11

Below are some of the practical statistical models that may be used to detect fraud and earnings manipulation. Some models are overlapping and complementary in nature. These models build on a theoretical foundation and have also been successfully used to detect fraud targets in a practical setting—either in their basic or altered form.

## 11.2 Beneish M-Score

A well-known practical model to detect financial fraud is the Beneish Model described in Beneish (1999). This statistical tool can be used to detect potential earnings manipulation within listed companies.

The M-Score uses eight financial ratios calculated from a company's accounting data. The model generates an M-Score, which indicates the risk of earnings manipulation. If the M-Score is less than −1.78, the target company is not anticipated to be manipulating earnings. The M-score is calculated this way:

1. **DSRI** (Days Sales in Receivables Index) is the ratio of days sales in receivables in period t compared to the previous period t-1. A significant increase in the value of DSRI is an indicator of revenue inflation.

$$DSRI = \frac{\frac{NetReceivables_t}{Sales_t}}{\frac{NetReceivables_{t-1}}{Sales_{t-1}}} \tag{11.1}$$

2. **GMI** (Gross Margin Index) is the ratio of the gross margin in period t compared to previous period t-1. A decrease in the value of GMI is an indicator of deteriorating margins. (COGS is Cost of Goods Sold)

$$GMI = \frac{\frac{Sales_{t-1} - COGS_{t-1}}{Sales_{t-1}}}{\frac{Sales_t - COGS_t}{Sales_t}} \tag{11.2}$$

3. **AQI** (Asset Quality Index) is the ratio of non-current assets apart from plant, property, and equipment (PPE) to the total assets. An increase in AQI points to a higher likelihood of capitalization of costs.

$$AQI = \frac{\frac{TotalAssets_t - CurrentAssets_t - PPE_t}{TotalAssets_t}}{\frac{TotalAssets_{t-1} - CurrentAssets_{t-1} - PPE_{t-1}}{TotalAssets_{t-1}}} \tag{11.3}$$

4. **SGI (Sales Growth Index)** is the ratio of sales in period t compared to period t-1. High sales growth can be a sign of aggressive revenue recognition.

$$SGI = \frac{Sales_t}{Sales_{t-1}} \tag{11.4}$$

5. **DEPI** (Depreciation Index) is the ratio of the rate of depreciation in period t compared to previous period t-1. A decrease in DEPI may indicate that the company has changed its depreciation policy to increase earnings.

$$DEPI = \frac{Depreciation_{t-1}/(PPE_{t-1} + Depreciation_{t-1})}{Depreciation_t/(PPE_t + Depreciation_t)} \tag{11.5}$$

6. **SGAI** (Sales, General and Administrative expenses Index) is the ratio of SGA (Selling, General, and Administrative Expenses) in period t compared to previous period t-1. An increase in SGAI indicates that the company might be recording revenues too soon or a too aggressive income statement classification.

$$SGAI = \frac{SGA_t/Sales_t}{SGA_{t-1}/Sales_{t-1}} \tag{11.6}$$

7. **LVGI** (Leverage Index) is the ratio of total debt to total assets. An increase in LVGI indicates an increase in debt which may be due to revenue inflation or aggressive recognition of intangible assets.

$$LVGI = \frac{TotalDebt_t/TotalAssets_t}{TotalDebt_{t-1}/TotalAssets_{t-1}} \tag{11.7}$$

8. **TATA** (Total Accruals to Total Assets) is a measure of the total accruals to total assets. A higher TATA value may indicate a higher likelihood of earnings manipulation.

$$\begin{aligned} TATA =& (Income\ from\ Continuing\ Operations_t \\ & - Cash\ Flows\ from\ Operations_t)/TotalAssets_t \end{aligned} \tag{11.8}$$

The M-Score is then calculated using these variables in the following formula:

$$M\text{-}Score = -4.84 + 0.92 \times DSRI + 0.528 \times GMI + 0.404 \times AQI + 0.892 \times SGI + 0.115 \times DEPI - 0.172 \times SGAI + 4.679 \times TATA - 0.327 \times LVGI \quad (11.9)$$

## 11.3 Montier C-score

Montier (2010) developed the James Montier C-score, which is a financial indicator developed to identify potential earnings manipulation within companies. The Montier C-score uses six measures calculated from a company's accounting data.

The model generates a C-score that indicates the likelihood of earnings manipulation. A C-Score of 0 suggests that there is no evidence of earnings manipulation, while a C-score of 6 indicates a high chance of earnings manipulation. The specific points in the score are calculated the following way. Where Δ denotes the change from the previous period.

1. An increasing discrepancy between net income and cash flow (1 point): If

$$\Delta NetIncome > \Delta CashFlowFromOperations \quad (11.10)$$

, then score = 1, else score = 0.

Higher accrual amounts tend to correlate with a higher risk of profit manipulation, indicating potential discrepancies in financial reporting.

2. Increasing receivable days (1 point): If

$$\Delta\left(\frac{AccountsReceivable}{Sales} \times 365\right) > 0 \quad (11.11)$$

, then score = 1, else score = 0.

If the average collection period for receivables rises substantially, it may be a sign that a company is prematurely booking revenue to artificially inflate earnings, potentially indicating aggressive accounting practices.

3. Increasing inventory days (1 point): If

$$\Delta\left(\frac{Inventory}{\text{Cost of Goods Sold}} \times 365\right) > 0 \quad (11.12)$$

, then score = 1, else score = 0.

A growing number of days inventory is held may point towards artificially inflated input costs or a slowdown in sales, both of which could be indicators of financial strain.

4. Increasing other current assets (1 point): If

$$\Delta \text{Other Current Assets} > 0 \tag{11.13}$$

, then score = 1, else score = 0.

Knowing that investors frequently scrutinize Accounts Receivable and inventory, companies might try to deceive investors by hiding issues in other current assets instead.

5. Drops in depreciation relative to gross fixed assets (1 point): If

$$\Delta\left(\frac{Depreciation}{\text{Gross Fixed Assets}}\right) < 0 \tag{11.14}$$

, then score = 1, else score = 0.

Companies have sometimes reduced depreciation expenses to artificially boost reported profits, which could be a sign of earnings manipulation.

6. Total asset growth in excess of 10% (1 point): If

$$\frac{\Delta \text{Total Assets}}{\text{Total Assets}} > 0.10 \tag{11.15}$$

, then score = 1, else score = 0.

Some firms adopt a strategy of continuous acquisitions, utilizing these mergers to create a misleading impression of their profitability. These cases are also known as roll-ups and described in Sect. 19.12.1.

## 11.4 The Sloan Accruals Ratio

Sloan (1996) invented the Sloan Accruals Ratio which measures earnings quality. The ratio might be used to detect potential accounting manipulations. The Ratio compares a company's net income with its cash flow. If the ratio is between −10% and 10%, the company is generally considered safe. However, a ratio outside this range may indicate accrual build-up, suggesting possible earnings manipulation. The simple Sloan Ratio calculation is done the following way:

$$SloanRatio = \frac{NetIncome - CFO - CFI}{TotalAssets} \tag{11.16}$$

where:

CFO is cash flow from operations

CFI is cash flow from investing

The advanced version of Sloan Ratio is determined by taking a company's discretionary accruals (net income less cash flow from operations) and dividing that number by the company's total assets.

$$SloanRatio = \frac{\Delta CA - \Delta Cash - \Delta CL + \Delta STD + \Delta TP - Dep}{TotalAssets} \tag{11.17}$$

where:

ΔCA is the change in current assets

ΔCash is the change in cash/cash equivalents

ΔCL is the change in current liabilities

ΔSTD is the change in debt included in current liabilities

ΔTP is the change in income taxes payable

Dep is depreciation and amortization expense

## 11.5 Dechow-Dichev model

The linear regression model developed by Dechow and Dichev (2002) assesses earnings quality by measuring the degree of accrual estimation errors. It provides empirical estimates based on the relationship between accruals and cash flows. This model helps the investor identify earnings manipulation and evaluate the quality of earnings.

The model is empirically measured as the unexplained portion of changes in working capital after accounting for the effects of past, current, and future operating cash flows using a firm-specific regression model.

The model can be represented as follows:

$$\Delta WC = \alpha + \beta_1 CFO_{t-1} + \beta_2 CFO_t + \beta_3 CFO_{t+1} + \varepsilon \tag{11.18}$$

where:

ΔWC represents the change in working capital.

CFO represents cash flow from operations.

α, β1, β2, and β3 are parameters to be estimated.

α (Intercept) is the expected value of the changes in working capital when all cash flows are zero.

β1 (Lag Coefficient) measures the relationship between changes in working capital and the previous period's operating cash flows.

β2 (Contemporaneous Coefficient) measures the relationship between changes in working capital and the current period's operating cash flows.

β3 (Lead Coefficient): measures the relationship between changes in working capital and the next period's operating cash flows.

ε is the error term.

The residuals from this regression (ε) represent the accrual estimation errors. A larger absolute value of ε indicates a larger estimation error and lower quality of earnings.

## 11.6 Jones Non-discretionary Accruals

This linear regression model by Jones (1991) is used to detect earnings management and potential manipulation. It does this by comparing a company's actual accruals to the accruals that would be expected based on the company's economic circumstances (as represented by its gross Property, Plant, and Equipment (PP&E) and changes in revenues and receivables). The difference between the actual and expected accruals (the residuals) are considered non-discretionary accruals. If the actual accruals are significantly higher than the expected accruals, it could be a sign that the company is engaging in earnings management.

For example, let us say a company has a substantial increase in its accruals but there is no corresponding increase in its PP&E or revenues. This could be a red flag that the company is manipulating its accruals to inflate its earnings. The Jones model would detect this by showing a significant difference between the actual and expected accruals.

The Jones Model comes in several versions, below the original and modified version. The original is calculated the following way:

$$TACC = \alpha_0 + \alpha_1 \frac{1}{A_{t-1}} + \alpha_2 \frac{\Delta REV_t}{A_{t-1}} + \alpha_3 \frac{PPE_t}{A_{t-1}} + \varepsilon_t \qquad (11.19)$$

where:

TACC is total accruals,

At − 1 is total assets at the end of year t − 1,

ΔREVt is the change in revenues from year t − 1 to t,
PPEt is gross property, plant, and equipment at the end of year t,
ϵt is the error term.

The Modified Jones Model by Dechow et al. (1995) was later introduced to improve the accuracy of the original model. The modification involves adjusting for changes in accounts receivable, which can be manipulated to manage earnings. The modified model is defined as follows:

$$NDA_t = \alpha_1 \frac{1}{A_{t-1}} + \alpha_2 \frac{(\Delta REV_t - \Delta AR_t)}{A_{t-1}} + \alpha_3 \frac{PPE_t}{A_{t-1}} \tag{11.20}$$

where:
NDA is normal, non-discretionary accruals,
ΔARt is the change in accounts receivable from year t − 1 to t2.

The Modified Jones model utilizes the equation parameters to determine non-discretionary accruals. To address the issue of managed credit sales potentially skewing the estimate of normal accruals in the event period, cash revenues can be considered in both stages.

## 11.7 Dechow F-Score

The Dechow F-Score is a model developed by Dechow et al. (2010) to estimate the probability of a company engaging in fraudulent financial reporting. It considers test data from Accounting and Auditing Enforcement Releases issued by the SEC in the period from 1982 to 2005.

$$F - Score = 2.020 + \left(0.327 * \frac{\Delta AR}{AvgTA}\right) + \left(1.209 * \frac{\Delta Sales}{AvgTA}\right) + \left(0.208 * \frac{\Delta ROA}{AvgTA}\right) \tag{11.21}$$

where:
ΔAR/AvgTA is change in Accounts Receivable divided by Average Total Assets. An abrupt and unexpected increase in AR may indicate attempts to inflate revenue through manipulation, which has not yet been converted to cash flow.

$\Delta$Sales/AvgTA is the change in Sales (Revenue) divided by Average Total Assets. Substantial changes in sales may indicate revenue recognition issues or overly aggressive accounting practices to boost earnings.

$\Delta$ROA/AvgTA is change in Return on Assets divided by Average Total Assets. Fluctuations in ROA might imply earnings management tactics as companies try to meet performance targets.

The interpretation of the F-Score is as follows:

- If F-Score > 1—indicates an above-average risk of earnings manipulation.
- If F-Score > 2.45—indicates a very high risk of earnings manipulation.

Though these scores may vary between industries, which should be taken into consideration using it in a practical setting.

## 11.8 Benford's Law

Benford (1938) outlines Benford's Law, which is also known as the First Digit Law. Basically, Benford's Law studies the frequency distribution of the leading digits in a dataset. From a practical fraud detection view it may be used to successfully detect several types of fraud including financial statement fraud.

The principle is that in many real-life numerical datasets (following a power-law distribution), the leftmost digit in a multidigit number is most likely to be small, with the digit 1 appearing about 30% of the time and the digit 9 less than 5% of the time, illustrated in Fig. 11.1.

Therefore, the law may be used to detect anomalies in financial and accounting data. Deviations from the expected distribution can indicate fraud. From a practical point of view, the law is e.g. very good when humans have fraudulently put in "random" fake numbers in financial data and accounting statements. The human made "random" numbers are often found not to be random, but follow patterns, like the practical placement of numbers on numeric keypads, or the "qwerty" keyboards.

In its simplest application Benford's Law can be mathematically expressed as follows:

The probability

$$P(d)$$

that the leading digit

$$d$$

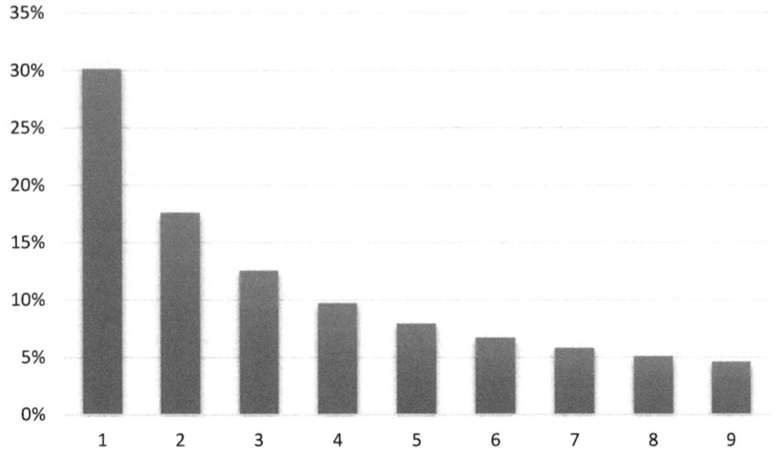


**Fig. 11.1** Illustration of the probability of a leading digit according to Benford's Law based on Benford (1938)

where

$$d$$

is an integer from 1 to 9) occurs in a dataset is given by:

$$P(d) = \log_{10}\left(1 + \frac{1}{d}\right) \tag{11.22}$$

This equation shows that the number 1 appears as the leftmost digit about 30% of the time, while 9 appears less than 5% of the time.

In Fig. 11.2, the fraudster chose to evenly distribute the leading number between 1 to 9. In that case the general mathematical expression follows a Discrete Uniform Distribution, followed by the specific example with 9 outcomes:

The Probability Mass Function (PMF) for a general Discrete Uniform Distribution is given by:

$$f(x) = \frac{1}{n} \tag{11.23}$$

where n is the number of outcomes.

For the specific example with 9 outcomes, the PMF becomes:

$$f(x) = \frac{1}{9} \approx 11.11\% \tag{11.24}$$

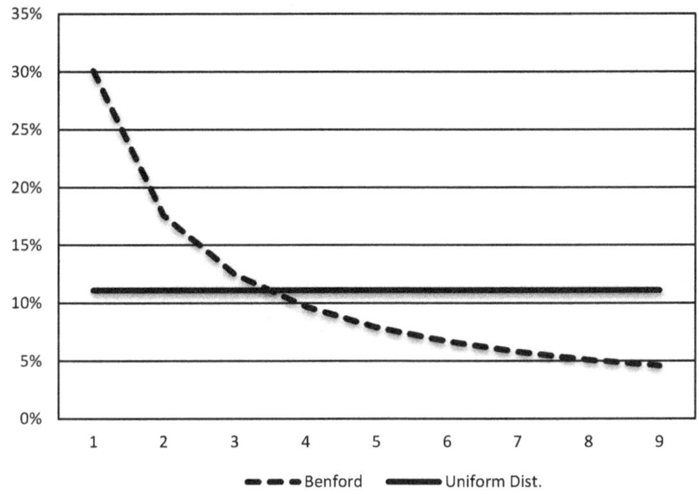


**Fig. 11.2** Benford vs. uniform distribution

In Fig. 11.2, it is shown that the Benford's Law distribution should look like the dotted line.

However, the Fraudster decided to fake the numbers by distributing them evenly across the 1 to 9 range following the solid line of the uniform distribution.

Benford's law is a principle that may be used on its own or in combination with other statistical methods.

## 11.9 AB-Score and ABF Score

In a study by Chakrabarty et al. (2024), the researchers building on Benford's law, and Dechow F-score tries to improve fraud detection metrics using the AB-Score, which is a more sophisticated score that also measures the deviation from Benford's Law. The score is designed explicitly to predict the likelihood of "misreporting" (i.e., fraudulent financial statements). The ABF-score integrates the AB-score and the Dechow F-Score. The aim is to create maximum accuracy in fraud detection and expand the kinds of situations where it can be applied. It performs well across alternative misstatement proxies and outperforms the benchmark F-score model, according to the research.

## 11.10 Other Statistical Models That Can Be Used as Building Blocks to Detect Fraud

Like Benford's law a multitude of general and basic mathematical and statistical principles may be used to detect financial and corporate fraud. A few examples include:

- **The Z-Score** developed by Gosset (1908), under the pseudonym Student. **The Modified Z-Score** created by Iglewicz and Hoaglin (1993) and **Extreme Value Theory** first outlined by Fisher and Tippett (1928) are all statistical methods that may be used to detect fraud anomalies in data. The methods look at how data is compared to the mean or median. For example, if a company's profit margin is substantially higher than the industry average, it might be a sign of fraudulent activity.
- **Chi-square test** conceived by Pearson (1900): This test compares observed data with expected data based on a hypothesis. If the investor has some preconceived idea or hypothesis about the data, the investor can test and potentially detect fraud that way. E.g. if we expect a Benford's law distribution, test for that.
- The original **Runs test** was developed by Wald and Wolfowitz (1940): This test examines whether a sequence of values is random or not, and may be used to detect fraud. It could be that suddenly, at the end of a period, numbers deviate from a random pattern, to "magically" meet targets. For insiders, like auditors, this could be daily sales numbers. For external investors, this could be e.g. a web-based company's unique visitor pattern. The public web statistics on unique visitors have followed a random pattern, but suddenly show e.g. a linear pattern, which meets or beats a visitors target number. That may be an indication that unique visitors are artificially boosted.
- **Multivariate analysis,** Anderson (1958), examines the relationship between multiple variables. It might be used to look at several variables to detect financial fraud. This method can be used to examine relationships between multiple variables in a company's financial statements. For example, if a company's revenue is growing, but its accounts receivable and inventory are not changing accordingly, it could be a sign of revenue recognition fraud.

## References

Anderson, T. W. (1958). *An Introduction to Multivariate Statistical Analysis.* Wiley.

Beneish, M. D. (1999). The Detection of Earnings Manipulation. 1 September 1999 Financial Analysts Journal Volume 55, Issue 5. Retrieved September 14, 2024, from https://www.calctopia.com/papers/beneish1999.pdf

Benford, F. (1938). The Law of Anomalous Numbers. *Proceedings of the American Philosophical Society, 78*(4), 551–572. Retrieved September 14, 2024, from http://www.jstor.org/stable/984802

Chakrabarty, B., Moulton, P. C., Pugachev, L., & Wang, X. (Frank). (2024). *Catch Me If You Can: In Search of Accuracy, Scope, and Ease of Fraud Prediction.* Retrieved September 14, 2024, from https://ssrn.com/abstract=3352667 or https://doi.org/10.2139/ssrn.3352667

Dechow, P. M., & Dichev, I. D. (2002). The Quality of Accruals and Earnings: The Role of Accrual Estimation Errors. *The Accounting Review, 77*, 35–59. Retrieved September 14, 2024, from http://www.jstor.org/stable/3203324

Dechow, P. M., Sloan, R. G., & Sweeney, A. P. (1995). Detecting Earnings Management. *The Accounting Review, 70*(2), 193–225. Retrieved September 14, 2024, from http://www.jstor.org/stable/248303

Dechow, P., Ge, W., Larson, C. R., & Sloan, R. G. (2010). Predicting Material Accounting Misstatements. Contemporary Accounting Research, Forthcoming, AAA 2008 Financial Accounting and Reporting Section (FARS) Paper. Retrieved September 14, 2024, from https://ssrn.com/abstract=997483

Fisher, R., & Tippett, L. (1928). Limiting Forms of the Frequency Distribution of the Largest or Smallest Member of a Sample. *Mathematical Proceedings of the Cambridge Philosophical Society, 24*(2), 180–190. https://doi.org/10.1017/S0305004100015681

Iglewicz, B., & Hoaglin, D. C. (1993). *How to Detect and Handle Outliers* (Vol. 16, p. 11). ASQC Quality Press.

Jones, J. J. (1991). Earnings Management During Import Relief Investigations. *Journal of Accounting Research, 29*(2), 193–228. Retrieved September 14, 2024, from https://doi.org/10.2307/2491047

Pearson, K. (1900). On the Criterion That a Given System of Deviations from the Probable in the Case of a Correlated System of Variables Is Such That It Can Be Reasonably Supposed to Have Arisen from Random Sampling. *Philosophical Magazine Series, 5*, 157–175. Retrieved September 14, 2024, from https://doi.org/10.1080/14786440009463897

Sloan, R. G. (1996). Do Stock Prices Fully Reflect Information in Accruals and Cash Flows about Future Earnings? *The Accounting Review, 71*(3), 289–315. Retrieved September 14, 2024, from http://www.jstor.org/stable/248290

Student. (1908). The Probable Error of a Mean. *Biometrika, 6*(1), 1–25. Retrieved September 14, 2024, from https://doi.org/10.2307/2331554

Value Investing—Tools and Techniques for Intelligent Investment by James Montier, 2010, Wiley.

Wald, A., & Wolfowitz, J. (1940). On a test whether two samples are from the same population. *The Annals of Mathematical Statistics, 11*, 147–162.

# 12

# Machine Learning Models to Screen Financial Statements for Fraud

## 12.1 Introduction to ML-Models to Screen Financial Statements for Fraud

A more advanced way to continuously screen a high volume of bulk financial reports and other corporate data points to detect corporate fraud, is utilizing ML models. While Sect. 34 will give a more general overview of utilizing ML models in practice, the below is dedicated to the application of Machine Learning detecting financial statement and corporate fraud. Starting with financial data models, where some may build on the top of statistical models from Sect. 11. The section will go from a simpler screening of only the quantitative data in financial reports to a more advanced holistic screening.

ML-models that are screening:

- The quantitative data in financial reports for fraud.
- The textual content of financial reports for fraud.
- The entire financial reports, both quantitative and textual content for fraud.
- A holistic perspective of the entire financial reports, plus other external data sources for fraud.

A literature review by Ashtiani and Raahemi (2022) offers a good comprehensive overview of the areas and types of many ML-Models and methods used in financial statement fraud detection that is available in the public domain. Below, only a few examples are shown.


J. Sørensen, *Shorting Fraud*, https://doi.org/10.1007/978-3-031-81834-9_12

## 12.2 ML-Models Screening Quantitative Data in Financial Reports for Fraud

Building these screening models looking solely on quantitative financial data may take on two practical approaches. One approach is building on top of the already tried and tested quantitative statistical models and fraud-related financial ratios like Benish M-score, Montier C-Score and Dechow F-Score etc. described in Sect. 11.

In the public domain this has been done by e.g. Hassanniakalager et al. (2022) building on Dechow Financial Ratios using a fraud detection ML model with 11 financial ratios like accruals, changes in inventory, Accounts Receivable, cash, etc. as predictors.

Another approach, which could be examined when building ML-models screening quantitative financial data is conducted by Zhao and Bai (2022), studying listed Chinese companies to detect fraud. Starting with 366 different quantitative indicators, and using five different types of ML models, the researchers ended up singling in on 13 main indicators and an ensemble model that combines two different types of ML-models.

A different quantitative data approach is building and training new explorative models based on a rawer financial data foundation. Like more raw data from income statements, balance sheets, cash flow statements.

Explorative ML-Models like these may be more applicable in real world settings. They may also develop new specialized insights on corporate fraud. Like multidimensional risk scores from big data sets that the human mind is not able to extract or understand at first glance.

While most of these new exploratory ML-Models, are private proprietary models and new corporate fraud metrics, developed internally in financial institutions, there are also examples of these attempts in the public domain, by a more raw and more exploratory approach to quantitative financial data.

This is done by e.g. Bao et al. (2020) looking at 28 raw financial data items like retained earnings, depreciation & net income for Publicly Traded U.S. Companies. The researchers discovered a new fraud related performance metric called Discounted Cumulative Gain at position k (NDCG@k). A metric, which may be used in a practical setting to actors that monitor fraudulent companies, but have limited resources to investigate, and need to prioritize the investigation of potential listed fraudulent companies. This is something that would benefit authorities, or in our case fraud short sellers.

## 12.3 ML-Models Screening Textual Content of Financial Reports for Fraud

Financial reports not only consist of financial numbers, but also textual content, which may be screened and analyzed. This textual content includes Management Discussion and Analysis, Footnotes to Financial Statements, Risk Factors, and Sustainability Reporting. In addition to Auditor's Report, Director's Report and Corporate Governance Report.

In contrast to quantitative financial statement analytics, NLP analytics of textual content is a relatively newer field, which is driven by Machine Learning. Here financial institutions and software vendors are busy building proprietary models to screen for corporate fraud. However, there are also examples of models in the public domain. Zhang et al. (2021) conducted a study and developed a new method to identify corporate fraud in listed companies based on text analysis of annual reports in listed companies.

The study scrutinizes the annual reports of 68 companies penalized for financial report fraud by the Chinese Securities Regulatory Commission between 2010 and 2019, alongside 68 corresponding non-fraudulent companies.

Their findings reveal that the textual content in the annual reports may detect fraudulent listed companies. It is demonstrated that text analysis can serve as a potent tool in identifying financial report fraud.

In short, the language difference between fraudulent and legitimate companies in their annual reports is the diversity and intentionality of the language utilized. Legitimate companies tend to use a wider and more varied vocabulary, while fraudulent companies are more cautious and deliberate in their usage of language.

More complex textual analytic models might be developed, taking into consideration the subparts and sections of the textual content in company reports. These models may build on e.g. the FinChain-BERT model described in Sect. 15.5.

## 12.4 ML-Models Screening Entire Financial Reports—Quantitative and Textual Content

A more advanced approach is to include both the quantitative aspects of the financial analytics and the qualitative aspect of the textual context, supplied by the management and others in the financial reports.

In this approach the ML-Models not only look at the anomalies in the quantitative measures and anomalies in the textual content isolated. Instead, the models analyze across the two areas. From a pragmatic point of view, the models analyze if what the management, auditors, chairman, etc. say about the company and its development, corresponds with the numbers presented in the report.

The clear-cut example is the CEO stating that things are good and have never been better, while the financials show that the company is experiencing a cash crunch, and the auditor report even questions a going concern. Sanity checking for inconsistencies in less clear-cut cases is possible, but very time consuming.

Reading and understanding the more subtle signs of fraud, and potential internal inconsistencies with financial results across thousands of companies, to detect corporate fraud, is not humanly possible without significant resources. ML-Models analyzing and screening for corporate fraud might therefore be a viable strategy to do this.

Proprietary models may be built using different methods. An example of models and research in the public domain that study the combination of financial ratios and text, includes Craja et al. (2020). They work with a combination of financials and textual content like the Management Discussion and Analysis section. Their study finds the combination of the financials and text is better to detect fraud than the methods used individually. The researchers also introduced a Hierarchical Attention Network (HAN) model. Here "red flag" sentences are highlighted by the model. This is a practical approach that may guide investors to focus their attention on the most suspicious areas of the report.

The next step is to include more indicators from outside the financial report, moving to a more holistic ML corporate fraud screening approach.

## 12.5 ML-Models Screening holistically—Financial Reports + Other External Data Sources

From a practitioner's view, in addition to WHAT (the content) is reported, it is also valuable to notice HOW, WHEN, and in WHAT context financial reports are published. All the various parts help paint a fuller, more holistic picture with important clues and potential red flags that may indicate fraud.

The more complex corporate fraud ML screening models move beyond only focusing on financial reports' quantitative and qualitative aspects. These screening models widen the horizon and consider other factors outside the financial report. These are factors like e.g., Corporate Governance, Equity Analyst Attention, Equity Analysts Reports, Delisting Pressure, Block shareholders, Related Party Shareholders, Media Exposure, Regulator Authority Activity, Auditor Types, etc.

Most of these advanced models are of course proprietary internal ML-models in financial institutions. However, there are examples in the public domain from which to draw inspiration.

Research conducted by Wu and Du (2022), studied more than 5,000 listed Chinese companies and developed advanced Deep Learning models. In addition to studying 58 traditional financial metrics, they studied 16 non-financial indicators, like Management & Ownership structure, and Auditor's Opinion. On top of that, textual analysis of the MD&A section was part of the model. In general, the study finds that a more holistic model based on deep learning and incorporating financial, non-financial metrics and textual analysis performs better.

Also, Bertomeu et al. (2021) have created a more holistic ML-model to detect material misstatements. On top of financial variables, the model includes a broader set of data. It includes capital market data like stock return volatility, bid-ask spreads, and short interest. In addition, governance issues like board of directors, management, and other corporate governance mechanisms. Finally, auditing and auditors' data variables, type of auditor and auditor qualifications. The researchers find that a model including more than financials is doing better than a model relying solely on financials.

Similarly, a fuller ML-Model to detect fraud by Wang et al. (2022) analyzes publicly listed companies in China, taking into consideration a more holistic approach also with multiple dimensions, like external analyst expectations, debt pressure, asset quality, industry competitive pressure, effectiveness of board, media exposure and regulatory disclosure. The researchers imply that their fuller model is performing better than traditional fraud detection models.

## References

Ashtiani, M. N., & Raahemi, B. (2022). Intelligent Fraud Detection in Financial Statements Using Machine Learning and Data Mining: A Systematic Literature Review. *IEEE Access, 10*, 72504–72525. Retrieved September 14, 2024, from https://doi.org/10.1109/ACCESS.2021.3096799

Bao, Y., Ke, B., Li, B., Yu, Y. J., & Zhang, J. (2020). Detecting Accounting Frauds in Publicly Traded U.S. Firms: A Machine Learning Approach. *Journal of Accounting Research*. Retrieved September 14, 2024, from https://doi.org/10.2139/ssrn.2670703

Bertomeu, J., Cheynel, E., Floyd, E., et al. (2021). Using machine learning to detect misstatements. *Review of Accounting Studies, 26*, 468–519. Retrieved September 14, 2024, from https://doi.org/10.1007/s11142-020-09563-8

Craja, P., Kim, A., & Lessmann, S. (2020). Deep Learning for Detecting Financial Statement Fraud. *Decision Support Systems, 139*, 113421. https://doi.org/10.1016/j.dss.2020.113421

Hassanniakalager, A., Ji, X., Perotti, P., & Tsoligkas, F. (2022). *A Machine Learning Approach to Detect Accounting Frauds*. Retrieved September 14, 2024, from https://www.researchgate.net/publication/360807113_A_Machine_Learning_Approach_to_Detect_Accounting_Frauds

Wang, Y., Ma, Z., Zheng, Y., Yuan, H., Zhang, Y., Liu, Y., & Xu, Z. (2022). *Application of Machine Learning Models in Detecting Financial Fraud in Publicly Traded Companies*. Retrieved September 14, 2024, from https://ssrn.com/abstract=4635606 or https://doi.org/10.2139/ssrn.4635606

Wu, X., & Du, S. (2022). An Analysis on Financial Statement Fraud Detection for Chinese Listed Companies Using Deep Learning. *IEEE Access, 10*, 22516–22532. Retrieved September 14, 2024, from https://doi.org/10.1109/ACCESS.2022.3153478

Zhang, X., Su, J., & Zhou, L. (2021). Identification of Financial Report Fraud Based on Text Analysis. In H. Meng, T. Lei, M. Li, K. Li, N. Xiong, & L. Wang (Eds.), *Advances in Natural Computation, Fuzzy Systems and Knowledge Discovery*. ICNC-FSKD 2020. Lecture Notes on Data Engineering and Communications Technologies, Vol. 88. Springer, Cham. Retrieved September 14, 2024, from https://doi.org/10.1007/978-3-030-70665-4_133

Zhao, Z., & Bai, T. (2022). Financial Fraud Detection and Prediction in Listed Companies Using SMOTE and Machine Learning Algorithms. In Perspectives and Prospects of Computer Recognition and Machine Learning in Signal and Image Processing, Selected Papers from PRML 2022 (Special Issue)

# 13

# Lie Detection Screening of the C-Suite with AI and ML

## 13.1 Detecting the Lies of the C-Suite

The seasoned practitioner in fraud detection might listen to a CEO and subconsciously know that something is not right. Not just because of what is said, but because of how it is said and how the CEO visually acts while saying it.

It could be the CEO's reaction to the equity analyst's challenging question. This is a mixture of the verbal and non-verbal cues given by the CEO. There are many books, articles and theories on deception and lie detection. Some with hard scientific evidence and some in the pseudo-science category. DePaulo et al. (2003) did a meta-analysis of the difference in behavior between people lying and people telling the truth and reduced it to 148 cues. Obviously, cues may be verbal, like the text content spoken and what is said. This may be analyzed with the methods of NLP or Natural Language Understanding (NLU) models treated in Sect. 34.3.

However, non-verbal cues like body language, tone and pitch of the voice, eye movement and facial expressions, might also be cues that can help detect if a CEO is lying. Or a combination of the verbal and non-verbal cues. Regardless of which methods are used, it most often boils down to if there are any behavioral inconsistencies that may act as an indicator of deception of the target.


J. Sørensen, *Shorting Fraud*, https://doi.org/10.1007/978-3-031-81834-9_13

If the investor looks there is a plentitude of both audio and video recordings of C-level staff conducting earning calls, annual general meetings, interviews on business media. Some with known corporate fraudsters blatantly telling lies. This audio and video data can be used to train AI / ML to detect the risk of deceptive and fraudulent behavior.

## 13.2 Lie Detection AI and ML Models in the Public Domain

Due to the natural interest from both law enforcement and the counterintelligence community, some of the innovative work regarding lie detection is naturally confidential, private, and not accessible to the public. However, some work is in the public domain and here are some examples to draw inspiration from, when building models to detect deception in relation to corporate fraudulent behavior.

## 13.3 Acoustic Features of the Voice

The application of acoustic features is interesting, since it may have the potential to be used for analyzing the voice of the executives on earnings calls, on a major scale.

Talaat (2023) created an Enhanced Recurrent Neural Network (ERNN). This is a type of AI that is good at recognizing patterns over time. The model analyzes voice features and speech patterns, focusing on "voice stress" which changes in pitch when a target is not telling the truth. The AI system analyzes the target's voice. It is looking for certain patterns or changes that might indicate the person is lying, changing pitch, when the target is not telling the truth. The model achieved an accuracy score of 97.3%, indicating that it correctly classified 97.3% of the total instances.

Another practical example to get inspiration from is Xue (2019) that trained a Neural Network to detect lies from the Acoustic Features of the voice. The method was found to be better to detect lies than humans are. The study found that the human accuracy in the laboratory experiment was 48%, while the max. accuracy achieved by the lie detector model is 55.8%. The Deep Learning Model is currently publicly accessible at GitHub.[1]

[1] http://web.archive.org/web/20240414041336/https://github.com/alicex2020/Deep-Learning-Lie-Detection.

## 13.4 Facial Expressions and Micro Signaling

Another type of visual cues in lie detection is facial expression and micro signaling. In the case of images, video footage or streaming. Facial expressions, voluntary or involuntary, convey emotional states. In lie detection, researchers focus on involuntary expressions, harder to control, potentially revealing deception. Micro-expressions are brief, involuntary expressions occurring when emotions are concealed or repressed. Lasting less than half a second, they are hard to recognize consciously for human beings.

Several researchers are working with AI models to detect lies from facial cues. For instance, Rodriguez-Diaz et al. (2022) had success training an AI in a controlled card game situation with intentional lying. Monaro et al. (2021) video recording facial expressions lying. The AIs were better than humans in detecting lies. This research may be the foundation and inspiration for training AI models to detect deception by facial expression and micro signaling in earnings calls, annual general meetings, or business interviews.

## 13.5 Acoustic Voice Features and Micro Signaling Combination

Bhamare et al. (2020) suggest a model that combines the acoustic voice features with micro signaling. Adding the layer of Micro Signaling on top of voice features. The algorithm analyzes visual cues such as eye movements, eyebrow raises, and lip movements. It combines audio-based cues such as changes in pitch or loudness. These cues are used to train the deep learning model. The combination of audio and visual cues improves the reliability of the system and the detection rate of deception considerably, according to the paper.

While these AI Audio Visual models may become valuable tools in the near future there still is one caveat. The challenge with a corporate fraud screening framework is that some of these studies are done in highly controlled environments.

Earnings calls and interviews might be more complicated to analyze, since it does not happen in the same highly controlled settings, especially with the visual settings. Like full frontal face recognition, etc.

## References

Bhamare, A. R., Katharguppe, S., & Nancy, J. S. (2020). Deep Neural Networks for Lie Detection with Attention on Bio-signals. In *2020 7th International Conference on Soft Computing & Machine Intelligence (ISCMI)* (pp. 143–147). Stockholm, Sweden. https://doi.org/10.1109/ISCMI51676.2020.9311575

DePaulo, B. M., Lindsay, J. J., Malone, B. E., Muhlenbruck, L., Charlton, K., & Cooper, H. (2003). Cues to Deception. *Psychological Bulletin, 129*(1), 74–118.

Monaro, M., Maldera, S., Scarpazza, C., Sartori, G., & Navarin, N. (2021). Detecting Deception Through Facial Expressions in a Dataset of Videotaped Interviews: A Comparison Between Human Judges and Machine Learning Models. *Computers in Human Behavior*. Retrieved September 14, 2024, from https://doi.org/10.1016/j.chb.2021.107063

Rodriguez-Diaz, N., Aspandi, D., Sukno, F. M., & Binefa, X. (2022). Machine Learning-Based Lie Detector Applied to a Novel Annotated Game Dataset. *Future Internet, 14*(1), 2. Retrieved September 14, 2024, from https://doi.org/10.3390/fi14010002

Talaat, F. M. (2023). Explainable Enhanced Recurrent Neural Network for Lie Detection Using Voice Stress Analysis. *Multimedia Tools and Applications*. Retrieved September 14, 2024, from https://doi.org/10.1007/s11042-023-16769-w

Xue, A. (2019). *An Acoustic Automated Lie Detector*. Princeton. (Thesis). Retrieved September 14, 2024, from https://www.cs.princeton.edu/sites/default/files/alice_xue_spring_2019.pdf

# 14

# Screening Auditors and Equity Analysts Traits Related to Corporate Fraud Risk

## 14.1 Screening Public Auditors' Characteristics Indicative of Corporate Fraud Risk

Public auditors are special stakeholders. They are supposed to be independent with a deep understanding of the corporation. However, despite this special insight they are still involved in major fraud scandals. Therefore, Public Auditors' involvement is interesting to explore when screening for corporate fraud risk.

### 14.1.1 Auditors' Role in Corporate Fraud Cases

One of the main participants in making the yearly and sometimes quarterly reports are the auditors. In a best-case scenario, auditors should be seen as an independent stakeholder, sanity checking and verifying financial statements and reports brought forward by the management of the company.

However, as the collapse of the former auditor giant, Arthur Andersen, previously one of the world's largest accounting firms shows, this does not always happen. Andersen's involvement in the Enron scandal led to its downfall. However, Arthur Andersen is far from alone to have been involved or missed to detect corporate fraud cases. Another recent example is EY that missed the Wirecard Fraud for more than a decade according to Storbeck (2021, October 25). Partridge (2020, September 17) reported that Deloitte was fined a record £15m for failings in the Autonomy case, and Deloitte also was involved in the currently ongoing Tingo case, described in


J. Sørensen, *Shorting Fraud*, https://doi.org/10.1007/978-3-031-81834-9_14

Sect. 18.6, according to Adeoye et al. (2023 December 24), Thomas (2023, October 12), BBC (2022, February 3) and Makortoff (2022, May 12) have reported on KPMGs involvement in the Carillion Collapse case in the UK. KPMG got two fines by The Financial Reporting Council (FRC). One fine (£21 million) for failures in its auditing and one fine (£14.4 million) for misleading FRC. The first fine was the result of the "number, range and seriousness" of issues in KPMG's work for Carillion. The FRC found problems with fundamental auditing principles. In addition to patterns of insufficient professional skepticism. KPMG overlooked multiple red flags indicating Carillion's manipulation of financial results. Specifically, auditors failed to challenge misleading management representations and neglected to investigate indicators of unsustainable practices designed to mask losses and inflate cash flow.

If the biggest and supposedly most sophisticated audit firms on the globe are missing fraud, all audit firms might miss it, either unintentionally or intentionally. The question is what factors regarding the auditors might influence the risk of them missing the fraud, which is discussed in the next sections.

### 14.1.2 Public Auditor Tenure and Corporate Fraud

The relationship between the length of time a Public Auditor has been auditing a publicly listed company and the risk of the audited company committing fraud is complicated.

As a practitioner there are two conflicting views of auditor tenure that Patterson et al. (2018) also deals with. Some argue that long-term auditor relationships may lead to complacency, reducing their effectiveness in identifying errors. Others believe that repeated audits enhance the auditor's understanding of the company, improving their ability to spot misstatements. However, the occurrence of long-term frauds of Wirecard, Enron, etc. with long time auditors attached, raises concerns about the impact of auditor tenure on fraud detection.

The tenure aspect has also been described by Fairchild (2007) in a Game Theory Model that examines the relationship between auditor tenure and the occurrence of managerial fraud. There are two opposing effects, as auditor tenure increases. The positive effect is the auditor's ability to detect fraud increases as time goes by, since they get a deeper understanding of the company. The negative effect is that as time passes, the auditors may also become more sympathetic towards management, potentially increasing the likelihood of condoning corporate fraud.

- **Short Audit Tenures:** On one hand it has been observed in fraud cases that companies which often change auditors may have problems with corporate fraud. These observations are in line with findings that the longer an auditor has been with a company the better the Audit Quality is.
- **Long Audit Tenures:** On the other hand, is the view that the longer the tenure with the audited company the greater the risk it loses its arm's length and objectivity. Like in the case of Wirecard.
- **A sweet spot audit tenure?** With this inconclusive nature of the tenure length, one might suggest that there is a sweet spot tenure, where the public auditor is still critical enough, and at the same time has a solid insight into the company.

### 14.1.3 Other Factors Regarding the Public Auditor and Corporate Fraud

Other factors have been observed from a practitioner's view and to some extent supported by academic research conducted by Khaksar et al. (2021).

This includes factors like the size of the audit firms. Larger audit firms often have more resources and expertise, which can help detect and prevent fraud. The specific red flags to look for are small auditing firms taking on major companies. The specialization of the auditor. If auditors specialize in a particular industry, they are more likely to understand that industry and look through frauds. Is auditing the core business and income stream. In some cases, auditing might only be a part of a one-stop service that the auditor firm is supplying the publicly listed company with. In addition, it supplies e.g. IT-consulting, Management Consulting, etc. In that case the auditor services would often be a minor income stream. In order not to jeopardize the other income streams, the auditor might be forced to turn a blind eye.

In addition, the researchers also found that psychological factors like auditor narcissism with regards to the individual auditor have been observed in fraud cases. Also, the lag between end-of-period and the financial report. What the practitioner should assess here is how long it took, how many auditors, to audit how much. Finally, the audit fee should be assessed. An abnormally high audit fee compared to what would be the norm could be an indicator of fraud risk.

Complex power relations between auditors and the company were found by Assem (2023) in a study on failures to detect and report fraud by public auditors. The auditors felt pressured and intimidated by the companies when the auditor raised fraud issues. Also, the fact that the audit fee is paid by the company that the auditor is supposed to control is a problem with regards to conflicts of interest. Even worse, the power structures within the audit firms with higher level partners who were found dishonest, might pressure the auditors into accepting fraud.

### 14.1.4 Public Auditors Helping Multiple Fraudulent Corporations

While there have been no wider studies found. From a practical case point of view, observations have been made that highly unethical or outright fraudulent companies appear to be clustering around certain specific auditors.

Why this clustering happens is of course not obvious without further research. However, it could mean that either these auditors are too incompetent to see the frauds, and then abused by corporate fraudsters. Another possibility is that these auditors simply do not care about the fraud and turn a blind eye. Finally in the worst-case scenario, the auditor specializes in auditing and helping fraudulent companies.

## 14.2 Screening Equity Analysts' Behavior and Corporate Fraud

Another important group of stakeholders with a special interest in the publicly listed company are equity analysts, covering the publicly listed company. How these equity analysts behave is interesting when screening for corporate fraud.

### 14.2.1 Equity Analysts

Besides the auditors having an inside look into the company, many publicly listed companies are followed by equity analysts.

Equity Analysts are financial analysts who research these publicly traded companies to assess their investment potential. Based on publicly available material, mainly the annual and quarterly reports. However, also analyzing industry and broader economic information. These analysts then publish reports with investment recommendations to investors. With recommendations on buying, selling, or holding the share. Also, they set a target price for the share. This is what the equity analyst thinks the company is worth, based on their estimation models.

The equity analysts, their insights, motives, and behavior are interesting in relation to fraud detection. First, since they cover a limited number of companies, they should have a special insight into the target company. Second, who pays the analysts? There are two types of equity analysts. Buy-side analysts that work for investors like Asset management firms, hedge funds, pension funds, insurance companies. Then there are sell-side analysts, that some way or another are paid by the company to cover the company.

### 14.2.2 Sell-side Equity Analysts

In theory sell-side analysts should be independent, but like auditors, sell-side analysts are paid by the company they analyze and report on. Either directly issuer-paid research or as part of investment banking package deals. Therefore, there is a risk they are not impartial, since they might be fired by the company if the company is not satisfied with the investment reports.

The behavior of equity analysts around fraudulent companies is diverse. Amongst other things it depends on the relations between the equity analyst and the fraudulent corporations.

### 14.2.3 Equity Analysts Dropping Coverage of a Company

A study by Young and Peng (2013) of Equity Analysts and fraudulent behavior in corporations suggests that if an analyst drops the coverage of a company, it could be an indicator of fraudulent behavior of the company. The researchers found that when a company is suspected of accounting fraud, analysts are more likely to stop covering that company rather than just downgrading their recommendations. The more serious the suspected fraud is, the quicker the analysts are to drop coverage of the company. Hence if the investor observes that analysts suddenly stop covering a company it could be a red flag of corporate fraud.

### 14.2.4 Equity Analyst Coverage impact on Earnings Management

While Earnings Management might not be illegal, it might still be viewed as a close relative to its "cousin" financial statement fraud. The conclusions on several studies from e.g. Almaharmeh (2022) and Yu (2008), suggest that the more coverage in quantity (number of analysts following a company) and the higher the quality of these analysts are, the lower the risk of earnings management is in general. In addition, Xu et al. (2013) found that in environments with less regulation and investor protection, more coverage in quantity leads to less earnings management.

## References

Adeoye, A., Quinio, A., & Aliaj, O. (2023, December 24). 'A Fiction': The Fall of a Fintech Star Accused of 'Massive Fraud'. *Financial Times*. Retrieved September 14, 2024, from https://www.ft.com/content/7825234e-d9aa-4274-bd64-949eea18fa88

Almaharmeh, M. I. (2022). Does Analyst Coverage Enhance or Curb Earnings Management? The Impact of Mandatory IFRS Adoption. *International Journal of Management Practice, 15*(2), 253–277. https://doi.org/10.1504/IJMP.2022.121150

Assem, R. (2023). Investigating the Black-Box of External Audit Practice: The Paradox of Auditors' Failure in Detecting and Reporting Fraud. *Journal of Accounting Literature (Early Access)*. Retrieved September 14, 2024, from https://oro.open.ac.uk/87423/1/jal-05-2022-0057.pdf

BBC. (2022, February 3). *Carillion: KPMG Hit with £1.3bn Government Lawsuit Over Audit*. BBC News. Retrieved September 14, 2024, from https://www.bbc.com/news/business-60243464

Fairchild, R. J. (2007). *Does Audit Tenure Lead to More Fraud? A Game-Theoretic Approach*. Retrieved September 14, 2024, from https://ssrn.com/abstract=993400 or https://doi.org/10.2139/ssrn.993400

Khaksar, J., Salehi, M., & DashtBayaz, M. L. (2021). The Relationship Between Auditor Characteristics and Fraud Detection. *Journal of Facilities Management*. ISSN: 1472-5967.

Makortoff, K. (2022, May 12). KPMG to Be Fined £14m for Forging Documents Over Carillion Audit. *The Guardian*. Retrieved September 14, 2024, from https://www.theguardian.com/business/2022/may/12/kpmg-fined-frc-audit-carillion.

Partridge, J. (2020, September 17). Deloitte Fined Record £15m for Failings in Autonomy Audits. *The Guardian*. Retrieved September 14, 2024, from https://www.theguardian.com/business/2020/sep/17/deloitte-fined-record-15m-for-failings-in-autonomy-audits

Patterson, E., Smith, J. R., & Tiras, S. L. (2018). *The Effects of Auditor Tenure on Fraud and Its Detection* (Kelley School of Business Research Paper No. 17–21). Retrieved September 14, 2024, from https://ssrn.com/abstract=2935224 or https://doi.org/10.2139/ssrn.2935224

Storbeck, O. (2021, October 25). EY and Wirecard: Anatomy of a Flawed Audit. *Financial Times*. Retrieved September 14, 2024, from https://www.ft.com/content/bcadbdcb-5cd7-487e-afdd-1e926831e9b7

Thomas, D. (2023, October 12). *Carillion: Record Fine for KPMG Over 'Exceptional' Failure*. BBC News. Retrieved September 14, 2024, from https://www.bbc.com/news/uk-67087757

Xu, B., Li, K., & Zhang, W. (2013). Empirical Research of the Relevance among Analysts Coverage, Institutional Environment and Earnings Management. In *The 19th International Conference on Industrial Engineering and Engineering Management* (pp. 95–102). Engineering Economics Management.

Young, S. M., & Peng, E. Y. (2013). *An Analysis of Accounting Frauds and the Timing of Analyst Coverage Decisions and Recommendation Revisions: Evidence from the US*. Fordham University Schools of Business Research Paper.

Yu, F. (2008). Analyst Coverage and Earnings Management. *Journal of Financial Economics, 88*, 245–271. Retrieved September 14, 2024, from https://ssrn.com/abstract=828484

# 15

# Screening Other Public Disclosures for Risk of Corporate Fraud

## 15.1 Detecting Suspicious News and Disclosures with Text Analyzing Machine Learning

We already looked at text analytics specific to company financial reports in Sect. 12.3. However, this is not the only way that text analytics might be used to detect corporate fraud. Also important, analyzing company reports for corporate fraud is a lagging screening indicator. The investor is mostly analyzing historic events of the past quarter or year. To address the delay in traditional fraud detection methods, the investor may turn to leading indicators like news, social media, or other disclosures about the company, to screen for early warning signs of corporate fraud.

To use more general public disclosures for fraud detection, one may use other types of ML models to analyze the textual content of the announcements. An example of such an ML model has been developed by Liu et al. (2020). The model is identifying fraudulently publicly listed Chinese companies by text analytics. By analyzing news and user generated content from financial media platforms, fraudulent listed companies are detected. This is done with implicit information in unstructured text data, by using a text classification model based on Systemic Functional Linguistics (SFL) theory. This captures the literal meaning of words and sentences, as well as the primary intentions and attitudes expressed in the text.

The method involves extracting Term Frequency-Inverse Document Frequency (TF-IDF) features, which basically shows the importance of words and phrases in a document set. Topic features, which represent main themes


J. Sørensen, *Shorting Fraud*, https://doi.org/10.1007/978-3-031-81834-9_15

discussed in a text. Finally, the Explosive News Quantity features that count rapidly appearing news on a topic are also used.

The empirical analysis was carried out by collecting texts on 124 companies using the Chinese financial information platforms - Eastmoney & JRJ.com.

Models like these may support investors screen and detect corporate fraud earlier, than traditional methods focusing on company reports.

## 15.2 Suspicious Patterns Around Material and Voluntary Disclosures

Material events are significant developments impacting the company's stock price and performance (e.g., mergers, lawsuits, leadership changes, product launches). Voluntary disclosures are information that companies choose to share, even though they are not legally required to do so. Like strategic plans, or other non-financial information.

It has been observed that these disclosures might be abused by fraudulent companies in several ways. A common objective of this is to send a distorted signal, supporting the management deceiving shareholders. This includes the timing of disclosures, the number of disclosures, and manipulating the content of disclosures.

Suspicious timing - Here the positive or negative statements are strategically timed in relation to other events. A practice reported by Aboody and Kasznik (2000), which found that executives timed the voluntary disclosures to maximize their own stock options benefits. Selectively, choosing to disclose good or bad news.

Another practice could be a high number of irrelevant positive spun disclosures that are not material in nature, even though presented so. For instance, the announcement of partnerships with little economic value has been observed in fraud cases.

Lang and Lundholm (2000) found that management may manipulate stock prices up with a growing number of disclosures leading up to a secondary offering. This relates both to the number of disclosures and the previous point about suspicious timing of disclosures. Manipulation is downplaying negative material events or overstating the material events positively.

First, the investor might use the general statistical methods from e.g. Section 11.10 to detect anomalies and see if there are suspicious patterns around the number of disclosures, and the timing of these disclosures.

Second, content analysis like Natural Language Processing (NLP), touched in Sect. 12.3 & 15.1 and treated in more detail in Sect. 34.3. may be used to analyze and screen these disclosures for indications of corporate fraud.

## 15.3 Suspicious Timing of Earnings Announcements

Like the timing of various types of disclosures, timing of earnings announcements is also a strategy that may be abused by fraudulent companies. Cheng et al. (2023) found that companies with fraudulent financial reporting are more likely to time their earnings announcements strategically.

In general, investors have different attention spans and focus, at different times. This can be abused as a tool by the fraudulent top management. For example, research by DellaVigna and Pollet (2009) finds inattention on Fridays to earnings announcements. Looking at the day of the week and the time of the day, Michaely et al. (2015) found that Friday evenings were used to publicize the worst earnings news of listed companies.

Also, Johnson and So (2017) found that there is a relationship between scheduling of earnings calls and the expected earnings result. Specifically, firms that schedule their announcements later than expected tend to deliver worse news compared to those that schedule earlier than expected.

Aggregation of these insights may help the investor build statistical models that can be used to analyze and screen for companies with suspicious earnings announcement behavior.

## 15.4 Suspicious Shareholder Meetings Activity

The management has control over the Annual General Meeting as well as extraordinary general meetings. Screening shareholder meetings is important since they may be abused by management to cover fraudulent activity.

A study by Gam et al. (2021) on the South Korean Stock market found that management of fraudulent companies strategically place their Annual General meetings on popular dates to avoid attendance of especially institutional investors, avoiding potential scrutiny. Another study by Li and Yermack (2014) found that management might place their physical annual general meeting in a remote location to avoid attendance and scrutiny. The study also found that despite most voting being done electronically before the meeting, voter participation decreased when meetings were conducted at unusual hours.

Working hands on with fraudulent companies it also appears from the field observation of cases (not found to be researched by academia yet), that usage of extraordinary shareholder meetings (ESM) with e.g. minimal notice appears to occur frequently in fraudulent companies. These ESMs may have changes in the articles of association, capital structure, and equity issuance activity mentioned in Sect. 15.6. The ESMs may happen in serial piecemeal style, with one or few point agendas, rendering it hard for investors to attend.

## 15.5 Screening Shareholder Meeting Content and Presentations by Executives & Directors

Written shareholder meetings material, which consists of more types of text material, might be screened by models based on FinChain-BERT, developed by Yang et al. (2023).

The FinChain-BERT is derived from Google's NLP model called Bidirectional Encoder Representations from Transformers (BERT). BERT uses transformers and bidirectional training to understand the context of each word in a sentence.

The FinChain-Bert is designed for financial fraud detection. The model presents an attention mechanism called the "Fraud Focus Filter," which is used in the initial stage of data input, where it highlights key information that might be connected to fraudulent behavior. This streamlines the processing and analysis of data, which allows a more targeted approach with regards to detection of corporate fraud.

Alternative, more general NLP model principles presented in Sect. 34.3. may be used for analyzing textual content from shareholder meetings. In addition, management oral and video captures of presentations might be screened and analyzed by the lie detection models described in Sect. 13.

## 15.6 Suspicious Equities Issuances Activity

It has been observed that fraudulent listed companies attempted and sometimes succeeded in multiple kinds of new share offerings or converting debt to equity. This to have the fraudulent company improve the cash or debt situation. While the management may carry the fraud forward with new capital, shareholders are hit by dilution of ownership.

These practical firsthand empirical observations are supported by research by Bonini and Boraschi-Diaz (2013). The study found that prior to a corporate scandal, companies issued more equity than their peers. Two years before the scandal they issued 7.7 times more equity than peers. One year before the scandal, 4.26 times more, dropping to 2.39 times more in the year of the scandal.

It means that screening for these abnormal equity issuances may be a leading indicator of corporate fraud up to two years before the scandal.

## 15.7 Suspicious Stock Splits and Reverse Splits

Another fraud indicator that the investor should look for are abnormal corporate actions, like stock splits and reverse stock splits. These may be abused by management and could be indicators of fraudulent activity.

This is supported by research by Titman et al. (2020) and Elnahas et al. (2016). The studies found that opportunistic stock splits may be related to fraudulent activities by management.

This includes manipulating Earnings Per Share (EPS), price tampering and avoiding delisting, etc. Especially retail investors may fall for these corporate action deceptions, not realizing that the value of the company has not changed.

## 15.8 Suspicious Share Buybacks

Strange share buybacks have been observed in investigations of potential fraud cases. Buybacks may be abused by the fraudulent management in several ways. This could be support for insider trading by management or more general deception of investors, which is documented by Wang et al. (2022) and Chan et al. (2010). The management may e.g. signal share buybacks, cancel it later, or follow up with token buybacks. Therefore, screening for abnormal buyback announcements and patterns of suspicious share buybacks may help detect fraudulent companies.

## 15.9 Corrections and Financial Restatements

In several fraud investigations it has been found that financial restatement was a red flag. This is supported by Fischer and Shumburger (2022). They found that most of the about 18,000 financial restatements in publicly listed companies in the US, in the period 1995 till 2020 were due to errors, like misapplication of GAAP, Clerical Issues, etc. However, still short of 2% (312) were classified due to fraud. This is about 13 confirmed cases a year on average in the US. Therefore, financial restatements are still a potential indicator when screening for corporate fraud. Also bear in mind that when investigating financial restatements, there might be a gray zone between errors and fraud. So, the number due to fraud could be higher, when a deep-dive investigation of a company's restatement is conducted.

The study also showed there might be industry related trends in restatements. Relating to e.g. intangible or fixed asset impairments, in addition to revenue recognition. This has been observed in actual cases with e.g. channel stuffing, where significant portions of the revenue disappeared year-over-year. These methods are described in more detail in Sect. 24.3.

## References

Aboody, D., & Kasznik, R. (2000). CEO Stock Option Awards and the Timing of Corporate Voluntary Disclosures. *Journal of Accounting and Economics, 29*(1), 73–100. Retrieved September 14, 2024, from Retrieved September 14, 2024, from https://doi.org/10.2139/ssrn.144589

Bonini, S., & Boraschi-Diaz, D. (2013). The Causes and Financial Consequences of Corporate Frauds. In *Entrepreneurship, Finance, Governance and Ethics* (pp. 295–314). Retrieved September 14, 2024, from https://doi.org/10.1007/978-94-007-3867-6_13. Retrieved September 14, 2024, from https://www.researchgate.net/publication/290896426_The_Causes_and_Financial_Consequences_of_Corporate_Frauds

Chan, K., Ikenberry, D. L., Lee, I., & Wang, Y. (2010). Share Repurchases as a Potential Tool to Mislead Investors. *Journal of Corporate Finance, 16*(2). Retrieved September 14, 2024, from https://ssrn.com/abstract=1485583 or https://doi.org/10.2139/ssrn.1485583

Cheng, X., Palmon, D., Yang, Y., et al. (2023). Strategic Earnings Announcement Timing and Fraud Detection. *Journal of Business Ethics, 182*, 851–874. Retrieved September 14, 2024, from https://doi.org/10.1007/s10551-021-05029-2

DellaVigna, S., & Pollet, J. M. (2009). Investor Inattention and Friday Earnings Announcements. *The Journal of Finance, 64*(2), 709–749. Retrieved September 14, 2024, from http://www.jstor.org/stable/20487983

Elnahas, A., Jain, P. K., & McInish, T. H. (2016). Stock Splits, Accounting Manipulation, and Unwarranted CEO Compensation. *Opportunistic stock splits.* Retrieved September 14, 2024, from https://doi.org/10.2139/ssrn.2800765

Fischer, M., & Shumburger, D. K. (2022). Corporate Financial Restatements From 1995 Through 2020. *Journal of Accounting and Finance, 22*(1). Retrieved September 14, 2024, from https://doi.org/10.33423/jaf.v22i1.4983

Gam, Y. K., Gupta, P., Im, J., & Shin, H. (2021). Evasive Shareholder Meetings and Corporate Fraud. *Journal of Corporate Finance, 66*, 101807. Retrieved September 14, 2024, from https://doi.org/10.1016/j.jcorpfin.2020.101807

Johnson, T. L., & So, E. C. (2017). Time Will Tell: Information in the Timing of Scheduled Earnings News. *Journal of Financial and Quantitative Analysis, 53(6),* 2431–2464.

Lang, M. H., & Lundholm, R. (2000). Voluntary Disclosure and Equity Offerings: Reducing Information Asymmetry or Hyping the Stock? *Contemporary Accounting Research, 17*(4), 623–662.

Li, L. Y., & Yermack, D. (2014). *Evasive Shareholder Meetings.* (NBER Working Paper No. w19991). Retrieved September 14, 2024, from https://ssrn.com/abstract=2413339

Liu, H., Tao, L., & Liu, M. (2020). Research on Financial Fraud Identification of Listed Companies Based on Text Data Mining. In *2020 International Conference on Image, Video Processing and Artificial Intelligence* (Vol. 11584, 115841X). SPIE. Retrieved September 14, 2024, from https://doi.org/10.1117/12.2581398

Michaely, R., Rubin, A., & Vedrashko, A. (2015). Further Evidence on the Strategic Timing of Earnings News: Joint Analysis of Weekdays and Times of Day. *Journal of Accounting and Economics.* (Forthcoming).

Titman, S., Wei, C., & Zhao, B. (2020). Stock Price Manipulation: Corporate Actions and the Exploitation of Retail Investors in China. Retrieved September 14, 2024, from https://doi.org/10.2139/ssrn.3569429

Wang, D. S., Li, X., Tang, H., & Sun, Y. (2022). Insider Trading and Fraudulent Share Repurchase. *Credit and Capital Markets, 55*(2), 227–260.

Yang, X., Zhang, C., Sun, Y., Pang, K., Jing, L., Wa, S., & Lv, C. (2023). FinChain-BERT: A High-Accuracy Automatic Fraud Detection Model Based on NLP Methods for Financial Scenarios. *Information, 14*(9), 499.

# 16

# Screening for Corporate Governance Factors and Adverse Media Signals Related to Corporate Fraud

## 16.1 The Board of Directors

There has been extensive research on corporate governance and corporate fraud. Velte (2023) did a review of 94 studies and found that several results were inconclusive. However, some corporate governance factors have been found viable and might be used to screen for corporate fraud.

In several jurisdictions it is possible to get more detailed information on the board members. With focus on different aspects like the board composition, board committees and internal audit functions. Variables such as board independence, expertise, gender diversity, and social ties are examined for their impact on financial reporting quality.

Western corporate governance studies From a US perspective by Abbot et al. (2000) found that active and independent audit committees on corporate boards are less likely to be sanctioned by the SEC.

Studying Financial Statements from publicly listed Saudi Arabian companies 2014 to 2019, Ebaid (2023) found that board independence and board size had an influence on Financial Statement Fraud. The bigger the board the higher the risk of fraud. The more independent the board is of the top management, the less risk of financial statement fraud.

Studies by Mousavi et al. (2022) and Rostami and Rezaei (2021) researched the relationship between Corporate Governance Structure, Fraud and Money Laundering. The research was conducted on all publicly listed companies on the Theran Stock exchange in the period 2013–19. The studies investigated factors such as the board's and the audit committee's independence, the board's financial expertise, the board's industry expertise, and


J. Sørensen, *Shorting Fraud*, https://doi.org/10.1007/978-3-031-81834-9_16

board members' effort put into the board's work. While some of these indicators are harder to screen for than others, they have been observed in actual fraud cases.

One of the most central risks and extensively studied is the CEO duality role. The cases where the CEO also serves as the chairman of the board. This means the CEO is overseeing herself. Here there is a significantly higher risk of corporate fraud. This is for the obvious reason that the control conducted by the board on the CEO is weakened if the CEO is chairman of the board at the same time. This risk of fraud is supported by Dechow et al. (1996) and Yang et al. (2017). In some countries and jurisdictions like Denmark, it is prohibited by law for listed companies that the chairman and CEO is the same person. In other jurisdictions it is common practice or de facto standards that the role is not held by the same person.

In Table 16.1 corporate governance indicators that may be used to screen for corporate fraud are listed. Some of them, like simple board size, are available directly from many company registrars or corporate data providers as raw data. Others must be processed in more advanced analytics. For instance, the number of board members with industry-specific experience can be done with professional network analysis and relationship mapping. To map out current and historic industry experience of the board members. This is possible on a larger scale if the data providers can supply the necessary data of adequate quality.

The Corporate Governance data might be found in sources like BoardEx that holds detailed information on board members, committees, and executive remuneration. There are several other vendors providing data on institutional ownership like Thomson Reuters, Morning Star, etc.

## 16.2 The CEO & C-level Management Fraud Risk Screening

Screening top management like CEOs, CFOs, and other C-level staff is a potential way to detect corporate fraud.

### 16.2.1 Executives' Participation in Criminal Cases and Civil Suits

First, looking at criminal cases, the courtroom activity is just the tip of the iceberg. In many jurisdictions, a significant number of criminal cases referred by law enforcement are dropped and will not see their day in court. Going

**Table 16.1** Select board factors from research and practical observations with suggested (proxy) variables

| Category | Factor | Explanation | (Proxy) Variable |
|---|---|---|---|
| Board Composition | Board Size | The bigger the board, the higher risk of fraud | Number of board members |
| | Independent Directors | Independent directors can take decisions without influence from management. Higher rate, means less fraud | Fraction of independent directors on board. Minority, Majority or Supermajority |
| | Independent Audit Committee | Independent audit committee equals less chance of fraud | Presence of an independent audit committee (Yes/No) |
| | Financial Expertise of Audit Committee | The audit committee has good financial expertise | Number of financial experts in the audit committee |
| Chairman | CEO/Chairman Duality | If role is split there is less likelihood of fraud than if it is not | CEO /Chairman the same person (Yes/No) |
| Directors | Attention to & understanding of Financial Matters | If directors pay attention / understand financial reporting, there is less likelihood of fraud | Number of board members with financial background |
| | Time and Energy Dedicated in Board Role | The more time and energy the directors focus on the specific company the less likelihood of fraud | Average number of boards a member serves on. Number of board meetings |
| | Understanding of Specific Industry | The better the board members understand the specific industry of the company the less likelihood of fraud | Number of board members with industry-specific experience |

through all jurisdictions on the globe is impossible. However, in the US, TRAC (2023) reports that for white-collar crime only 38% of law enforcement agency referrals of natural persons are prosecuted. For cases involving corporations, a little more than 5% were prosecuted in the US in 2022. So, the risk of a penal case is low, and this is a downtrend.

The civil courtroom activity is even more opaque. Here out-of-court settlements may be conducted. This means for every case the executive has been involved in, there is a chance that the case never went to any type of court and was kept under wraps.

Depending on the jurisdiction it is also different what will be publicized about the case. In some courts nothing, in other courts, documents may be found, but with a heavy workload, sometimes only manually.

However, in some parts of the world, in addition to news articles, court databases are digitized and accessible for research, background checks and investigations.

There is a natural tendency to focus on whether the executive has been a defendant in a case. However, it may also be of interest if the executive has been a plaintiff and even on the witness list of a case. One complex fraud case was revealed by looking at the witness list of another major fraud case. In many white-collar crime cases the criminals do not work in isolation, but in networks, where they support each other. So, an executive being a witness, e.g. supporting a white-collar criminal is also an interesting indicator when screening for corporate fraud.

One might tend to specifically look for and focus on financial crime cases. However, misdemeanors and violations in unrelated areas are also interesting when screening executives, since they tell something about the character of the person. Even petty theft from a grocery store is telling on the nature of the executive. If an affluent executive is willing to incriminate herself for a few dollars of petty theft, there is a natural risk that she would do the same for a couple of millions.

### 16.2.2 Top-Management Involvement in Past Bankruptcies

As was seen in Sect. 7.1.1, a high number of bankruptcies might be related to corporate fraud. In the practical setting it has also been observed that there is a relationship between the risk of corporate fraud and the bankruptcy history of the individual top manager. In the most extreme case observed, the top manager was previously involved in 30 bankruptcy cases in private companies. While it is not a crime to be involved in a bankruptcy case, when screening for executive involvement in historic bankruptcy cases, the number and nature of the bankruptcies is relevant.

### 16.2.3 The CEO's Age and Risk of Fraud

Schneider and Brühl (2023) found that CEO age and risk of financial statement fraud follows a u-shaped curve. With the highest risk of fraud with a young CEO, and a risk dropping until the age of 60 years and then rising until the age of 70. This is supported by cases observed in a practical setting. The most extreme cases observed were conducted by fraudsters in the age range 25–35. Speculating in the motives, these young CEOs appear determined to show how big a success they are. Show success no matter what it takes. At the other end of the age scale, the CEO might fall behind, and turn to unorthodox methods to keep up, at least on the surface.

### 16.2.4 CEO Gender and risk of Fraud

This is an interesting field of study. Previously, research by Weeks et al. (1999) and Ho et al. (2015) have suggested that female CEOs are less likely to commit fraud. However, more recent research by Schneider and Brühl (2023) found a weak association between female CEOs and accounting fraud. Note that the researchers say it should be taken with caution because of the small amount of data in the sample.

This is interesting from a fraud screening perspective and general perception of female CEOs with regards to fraud. Previously the general notion was that female CEOs were especially trustworthy, compared to male CEOs. However, could it be that equality and gender neutrality with regards to the CEO position over time has erased that special characteristic of the female CEO.

In actual fraud cases, it has been observed this notion of a more trustworthy female CEO has been actively abused by female fraudsters, because the guards are down with investors and financiers.

This is due to the social construct and the public image of the stereotypical fraudsters are the white executive males of Enron, WorldCom or Wirecard.

However, far from all convicted or potential corporate fraudsters fit the profile of white middle-aged males. One of the most prominent current examples is the founder and CEO of OneCoin Ltd., Ruja Ignatova. A fugitive, she is currently number three on the FBI Ten Most Wanted Fugitives list, according to Federal Bureau of Investigation (2024).

Other examples mentioned in Sect. 8.5 are the convicted Elizabeth Holmes and the indicted and by DOJ alleged corporate fraudster and CEO, Charlie Javice. At the time of writing Ms. Javice is awaiting trial on charges of e.g., securities fraud, wire fraud, bank fraud. Ms. Javice is pleading not guilty.

There is a chance that the stereotypical view of the middle-aged white male white-collar criminal may lead to less focus on female corporate fraudsters and lead to less charges against them. This biased view may also be observed in the justice system regarding female white-collar criminals. Female white-collar criminals experience more lenient sentences compared to male criminals for white-collar crime according to Hagan et al. (1980) and Turner (2023).

The female corporate criminal at executive level is an area that is underrepresented in research. The focus has been on pink-collar criminals, which are women in lower corporate positions conducting financial crime, not women executives conducting material corporate fraud.

### 16.2.5 The CEO Tenure, Entrenchment and Risk of Fraud

There is different research on the tenure of executives and corporate fraud risk. Nothing is conclusive with regards to the simple time factor in the form of tenure. Latest research by Schneider and Brühl (2023) suggests that the risk of fraud by the CEO is highest in the first years, leveling off in year 3–4, but with a high variance in the subsequent years, when looking at the time factor alone.

### 16.2.6 C-Level Churn Rate and Risk of Fraud

From a practitioner's point of view, a high churn rate on executives below the CEO has been observed as a red flag. While no current academic research has been found, it appears that frequent changes in the C-level two and senior management level may be a red flag, in the case of the CEO orchestrating the fraud.

The CEO may frequently change CFO and other senior level positions when these executives start to get a notion of the fraud or start to push back on the fraud. Short C-level stints and high churn rate, many C-level replacements. Therefore, top management average tenure of C-level is interesting when screening, for the risk of corporate fraud.

## 16.3 Public Record Activity of Corporations and all Corporate officers

Corporations and corporate officers will have a public track record of public activity. From a fraud perspective many of these might be interesting. However, four of these activity areas have been found to be mostly interesting. Most importantly are legal actions. The others are lobbyist activity, political contributions, and charity contributions.

### 16.3.1 Screening For Legal Actions

This is one of the most critical areas to screen for. While one could screen the entire world for all types of violations of laws and regulations, focusing on corporate fraud, the following areas have been found to be mostly relevant.

**Criminal Law:**

- **Felonies:** Serious crimes like embezzlement or securities fraud should be on the top of the radar.

**Civil Law:**

- **Contract Disputes** - Fraudulent companies have been observed to be involved in activities like breach of contract. Relating to agreements between the company, suppliers, customers, and financiers.
- **Intellectual Property Disputes** - Corporate fraudsters may misuse intellectual property, such as stealing trade secrets or abusing others' intellectual property without paying proper licensing fees, etc.
- **Employment Law** - If a company engages in fraudulent practices that affect its employees, such as wrongful termination or wage problems, it could be an indicator of something bigger going on.
- **Tort Law:** Similar if a company's activities cause harm or financial loss to others, it could be a sign of corporate fraud is going on.

**Other Areas:**

- **Bankruptcy Law:** Involvement in bankruptcies as described in detail in Sect. 7.1.1. If a company fraudulently hides assets or misrepresents its financial status during bankruptcy proceedings in subsidiaries, etc.

- **Administrative Law:** Companies may violate laws governing the procedures and decision-making of government agencies, such as securities regulations.
- **Tax Law:** Companies committing fraud often engage in tax evasion too. So, tax cases might be an indicator that something else is going on related to corporate fraud.

### 16.3.2 Screening Political Lobbyist Activity

Corporate fraudsters do not play by the rules. Therefore, they might even try to change the rules, so they fit the corporation and its modus operandi better.

A study by Yu and Yu (2011) found that firms that engage in lobbying are less likely to be detected for fraud and can evade detection for about 120 days more than average. Regulators are 38% less likely to detect these firms. These fraudulent firms tend to spend significantly more on lobbying, especially during fraudulent periods. It means that when hunting for fraud, screening, and analyzing data from lobbyism databases could be a way to find companies with substantial risk of corporate fraud.

If we look at the VW Dieselgate scandal explained in Section 5.4.2.1. The German car making industry, which VW is the dominant part of, was aggressively lobbying German, European and US political systems for less strict rules on diesel before the fraud was revealed, as reported by King (2015) and Ewing (2015). Therefore, looking at lobbyism and aggressively lobbying companies, might detect some fraudulent companies.

### 16.3.3 Screening for Political Contributions and Influence

It has been observed that corporate fraudsters are actively engaging in political influence and contributions. Like in the recent case of Sam Bankman-Fried mentioned in Section 5.3.2.1.

Corruption, bribery, and political contributions may be an indicator of corporate fraud. An example case is the major Odebrecht case reported by Chavkin (2019) and Gallas (2019). The case was a massive corruption scandal of bribery and political influence, involving 12 countries. However, the case also involved multiple different corporate fraud practices, including false accounting, financial misstatements, inflating project costs and bid rigging.

To screen for political contributions, it is important to understand the setting. The type of governments varies across the many jurisdictions which harbor the 60,000 listed companies. Both on national, regional, and local level. If we look from a traditional break down of government in three branches, which is the case in many of the world's countries that has stock exchanges, it consists of:

- **Legislative branch** responsible for creating the laws. Usually made up of a parliament or congress, elected by the people
- **Executive branch** responsible for executing the laws. Usually headed by a president or prime minister, who is also elected by the people or indirect by the parliament.
- **Judicial branch:** responsible for interpreting the laws. Commonly headed by a high or supreme court, where judges are appointed by the executive branch, elected by the legislative branch, or elected by the people.

This means that all these, some of these or none of these might be elected by the constituents.

It means that both the persons making the laws (politicians), the one executing the laws (prosecutors, state attorneys, district attorneys, and even law enforcement agents), the one interpreting the laws (judges) might be up for election and run campaigns that cost money to conduct.

The company's and executives' contributions are not only to the lawmakers in the legislative branch, but also to persons in the executive branch and judicial branch. The two latter are especially interesting with regards to fraud.

Since supporting the executive branch might have influence on the prosecution and the judicial branch influence on the final verdict of specific cases that the fraudulent company is involved in.

There are different disclosure rules in different jurisdictions. In some places these are directly available in public databases that might be used for screening for fraudulent companies. In other jurisdictions, activist groups, and Non-Government Organizations (NGOs) might have collected and aggregated these in databases or lists.

It is especially interesting to screen and observe contributions from a betting perspective. Betting on a winner. Is the corporation making blanket contributions to all parties, playing on all horses, in elections with uncertainty about the outcome? Is the corporation making contributions to a single candidate that already has a high likelihood of being elected. Is the corporation making huge contributions to an underdog in the race, in hopes of the candidate being elected.

From the perspective of the actively fraudulent company, these contributions should be seen as a kind of indirect, latent dormant bribery or obstruction of justice.

This is somewhat supported by research as seen below. While no research directly addressing corporate fraud and political donations has been found, there is other related research. E.g. of corporate interactions between campaign contributions and the benefit to the contributing company from the legislative branch, like in presidential or general elections. In addition, they focus on the financial benefits to the company of supporting the winner. A study of Brazilian election by Claessens et al. (2008) found companies that financially supported the campaigns of elected federal deputies experienced improved stock market performance. In addition, the study found donor firms raised their bank leverage after the election, implying that access to bank finance was a key advantage of political connections.

Similarly, a study in the US conducted by Huber and Kirchler (2013) found that firms that made larger contributions to the winning candidate in US presidential elections from 1992 to 2004 experienced above normal positive returns on their stocks, post-election.

Finally, a study conducted as an experiment (legislative branch) by Kalla and Broockman (2016) found that a person's access to the elected senior representatives was between three or four times more likely for a political donor.

### 16.3.4 Screening Charity Contributions

An interesting observation with fraudulent companies and corporate executives is their contributions to charities and similar.

On top of political donations, Cha (2002) found that many fraudsters, like Bernard Ebbers (WorldCom), Jeffery Skilling (Enron) and Bernie Madoff, donated their ill-gotten gains to charities, universities, museums, etc. In the Madoff case, some of the money he stole from the charity funds investing with him, he gave away to other charities.

The motives for charity donation may vary. It could be a manipulative tool to appear as a model citizen or fueling the fraudster's ego. It may also be to butter up other stakeholders that have a personal interest in the specific charity. Another possibility is the personal redemption of the fraudster. The fraudster is trying to redeem the evil done in one place with good deeds in another.

One of the more abnormal charity contributor cases of corporate fraudsters, is Robert Allen Stanford, serving 110 years for a major $7 billion Ponzi scheme as reported by Brubaker and Harris (2012). Stanford's extravagant charity activities included everything from community projects, educational support, museum donations, healthcare, disaster relief efforts, and most prominently funding major international sports events within cricket. This case may be studied in detail for abnormal charity contributions when setting up screening methods for corporate fraudsters abuse of charity contributions.

There was no targeted academic research found describing fraudsters' usage of charities, but it is an interesting field of future study.

## 16.4 Broad Adverse Media Screening for Fraud Signals

This chapter explores the use of Adverse Media Screening (AMS) for corporate fraud detection. Traditionally used in financial crime for due diligence, AMS can also be used in a broader scope to identify potential corporate fraud.

### 16.4.1 Adverse Media Screening for Corporate Fraud Detection

Adverse Media Screening (AMS) is a well-known discipline within Financial Crime areas. These are used for e.g. Know your Customer (KYC) processes in relation to onboarding customers onto financial institutions or as ongoing due diligence of the customer base. This is to counter that customers or potential customers of the financial institutions are engaged in known dubious or criminal behavior, which might become a risk to the financial institution. However, adverse media screening might also be conducted in a more dragnet style, looking for signals related to corporate fraud.

### 16.4.2 Simple Setup of Adverse Media Screening

A simple but still effective way to screen for fraud candidates is screening:

- Mainstream media,
- Special business media
- Social media

The investor may screen for certain types of articles and hit words related to fraud. This may be done with tools like Really Simple Syndication (RSS) readers, or tools that combine RSS readers with news monitoring, keywords, and key phrases monitoring. Tools like Feedly, Inoreader or NewsBlur, aggregate and organize content from various channels in one central place. This includes sources like news websites, blogs, social media, and newsletters. These tools allow users to subscribe to specific personally tailored "Corporate Fraud Risk" news.

Some of the tools also offer features like highlighting certain phrases and removing duplicate news. It means that the investor may follow hundreds of news sources and only get the most relevant news hits shown. The trick is calibration - to get only the relevant hits.

Finding targets with these simple screening tools is effective from a practical adverse media screening point of view if the investor spends time on calibrating them to look for fraud signals only.

### 16.4.3 Advanced Adverse Media Screening tools

Another option is to acquire off the shelf or customized tools built by companies like Thomson Reuters, Bureau van Dijk, Refinitiv, etc. If the investor has the funds, these tools might be customized specifically to her special needs, screening the live news streams specifically for indicators of corporate fraud.

Alternatively, the investor might also use the big data feeds provided by these institutions in their own customized Natural Language Understanding (NLU) models to specifically screen for indicators of corporate fraud.

### 16.4.4 Which AMS Approach to take?

The investor will encounter potential fraud targets in the simple setup. However, success depends on the investor's ability to pick the correct news sources and how to calibrate the system.

The main problem is how to integrate AMS to other processes and tools the investor uses in the overall framework. The more Advanced Media Screening data and aggregator providers might offer almost plug- and-play integrations to other tools used. E.g. professional deep-dive investigative OSINT tools like Maltego, Blackdot Videris, or integrate to supportive ML tools.

## References

Abbott, L. J., Park, Y., & Parker, S. (2000). The Effects of Audit Committee Activity and Independence on Corporate Fraud. *Managerial Finance, 26*(11), 55–68. Retrieved September 14, 2024, from [https://www.emerald.com/insight/content/doi/10.1108/03074350010766993/full/html]

Brubaker Calkins, L., & Harris, A. (2012, June 15). Stanford gets 110-year Sentence for $7 Billion Fraud. *1 Bloomberg*.

Cha, A. E. (2002, September 15). Corporate Scandals Tainting Donations. *The Washington Post*. Retrieved September 14, 2024, from https://www.washingtonpost.com/archive/politics/2002/09/15/corporate-scandals-tainting-donations/7f6e5d2b-aa79-4c87-ac08-c63d4514d677/

Chavkin, S. (2019). The Leaked Odebrecht Documents That Helped ICIJ Uncover the Truth. *International Consortium of Investigative Journalists [ICIJ]*. Retrieved September 14, 2024, from https://www.icij.org/investigations/bribery-division/the-leaked-odebrecht-documents-that-helped-icij-uncover-the-truth/

Claessens, S., Feyen, E. H. B., & Laeven, L. A. (2008). Political Connections and Preferential Access to Finance: The Role of Campaign Contributions. *Journal of Financial Economics, 88*(3). Retrieved September 14, 2024, from https://ssrn.com/abstract=945196

Dechow, P. M., Sloan, R. G., & Sweeney, A. P. (1996). Causes and Consequences of Earnings Manipulation: An Analysis of Firms Subject to Enforcement Actions by the SEC. *Contemporary Accounting Research, 13*, 1–36.

Ebaid, I. E. (2023). Board Characteristics and the Likelihood of Financial Statements Fraud: Empirical Evidence from An Emerging Market. *Future Business Journal, 9*(47). Retrieved September 14, 2024, from https://doi.org/10.1186/s43093-023-00218-z

Ewing, J. (2015, September 28). Volkswagen Scandal Highlights European Stalling on New Emissions Tests. *The New York Times*. Retrieved September 14, 2024, from https://www.nytimes.com/2015/09/29/world/europe/volkswagen-scandal-highlights-european-stalling-on-new-emissions-tests.html?_r=0

Federal Bureau of Investigation. (2024). Ruja Ignatova. *FBI Ten Most Wanted Fugitives*. Retrieved September 23, 2024 from https://web.archive.org/web/20240910053521/https://www.fbi.gov/wanted/topten/ruja-ignatova.

Gallas, D. (2019). Brazil's Odebrecht Corruption Scandal Explained. *BBC News*, Retrieved September 14, 2024, from https://web.archive.org/web/20240524154008/https://www.bbc.com/news/business-39194395

Hagan, J., Nagel, I. H., & Albonetti, C. (1980). Differential Sentencing of White-Collar Offenders in Ten Federal District Courts. *American Sociological Review, 45*(5), 802–820.

Ho, S. S. M., Li, A. Y., Tam, K., & Zhang, F. (2015). CEO Gender, Ethical Leadership, and Accounting Conservatism. *Journal of Business Ethics, 127*, 351–370. Retrieved September 14, 2024, from https://doi.org/10.1007/s10551-013-2044-0

Huber, J., & Kirchler, M. (2013). Corporate Campaign Contributions and Abnormal Stock Returns after Presidential Elections. *Public Choice, 156*(1–2), 285–307. Retrieved September 14, 2024, from https://link.springer.com/article/https://doi.org/10.1007/s11127-011-9898-4

Kalla, J. L., & Broockman, D. E. (2016). Campaign Contributions Facilitate Access to Congressional Officials: A Randomized Field Experiment. *American Journal of Political Science, 60*(3), 545–558. Retrieved September 14, 2024, from https://www.jstor.org/stable/24877480

King, T. (2015, September 24). Beware Europe's Automotive-Political Complex. *Politico.* Retrieved September 14, 2024, from https://www.politico.eu/article/europes-automotive-political-complex-volkswagen-scandal-eu/

Mousavi, M., Zimon, G., Salehi, M., & Stępnicka, N. (2022). The Effect of Corporate Governance Structure on Fraud and Money Laundering. *Risks, 10*(9), 176. Retrieved September 14, 2024, from https://doi.org/10.3390/risks10090176

Rostami, V., & Rezaei, L. (2021). Corporate Governance and Fraudulent Financial Reporting. *Journal of Financial Crime*, ISSN: 1359-0790. Retrieved 24 May 2022.

Schneider, M., & Brühl, R. (2023). Disentangling the Black Box around CEO and Financial Information-Based Accounting Fraud Detection: Machine Learning-Based Evidence from Publicly Listed U.S. Firms. *Journal of Business Economics, 93*, 1591–1628. Retrieved September 14, 2024, from https://doi.org/10.1007/s11573-023-01136-w

Transactional Records Access Clearinghouse. (2023, January 19). Corporate and White-Collar Prosecutions Hit New All-Time Lows in FY 2022. *Transactional Records Access Clearinghouse.* Retrieved September 14, 2024, from https://trac.syr.edu/reports/708/

Turner, S. (2023). White-Collar Crime, Sentencing Gender Disparities Post-Booker, and Implications for Criminal Sentencing. *JCLC Online, 19.* Retrieved September 14, 2024, from https://scholarlycommons.law.northwestern.edu/jclc_online/19

Velte, P. (2023). The Link between Corporate Governance and Corporate Financial Misconduct. A Review of Archival Studies and Implications for Future Research. *Management Review Quarterly, 73*(1), 353–411

Weeks, W. A., Moore, C. W., McKinney, J. A., & Longenecker, J. G. (1999). The Effects of Gender and Career Stage on Ethical Judgment. *Journal of Business Ethics, 20*, 301–313.

Yang, D., Jiao, H., & Buckland, R. (2017). The Determinants of Financial Fraud in Chinese Firms: Does Corporate Governance as an Institutional Innovation Matter? *Technology Forecasting and Social Change, 125*, 309–320. Retrieved September 14, 2024, from https://doi.org/10.1016/j.techfore.2017.06.035

Yu, F., & Yu, X. (2011). Corporate Lobbying and Fraud Detection. The *Journal of Financial and Quantitative Analysis, 46*(6), 1865–1891. Retrieved September 14, 2024, from http://www.jstor.org/stable/41409670

# Part IV

## Deep-Dive Investigations of Potential Fraudulent Corporations

# 17

# Fraud Investigation, Deep-Dives & Due Diligence

## 17.1 The Practitioner's Perspective on Deep-Dive Investigations into Corporate Fraud

In the previous sections the interest was all the 60,000 listed companies in the world, to spot potential fraud targets. In this section we focus on the individual potential target.

During screening, the investor has already gotten hits from several red flag indicators of potential fraud targets. These red flags may of course be used directly in the final report. However, undoubtedly there is a necessity to scrutinize the fraud target in depth before writing the final report.

The author has worked with more than a hundred actual fraud cases from small startups to major corporations. Successfully detecting and stopping many of them early. The experience of deep-dives is drawn from three main areas and different perspectives of financial services:

- The first perspective is buy-side and asset management. Fraud Analytics of publicly listed companies (the focus of this book). However also e.g. private placement and co-investments alongside private equity funds.
- The second side is fraud due diligence from the sell-side perspective of Corporate Finance and Investment Banking. Having conducted fraud due diligence of Initial Public Offerings (IPOs) and other types of transactions.
- The final perspective is the Corporate Banking perspective, especially of publicly listed companies.



J. Sørensen, *Shorting Fraud*, https://doi.org/10.1007/978-3-031-81834-9_17

Corporate Fraud lessons may be drawn from all three financial service areas and viewpoints. However, the Corporate Banking of publicly listed companies will give you the most complete insight to learn from.

Not only do you have access to the public financial statements, but also the hundred thousand or more transactions going in and out of the bank accounts of the corporation's subsidiaries.

If you at the same time cover 90% corporations on the main index of a stock exchange and 50%-60% of the rest of the corporations in a geographical area you get an intuitive understanding of how normal and abnormal patterns should look like in a corporation. With access to big data analytics tools, you may study these transactions from a Corporate Fraud perspective and compare them to public disclosures and public financial reporting.

At some point you will have a better overview than the executives of the corporation, regarding the financial situation of the corporation. You have access to the actual cash flows that happened only minutes or hours ago, not the consolidated quarterly reports, months later.

## 17.2 How to Choose Fraud Targets to Deep-Dive in

One of the challenging questions is always when do red flags encountered during the broader screening justify a deep-dive investigation of a potential target.

This is a judgment to be conducted by the individual investor, based on several factors like how severe the red flags are, how many red flags are there. Also, how accessible, and applicable is the fraud short investment strategy from a practical point of view. If the investor cannot practically conduct a fraud short investment strategy, the investor may report the red flags to authorities and move on to other more ripe targets. On a more general scale the number of targets to deep-dive into depends on the investor's maturity, competencies, and capabilities with regards to areas like:

- Manpower available to do manual research, analytics, and due diligence of the target company.
- Machine power available to support the manpower with automatization, statistical and AI models.
- Materials available like quantitative financial statement data and qualitative company news data.

Before jumping into deep-dive investigations, it is suggested to look at some foundational concepts of research and investigations, specifically regarding companies.

## 17.3 Triangulation and Sanity Checking

The research, investigation, and analytical process behind hunting for fraud often means investors do not have the full picture from the beginning, and seldom will obtain it as an outsider.

From a practical point, in complex investigations, the concept of triangulation, known from social sciences, has been found to be a fruitful approach, detecting corporate fraud. Sociologist, Denzin (1970), argued that no single method, dataset, or observer can capture the entire truth. Denzin explained the concept of triangulation by identifying four distinct types:

- **Data Triangulation** is the collection of data via multiple sampling strategies. The aim is to gather diverse data slices from different times, social contexts, and a range of individuals. This approach ensures a more comprehensive and diverse dataset. Triangulation could be cross-referencing financial statements with public import/export data from the company, exposing inconsistencies.
- **Investigator Triangulation** refers to the deployment of multiple investigators on a single case. Each investigator collects and interprets data independently. The strategy enhances the reliability and interpretation by reducing individual biases of the investigator. While there might not always be two or more investigators for one case, techniques like peer-review could also be used.
- **Theoretical Triangulation** involves the application of multiple theoretical perspectives to interpret the data. Investigators may gain a more nuanced understanding of the cases by viewing the data through different theoretical lenses. Like one theory that financial statement fraud is used to hide embezzlement, another theory the fraud is for keeping the corporation afloat.
- **Methodological Triangulation** is the use of different methods to collect data. Using various methods, investigators can cross-verify and validate findings. Enhancing the robustness of the research. Like using forensic accounting techniques combined with in-depth interviews of ex-employees may disclose a better understanding of the company.

Figure 17.1 illustrates how triangulation works in the corporate fraud case.

These four forms of triangulation, as proposed by Denzin, may help the investor move forward on a practical level when deep-diving into a corporate fraud case. While there might be practical limitations when investigating a potential fraud case, it is always good to have different perspectives in mind.

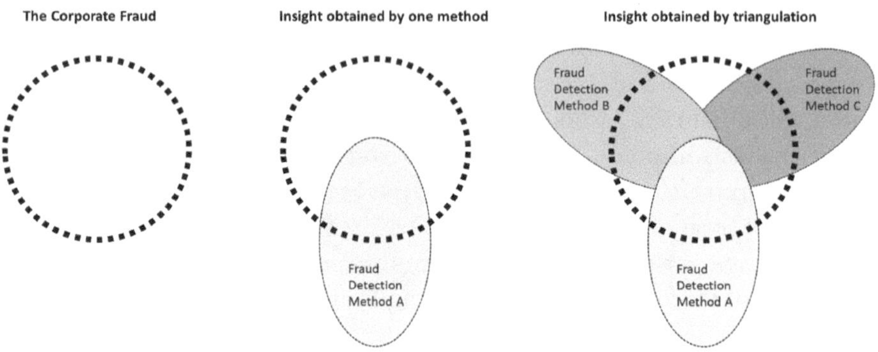


**Fig. 17.1** Illustration of triangulation method in fraud detection

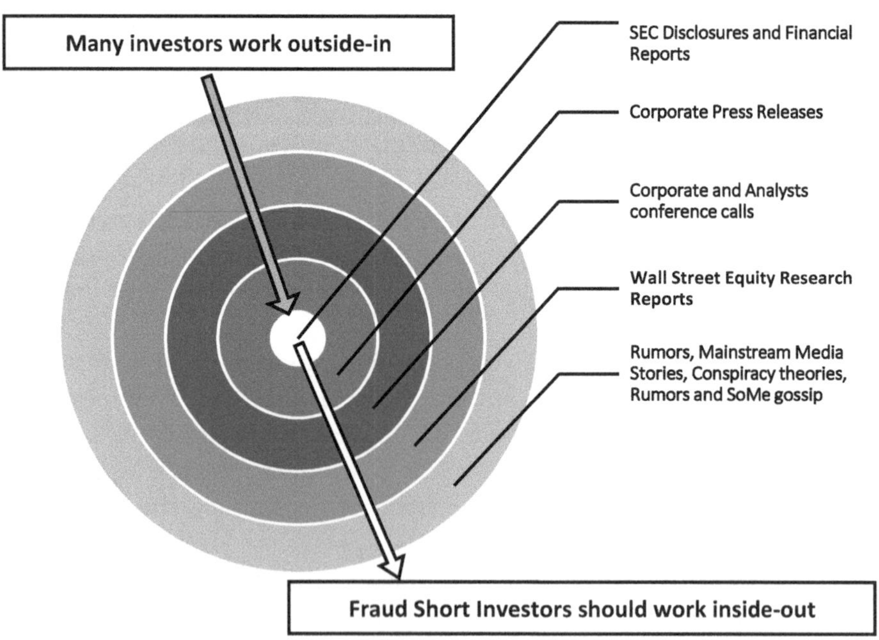


**Fig. 17.2** The fraud onion idea—illustration inspired by Jim Chanos' talks

## 17.4 Importance of Primary Sources, Primary Research and the Jim Chanos Onion

In fraud investigation cases it has been found productive to use as many primary sources and as much primary research as possible. Always bear in mind that the target company might have successfully deceived professional equity analysts and other pundits already. These experts have now become "Useful Idiots" according to the old Lenin term.

The Short Seller Jim Chanos has discussed the "onion" concept on several occasions, e.g. in Grant (2018). The onion concept (illustrated in Fig. 17.2) emphasizes the importance of primary research of target companies. Working hands on with corporate fraud cases, this "onion" concept has been found to be solid. The onion captures how stakeholders may look at and conduct research on a publicly listed company. Chanos highlights that many investors tend to rely on secondary sources of information, such as press releases, conference calls, and Wall Street research reports. While such sources may provide valuable insights, they often reflect a filtered interpretation of the company's true performance and underlying risks. By researching primary documents, and doing their own primary research, investors can directly access the company's raw data and unfiltered narrative, gaining a more comprehensive understanding of the business.

Chanos underscores the effectiveness of this approach by citing historical examples, such as the Enron scandal and Valeant Pharmaceuticals' accounting irregularities. Here, investors who relied on secondary sources of information were misled, while those who engaged in primary research were able to see the underlying deception.

## 17.5 Deep-Dive Investigations—Content, Context and Process

In contrast to screening, deep-dive investigations are much more targeted. They are in-depth investigations on the individual target company, the executives, the owners, and other stakeholders. From a practical point of view, these investigations can be looked upon as consisting of three interrelated dynamic aspects—the investigation's content, context, and process.

### 17.5.1 Investigation Content Analytics

First, the content is the material to be analyzed in a deep-dive. It may be compared to finding pieces of a jigsaw puzzle. This information is gathered using Open-Source Intelligence (OSINT). It includes finding and analyzing adverse media, legal documents, permits, company registrars, Stakeholder Background Reports, business model, financial statements, public disclosures, etc.

### 17.5.2 The Contextual Analysis of the Content

The second aspect is the context that the above content is going to be analyzed in. While the content is the little pieces of evidence (or pieces in the jigsaw puzzle), the contextual analysis is about putting the puzzle together, connecting the dots. Analyzing the relationships, connections, and links between pieces of content, like for instance links between legal entities and natural persons. This may be visualized by the physical evidence board known from crime movies (and actual criminal investigations) with suspects, sticky notes, newspaper clippings—all tied together with yarn around push-pins on the board. In Section 28 we will work in detail with the context from a network theory perspective and in Sect. 28.2.11 we will look at the modern virtual version of this physical evidence board.

### 17.5.3 The Corporate Fraud Investigation Process

In a perfect world one could set up a process to go through. Starting with step A and ending with step Z. However, the practical investigation process in corporate fraud cases is found to be hard to streamline like this. Each case might start from a different angle. With different puzzle pieces of content or a different type of contextual setting. The investigator will often be led in different directions during the investigations.

While efforts may be conducted to make standard operational procedures, many times these investigation cases do not follow a Fredric Taylor sequential "conveyor belt" logic. The process is about thinking out of the box, piecing all types of unrelated pieces of content together to paint a fuller picture of the corporate fraud.

It is like solving a jigsaw puzzle. If you turn the box with 10,000 puzzle pieces out on the table, it is unlikely you will solve the same puzzle the same way twice. Start with the same piece and put it together, in the exact same order. You might have a general strategy starting with the edges or similar, but even then, it is unlikely you pick up the edge pieces in the same way each time.

### 17.5.4 The Process, Content, and Context Analytics in Real-World Investigations

This book, for practical purposes, shows types of content to look at, and subsequently the context in which it is described. It must be emphasized that this should not be understood in sequential chapter order, where the first chapters should in all cases come before later chapters. Each case may start with an arbitrary single piece of content and work in various directions in random order.

In the real world, going through the investigation process, pieces of content will be woven together in a contextual setting, through a sometimes-chaotic process. In real world settings content and context analytics are interrelated and simultaneously used in parallel, which is hard to illustrate in a book.

## References

Denzin, N. K. (Ed.). (1970). *Sociological Methods: A Sourcebook*. Aldine.

Grant, J. (2018). Real Vision Jim Chanos [Video interview]. Real Vision. Retrieved September 14, 2024, from https://www.realvision.com/shows/the-archives-from-real-vision/videos/jim-chanos-re-release-pn1L?t=3053

# 18

# Investigating the Company Basics

## 18.1 Basic Areas of Investigation for Potential Corporate Fraud

Investigating the target company can be done in many ways. One should always consider looking at least at the following areas:

- The company basics
  - o What regions, countries, and industries do the company operate in?
  - o What life stage is the company at?
  - o What is the organizational size and legal entity setup of the company?
  - o Actual physical location of the company, compared to the virtual counterpart description?

## 18.2 Geography and Risk of Corporate Fraud

Fraud surveys from the ACFE (2022) report gives an indication of how corporate fraud is distributed in various geographical regions, illustrated in Fig. 18.1. However, keep in mind it might be skewed due to the number of registered Certified Fraud Investigators surveyed in each region & the total number of companies in the regions.

Another supportive source is the yearly CORRUPTION PERCEPTIONS INDEX (CPI) as e.g. seen in Transparency International (2022). The CPI ranks countries based on perceived public sector corruption. It uses expert


J. Sørensen, *Shorting Fraud*, https://doi.org/10.1007/978-3-031-81834-9_18

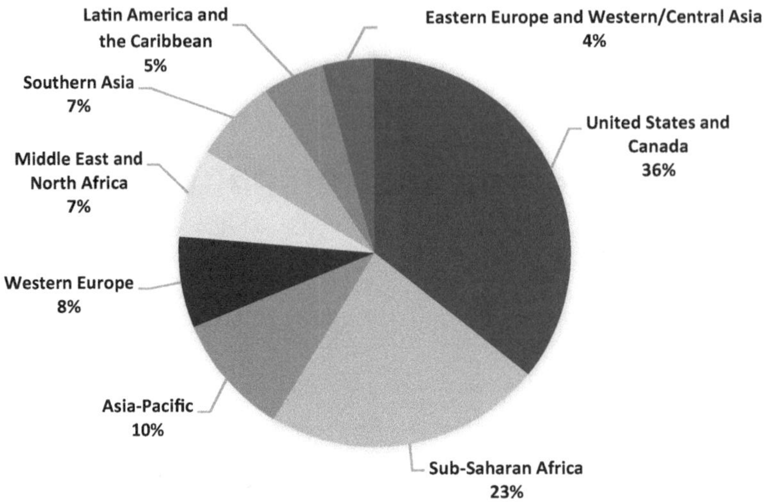


**Fig. 18.1** Fraud case distribution by region—based on data from ACFE (2022)

assessments and opinion surveys, scoring countries from 0 (high corruption) to 100 (low corruption). While public sector corruption and corporate fraud is not the same, the CPI may be used as a practical proxy indicator, for lack of better. One may analyze the individual country as one of the factors when analyzing corporate fraud. To get an initial baseline understanding, Table 18.1 shows the ten least corrupt countries and the ten most corrupt countries.

When analyzing the company this can be used to assess the background risk of corporate fraud in the company based on the country of the company. Also having the Corporate Fraud Premium perspective and the Canadian Paradox from Sect. 3 in mind, when analyzing.

**Table 18.1** Least & most corrupt countries in the world—based on data from transparency international (2022)

| Ten Least Corrupt Countries | Ten Most Corrupt Countries |
|---|---|
| 1. Denmark | 171. Equatorial Guinea |
| 2. Finland | 172. Haiti |
| 3. New Zealand | 173. North Korea |
| 4. Norway | 174. Libya |
| 5. Singapore | 175. Burundi |
| 6. Sweden | 176. Yemen |
| 7. Switzerland | 177. Venezuela |
| 8. Netherlands | 178. South Sudan |
| 9. Germany | 179. Syria |
| 10. Ireland and Luxembourg | 180. Somalia |

## 18.3 Industries and Corporate Fraud

Data collected by ACFE shows that corporate fraud may happen in any industry or sector. However, some industries are more likely to experience fraud than others. If we approach the corporate fraud problem from a risk-based approach, we can see from Fig. 18.2 which industries have reported the most cases of fraud.

This gives a good indication of the general risk of fraud in the industries. However, notice that certain industries have more corporate entities than other industries. Also, bear in mind that private companies and government entities are included, which may be skewed compared to publicly listed companies.

### 18.3.1 High Complexity Industries

All companies and industries are not equally complicated to understand. Investors, investing in complex industries, face the principal-agent problem described by Jensen and Meckling (1976). Investors encounter the principal-agent problem where the agent CEO/Executive/Management (Agent) has a better understanding of the company, its products, and services than the shareholder (principal). This is more prevalent in some industries than others.

This principal-agent problem has also been observed with regard to corporate fraud. In extraordinarily complex areas like biotech, artificial intelligence,

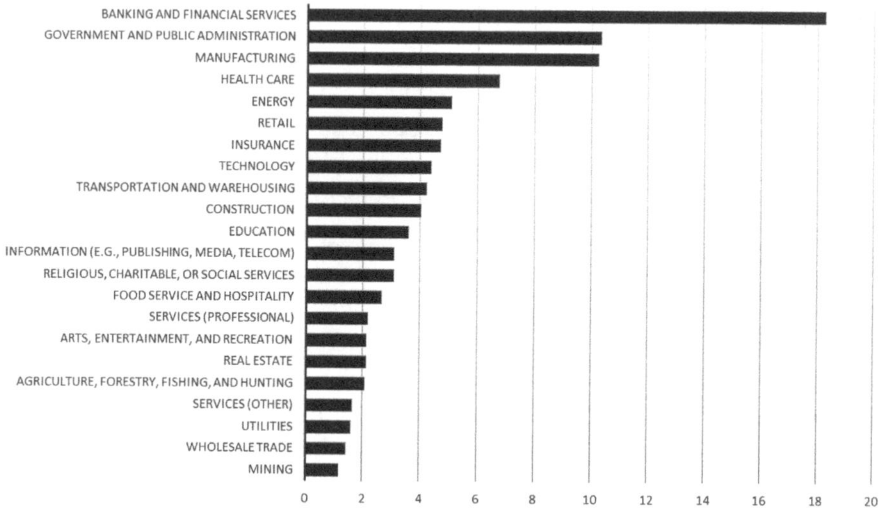


**Fig. 18.2** Percent of fraud cases by Industry—based on data from ACFE (2022)

quantum computing and blockchain/DeFi, the management often has a much deeper knowledge of the area than most professional investors.

The asymmetry between management and shareholder could disappear if the investor put more effort into analyzing the company. However, it has been observed this does not happen with corporate fraudsters for two reasons. The first reason is that professional investors might not want to invest the necessary time in understanding the complex industry—a laziness factor. The second is that the investors do not ask tough questions on what the AI does or how the biotech works for fear of losing face and looking incompetent. Both factors are abused by corporate fraudsters.

A great example of this is the corporate fraud case of the unlisted company Theranos. In that case many of the professional investors who invested in the company had no insight into the basics of the industry of Theranos. Hence, they were easily strung along by Elizabeth Holmes. According to Thomas (2022), the basic idea of Theranos had been debunked by Professor Phyllis Gardner, a professor of medicine at Stanford University, as impractical and undoable years before. However, none of the investors or board members appeared to have understood the basics of the technology, or industry of laboratory diagnostics. Instead, they give the impression of having been trophy board members, as described in Sect. 21.

Another recent interesting publicly listed (evolving at time of writing) case to study, is the $40 million settlement case between the SEC, Cassava Sciences Inc (SAVA), its former CEO, Senior Vice President of Neuroscience and a related researcher, as reported by SEC (2024, September 26).

SEC charged the former executives for misleading investors about the results of Alzheimer's clinical trials done by the researcher. After the publication of the reported misleading positive results of the clinical trials on the drug, the share price of SAVA soared from around $3 in the start of September 2020 to peaking at around $120–140 in the summer of 2021.

In August 2021, a Citizen Petition to the FDA asking them to halt the clinical Alzheimer's studies were submitted, according to FDA (2021). Also, an activist short seller campaign by Quintessential Capital Management was conducted, as reported in QCM (2021). This resulted in the share price of SAVA plummeting to the range of $10-$40 since then.

To sanity check these types of hard-to-understand companies or industries, one should either deep-dive to understand the industry and the complex company or hire a second opinion by one or more seasoned independent industry professionals.

### 18.3.2 Hyped Industries and Corporate Fraudsters

It has been observed in practice that hyped industries attract fraudsters, like moths, to a flame. These trends might be driven by several factors like the political agenda of sustainability, technological innovations such as AI, or new social trends, like the rise of vegan food. These are often industries with new advanced products and services, considered the next big thing. Industries that the general population may not really understand yet. In the 90's it was the internet, in 2025 it is e.g. AI and DeFi.

### 18.3.3 The Fear of Missing Out

The Fear of missing out (FOMO) has been observed as an underlying driver of many types of corporate fraud cases. FOMO is directly related to greed. People, especially within the investment community do not want to miss out on something great, the next big thing. This is something that the fraudsters are aware of and actively abuse.

Some professional investors like angel investors may expect a 100 × multiple of their investment, and later venture capitalist investment rounds may expect a 10–15 × multiple. Outside angel and VC, normally you only see these ROI numbers in simple crypto investment scams, get rich quick schemes and corporate frauds.

With the fear of missing out on a big win, even professional investors can have their guards lowered by corporate fraudsters. It has been observed that professional investors and experienced investment bankers will engage in highly doubtful investments or projects, if the promised payoff is big enough. This even after having been explicitly warned about the potential risk of fraud and other financial crimes.

Some of the hardest people to convince are professional investors in denial, suffering from delusion regarding an investment target. These may frequently be observed by the fraud short investor and are the investors on the long side of the short trade. These investors see a huge upside potential in the company. The Table 18.2 matrix gives an overview of the relationship between corporate fraud risk and industry type.

**Quadrant I)** has the highest risk. The investors' fear of missing out on the next big thing, while this next big thing is hard to understand, makes it a perfect environment for pulling off a corporate fraud.

**Quadrant II)** is in second place. The extreme hype can make the investors close their eyes and believe in a simple business model that are not sustainable

**Table 18.2** The industry fraud matrix

| | Low Complexity Industry | High Complexity Industry |
|---|---|---|
| Hyped Industry | **II)** Industries that are easier to understand, but trending and overly popular. Examples are car ridesharing, electric scooter / bike shares, food delivery services and online retail | **I)** These could be trending industries that require specialized knowledge to understand. Examples are crypto industry, AI, and electric vehicle industry. |
| Mundane Industry | **III)** These could be industries that are easy to understand and are not currently in the spotlight. An example could be the ordinary retail industry | **IV)** Industries that are complex but have no hype around it. An example could be the Oil and Gas, or engineering |

in the long run. This is based on the sole fear of missing out. So, hype might be abused and beat any business logic, if conducted by the skilled fraudster.

**Quadrant IV)** comes in third. These are often established, highly regulated industries. While they are complex, they have been around for a while. This makes it harder to pull off corporate fraud, since there are often established peers and analysts that will point out the problems. Also, without the FOMO factor, investors often take their time to do more due diligence.

**Quadrant III)** has the lowest risk. While not impossible it is harder to pull off a fraud in the established ordinary retail industry. Few investors fear missing out on the next ordinary supermarket chain, and most people understand the basics about how a supermarket works.

There are of course exceptions to the rules and quadrants should not always be seen in a static way. Corporate fraudsters might abuse mundane and low complexity industries by propping them up to fit into e.g. hyped quadrants.

This can be done by leveraging and opportunistically abusing political, social, or technological trends of the moment to suit the fraudsters' agenda.

In one case, it was observed that the person of interest, a CEO and founder over a period, clung on to whatever was the big thing in that specific moment in the media to promote herself and the company. Things like MeToo, diversity, sustainability, etc. A chameleon, shapeshifting approach like this, is a major red flag. AI one day, women's rights the next, then supporting the poor, etc.

Also, a mundane, traditional industry competitor, rebranding itself as hyped, positioning the company in a quadrant where it does not belong. It could be dressing up a company in a highly polluting industry in sustainability clothes. It could also be rebranding a traditional mundane industry as high tech scalable.

A good example in the public domain, of moving a low complex, mundane company up into the hype and complexity quadrant, is the company WeWork. The basic business model for WeWork was a co-working space leasing company. However, in several places WeWork was marketed as a tech company. E.g. in WeWork's S-1 filing, as seen in SEC (2019, Aug. 14th), WeWork Technology or Technologies are mentioned 119 times. According to Govindarajan and Srivastava (2019), WeWork could not be labeled as a tech company. Despite its tech claims, WeWork is essentially a real estate company. It lacks key tech company features, like low variable costs and low capital investments. Unlike tech companies that utilize scalable models, WeWork has significant operating expenses and thin profit margins. It also requires high capital for developing and furnishing rented premises. Its ability to generate free cash flow is questionable, in contrast to tech companies that generate huge profits with relatively low reinvestment requirements.

### 18.3.4 Virtual and Intangible Industries

Another group of high-risk companies are in virtual or intangible industries. These are the industries where there is often no physical product. It is all based on software, and often supported by a subscription model. Some of these might be the online games industry, the social media platforms, fintech, etc.

These are business models that are highly scalable with little production costs, when first set up. Here a problem observed is that it is quite easy to tamper with users, players, or subscribers. Especially in a freemium business model, where some users pay, and some do not. Additionally, in cases where online ad revenue is involved in the business model, fake visitors, click farms and spambots pose a problem of corporate fraud.

While the technology of most of these companies with virtual products and business models may be replicated very easily, from a technical point of view. One may build her own Social Media Platform within a few days. The potential user engagement and revenue streams are harder to replicate. One may copy much of the technological setup of Facebook fast. However, not the visitors, engagement, and revenue streams.

Analyzing companies in these virtual industries includes sanity checking traffic numbers, looking for signs of artificially pumped visitors or players. Traffic and interaction might be conducted by click farms, where fake users are paid to use the platform, or programmatic by bots that are interacting with the platform and tampering with the number of visitors, or even more basically just fabricating fake users.

An alleged potential example of the latter in the public domain, is the ongoing $175 million corporate fraud case with Charlie Javice and the Frank Platform initiated by DOJ (2023, April 4). The Frank platform was supposed to be a free online platform helping students with effortless application for student aid, scholarships, affordable courses, etc. However, the problem was it allegedly lacked actual users. User lists were then allegedly fabricated, so the company would appear much more successful than it was.

Corporate fraud cases with fabricated users and traffic are not a rarity. Outside the public domain, several corporate fraud cases and fraud attempts have been observed. These included either totally fabricated or artificially inflated customer lists. Fraudsters e.g. inflating visitors by counting the same visitor multiple times as different visitors and not as unique visitors, etc.

## 18.4 The Company's Investment Lifecycle

Just like a company's product might be at a specific phase within a product life-cycle model, the company itself might also be at different stages in an investment life-cycle model. While different types of corporate fraud might be observed in companies, at all life stages, we are mainly interested in the public life stage and beyond in Table 18.3.

Different life stages will see different types of risks of fraud associated with them. For instance, the startup is unlikely to see a lot of corporate fraud related to M&A and roll-ups. It is more likely to encounter simple embezzlement of money from the angel investors, lining the CEO and founder's pockets.

Investing in public companies, the first thought might be why even care about earlier life stages of the company? The investors need to care since the groundwork and architecture of the corporate fraud may already have been designed in the early stages. What is particularly interesting with regards to

**Table 18.3** Company life stage and fraud types observed

| Life Stage | Startups | Scaling | Maturing | Public | Stabilized |
|---|---|---|---|---|---|
| Source of Funds | Angel & Seed | Venture Capital | Private Equity | IPO | 2nd + M&A |
| Fraud Example Types | Misuse & embezzling of Seed Funding | Overstated Valuations | Asset Misappropriation | Financial Statement Fraud | Roll-ups |

corporate fraud, is if a company is suspiciously mature for its life stage, or there are signs of minor frauds early on.

If a company has managed to move ahead and skip two or three stages compared to its true underlying life stage, it might be a startup masking itself as a mature company ready to go public. While most of these will be prevented from IPOing - a few will enter. Especially through the back door via Special Purpose Acquisition Companies (SPACs) and reverse mergers, etc. treated in Sect. 18.10.

In some cases, suspecting fraud and blocking questionable IPOs was not successful. However, following the IPOs subsequently has been educational. The cases entered with high valuations and subsequently imploded in the following 2–3-year period, ending with either a de-listing or bankruptcy after losing 95%-99% of the IPO-value.

Companies IPOing, suffering from these delusions of grandeur are especially interesting from a fraud shorting perspective.

## 18.5 The Physical Location of the Company and Subsidiaries

A very low practical, but highly effective "acid test" which has been used to expose several fraudulent companies in a few seconds, is to check if the company is actually located where it says it is. Also, if this location makes any sense. By using simple free tools like Google Earth, or Google Street View, (or private satellite services), you can quickly find out where on the globe the company is located and if the company's locations make sense. Big red flags include locations in residential areas, office hotels, wrong type of business zone, post office, post box and mail forwarding locations, etc. If the company is trying to piggyback on a prominent address, try sending physical mail to the address. See if it is delivered or returned to the sender.

Besides satellite and street view, the investor might also hire boots on the ground in the form of private intelligence companies to sanity check. By visiting the corporate sites and determining the activity at the corporate sites. Does the number of employees arriving and leaving make sense? Do the deliveries make sense, etc.?

One would believe that these fake addresses would only relate to small unlisted scam companies. However, they are not. In the Wirecard case, subsidiary addresses were located at residential addresses and other at unrelated companies, like a bus-tour company according to McCrum (2020).

## 18.6 Business Certificates, Permits, Customs Documents and Official License to Operate

Another fast way to expose fraudulent companies in minutes, is to check if the company has all the different certificates, permits and licenses required to operate, where they claim to operate. Are they officially allowed to handle the products and services they claim to provide?

Especially in a company with a multi-jurisdictional setting, or transnational companies, this is a particularly good way to determine if the subsidiaries are active entities or shell or front companies, without real activity. Having the right web browser plugins and tools to translate foreign languages is a fast way to sanity check.

An example could be a hearing aid company that claims to export to several countries. However, the company does not have the proper official medical device permits issued by the authorities. Therefore, it may not even be allowed to sell the devices in those specific countries, where it claims to have revenue, which is a red flag.

Similarly, when trading between countries, customs declaration documents often are needed. These public authority databases are in some jurisdictions open for anyone to sanity check free of charge, or for a token amount to check.

A recent ongoing high-profile example is the publicly listed company Tingo (TIO) listed on NASDAQ and indicted by US authorities according to DOJ (2024) & SEC (2023). Already earlier in 2023, activist Short Seller Hindenburg Research (2023), alleged that Tingo Mobile did not hold any license to do mobile phone service in Nigeria as it claimed in its SEC Filings.

## 18.7 The Organizational Size, Number of Employees, Departments and Business Units

Working hands-on with corporate fraud detection, it has been observed that there are two contradictory forces with regards to the size of the company and corporate fraud.

On the one hand, in small organizations, it is faster to get an overview of what happens. However, control mechanisms might not be as evolved, there is less segregation of duties, and dependance on key employees.

The executives, especially the founder(s) may get away with a lot, before it is detected and stopped. Especially in young organizations, early in their life cycle that are founder driven, the founder is often admired as a new messiah by employees.

As organizations grow bigger, so do control, compliance, and audit mechanisms, both internally and externally. On the flip side as organizations grow, they become harder to get an overview of and processes may be decentralized, and harder to get a full impression of.

From a corporate fraud perspective analyzing the organizational size, one should look at the size and assess if there is a natural fit between the actual undertaking of the company and the size of the company. Are there too many or too few employees, too many or too few departments and organizational units, compared to what should be expected. This type of investigation is hard to set up some rules of thumb for. However, the experienced investor will gradually learn to look at this factor.

## 18.8 The Quality, Remuneration and Composition of the Workforce in the Company

One way to analyze the organization is by looking at the number and quality of the company's workforce. Though some of the following may come off as politically incorrect in today's diversity discussion, looking at the overall quality and composition of the workforce will often reveal something is not right.

Especially if the investor combines the experience with remuneration structure and pay scale. These are available from Glassdoor, LinkedIn, and similar websites. A red flag can be an inexperienced, young workforce, which is getting paid well above the experience level.

A staff in that situation, with well-paid jobs beyond anything they can get elsewhere, will be encouraged to let things slide for longer before they draw a line with regards to corporate fraud. While not directly bribes, the above-normal salary works as de facto "hush money." The employee may show up at the company and get paid hefty for not doing anything creating shareholder value.

Also, heavy focus on time-vesting equity payment might have the employees linger in a fraudulent company. Many corporate frauds are marketed as the next big thing. If the employees resign voluntarily or are fired due to questioning the management on fraud, they might lose the ticket to this next big thing.

While employment of immigrants is healthy for the workforce of a sound company, in fraudulent companies it may be the opposite. The employment of migrant workers may play a more sinister role in fraudulent companies, where they are skillfully abused in the corporate fraud. Especially where the employee visas are closely related to the company. The threat of repatriation or deportation to a country with lower living standards is a natural incentive to condone or cover for corporate fraud. Especially if the country of origin of the employees is a high-corruption country.

Other things to look for are the professional composition of the workforce and staff expertise. For instance, in a biotech company developing new drugs, the investor should expect that there is a predominance of scientists with a background in development of drugs. If there is a predominance of other skills, especially soft skills like management consulting, business analysts, etc. it could be a red flag. Similar in the software industry. If there is a predominance of consultants, managers, coaches, coordinators, and other types of talking heads, compared to hardcore software developers, programmers, and engineers, it is a red flag.

## 18.9 Companies Focus on Unrelated Activities

What has been observed in corporate fraud cases is that companies might suddenly focus on unrelated activities. This might come as unrelated conglomerate business activities outside core business areas as described in Sect. 19.12.2 or philanthropist activities as described in Sect. 4.3.2 and Sect. 16.3.4 These unrelated activities are used to compensate for core business failings and hence a major red flag.

## 18.10 Blank Check Companies, SPACs and Reverse Mergers

In the 1980s *"Blank Check Companies"*, which are basically empty shell entities, with no predetermined business plan were listed in the penny stock market. These Blank Check companies were commonly abused by criminals in multiple types of securities fraud. Therefore, Blank Check companies were later curtailed by regulation, as described by Castelli (2009).

### 18.10.1 Special Purpose Acquisition Companies (SPACs)

In recent years, the SPAC structure has been used and abused by fraudsters as a fast-track "back door" for publicly listing a private company as an alternative to the traditional IPO. From a securities fraud perspective, the SPAC structure is similar in many ways to the "Blank Check" companies of the 1980s. SPACs are (continuously) regulated tighter by the FSAs around the world as seen by e.g. SEC (2024). However, SPACs still present an elevated risk of potential securities fraud, because of two reasons.

First, SPACs appear to attract white-collar criminals that could not pass the scrutiny and sanity test of a real IPO's due diligence. SPACs have had a relatively high number of public fraud cases. These are just the tip of the iceberg. In addition to companies gone public through a SPAC merger, more problematic companies have not. Behind the scenes, more companies with risk of fraud were prevented from going public by de-SPAC reverse merger. These de-SPAC targets could not even meet lower SPAC due diligence standards. Some of the questionable or fraudulent SPAC examples that caught authorities' attention are listed in Table 18.4.

In addition to the concrete examples of SPACs in Table 18.4, SPACs raised general concerns with the SEC. This resulted in the SEC reactions; SEC (2021, March 31) & SEC (2021b, May 25).

Research by Klausner et al. (2022) has scrutinized and questioned SPACs, and found that due diligence was less rigorous, there was an absence of underwriter liability and a more lenient treatment of forward-looking statements in SPACs compared to IPOs. If one looks at these factors from a corporate fraud point of view, they are beneficial for actors who want to commit corporate fraud.

Also, with regards to securities class actions litigations, Cornerstone Research (2022) & Cornerstone Research (2024) found that SPAC litigations grew sixfold between 2020 and 2021, then were stable with a downward trend from 2021 to 2023. Other types of securities class actions were mostly stable or down trending. For the period 2019 to 2021 there was a litigation rate of 13% of the total number of SPACs. This was above the litigation rate of year two cumulative litigation rate of IPOs.

### 18.10.2 The Reverse Merger

The reverse merger is comparable to the blank check company and SPAC. A reverse merger also bypasses the scrutiny of the IPO and lists a company without a due diligence.

**Table 18.4** Questionable Spacs that caught the attention of the authorities—Sources SEC (2022, Sep. 21), SEC (2024, January 4), SEC (2024, February 29), SEC (2023, September 28), SEC ( 2023, August 4), SEC (2023, September 26)

| Company | Listing Year | Fraud Accusation Year | Description |
|---|---|---|---|
| Nikola Corporation | 2020 | 2020 | The electric truck company went public through a SPAC merger. Nikola faced allegations of misrepresenting its technology and capabilities, leading to investigations by the SEC and DOJ. Its founder, Trevor Milton, was eventually found guilty of fraud |
| Lordstown Motors | 2020 | 2021 | Another electric vehicle company that went public via a SPAC, Lordstown Motors was accused of exaggerating pre-order numbers and the development progress of its trucks. They remain under investigation. SEC filed a claim of $45 million violating securities laws |
| XL Fleet | 2020 | 2023 | SEC charged the company for Misleading Revenue Projections Ahead of SPAC Merger |
| Canoo Inc | 2020 | 2023 | SEC charged Electric Vehicle Company and Former CEO and CFO for Misconduct Related to SPAC Transaction |
| Hyzon Motors, Inc | 2021 | 2023 | SEC charged the company and two former executives for misleading investors |

The tactic from the white-collar criminal is finding a struggling, defunct publicly listed company to merge with its fraudulent private entity. Thereby avoiding professional scrutiny done by doing a full IPO. This happens with the private company taking control of the majority of shares in the already publicly traded company.

SEC (2011, June 9) warned about the reverse merger and their potential role in multiple corporate and securities fraud cases, subsequently following a string of fraud cases.

A recent example of a potential reverse merger abuse is the case of Tingo Inc. that conducted not just one reverse merger, but two subsequent mergers eventually publicly listing Tingo on NASDAQ.

First, Tingo did a reverse merger with iWeb Inc. as reported by Web Inc. (2021). This reverse merger "listed" Tingo on the OTC Markets in August 2021. Subsequently, Tingo did a reverse merger, which moved it from the OTC Market to the NASDAQ market in December 2022 as reported by MICT, Inc. (2022, November 9).

Later, SEC (2023, December 19) charged Tingo Mobile Founder and three Tingo Entities with Massive Fraud. SEC charges claimed that profits, revenues and cash balances were overstated by hundreds of millions of dollars. The case is still ongoing at the time of writing and the CEO has denied the allegations from the US authorities.

## References

ACFE. (2022). Occupational Fraud 2022: A Report to the Nations. Association of Certified Fraud Examiners. Retrieved September 14, 2024, from https://acfepublic.s3.us-west-2.amazonaws.com/2022+Report+to+the+Nations.pdf

Castelli, T. (2009). Not Guilty by Association: Why the Taint of Their "Blank Check" Predecessors Should not Stunt the Growth of Modern Special Purpose Acquisition Companies. B.C.L. Review, 50, 237. Retrieved September 14, 2024, from https://lira.bc.edu/work/sc/c1b43a74-5b6a-4d24-8996-ae45b0bf7eca

Cornerstone Research. (2022). Securities Class Action Filings—2021 Year in Review. Retrieved September 14, 2024, from https://www.cornerstone.com/wp-content/uploads/2022/02/Securities-Class-Action-Filings-2021-Year-in-Review.pdf

Cornerstone Research. (2024). Securities Class Action Filings—2023 Year in Review. Retrieved September 14, 2024, from https://www.cornerstone.com/wp-content/uploads/2024/01/Securities-Class-Action-Filings-2023-Year-in-Review.pdf

DOJ. (2023, April 4). Former Start-Up CEO Charged In $175 Million Fraud. U.S. *Department of Justice*. Retrieved September 14, 2024, from https://www.justice.gov/usao-sdny/pr/former-start-ceo-charged-175-million-fraud

DOJ. (2024). U.S. v. Mmobuosi Indictment. Retrieved September 14, 2024, from https://www.justice.gov/d9/2024-01/u.s._v._mmobuosi_indictment.pdf

FDA. (2021). U.S. food and Drug Administration. Docket FDA-2021-P-0930. Regulations.gov. Retrieved September 27, 2024, from https://www.regulations.gov/docket/FDA-2021-P-0930

Govindarajan, V., & Srivastava, A. (2019). No, Wework Isn't a Tech Company. Here's Why that Matters. *Harvard Business Review*. Retrieved September 14, 2024, from https://hbr.org/2019/08/no-wework-isnt-a-tech-company-heres-why-that-matters

Hindenburg Research. (2023). Tingo Forges Ahead with its Brazen Scam As $725 Million in Claimed Cash Disappears from its Balance Sheet in One Quarter. Retrieved September 14, 2024, from https://hindenburgresearch.com/tingo-scam-forges-ahead/

Jensen, M. C., & Meckling, W. H. (1976). Theory of the Firm: Managerial Behavior, Agency Costs and Ownership Structure. *Journal of Financial Economics, 3*(4). Retrieved September 14, 2024, from https://ssrn.com/abstract=94043 or https://doi.org/10.2139/ssrn.94043

Klausner, M., Ohlrogge, M., & Ruan, E. (2022). A Sober Look at SPACs. *Yale Journal on Regulation, 39*(1). (Stanford Law and Economics Olin Working Paper No. 559. NYU Law and Economics Research Paper No. 20–48. European Corporate Governance Institute—Finance Working Paper No. 746/2021).

McCrum, D. (2020). Wirecard and Me: Dan McCrum on Exposing a Criminal Enterprise. *FT Magazine*, September 3, 2020. Retrieved September 14, 2024, from https://www.ft.com/content/745e34a1-0ca7-432c-b062-950c20e41f03

MICT, Inc. (2022, November 9). MICT Scheduled to Complete Acquisition of Tingo, Inc. Operating Business and Assets Prior to November 30, Following Filing of Tingo Definitive Information Statement [Press release]. Retrieved September 14, 2024, from https://www.sec.gov/Archives/edgar/data/854800/000121390022070832/ea168333ex99-1_mictinc.htm

QCM. (2021). Cassava sciences (SAVA): Quintessential Capital Management. *Game over!*. Retrieved September 27, 2024, from https://www.qcmfunds.com/cassava-sciences-sava-game-over/

SEC. (2011, June 9). SEC Issues Bulletin on Risks of Investing in Reverse Merger Companies. Securities and Exchange Commission Retrieved September 14, 2024, from https://www.sec.gov/investor/alerts/reversemergers.pdf

SEC. (2019, Aug. 14th). Form S-1—Registration Statement—Under—The Securities Act of 1933—The we Company. Retrieved September 14, 2024, from https://www.sec.gov/Archives/edgar/data/1533523/000119312519220499/d781982ds1.htm

SEC. (2021, March 31). Financial Reporting and Auditing Considerations of Companies Merging with SPACs. By Munter, P. U.S. Securities and Exchange Commission. Retrieved September 14, 2024, from https://www.sec.gov/news/public-statement/munter-spac-20200331

SEC. (2021, May 25). What You Need to know About SPACs—Updated Investor bulletin. U.S. Securities and Exchange Commission. Retrieved September 14, 2024, from https://www.sec.gov/oiea/investor-alerts-and-bulletins/what-you-need-know-about-spacs-investor-bulletin

SEC. (2022, September 21). SEC Charges Nikola with Defrauding Investors. U.S. Securities and Exchange Commission. Retrieved September 14, 2024, from https://www.sec.gov/news/press-release/2022-09-21

SEC (2023). *SEC charges Tingo Mobile Founder, Three Companies with Massive Fraud and Obtains EEmergency Relief* (Press Release No. 2023–254).

SEC. (2023, August 4). Case No. 23-cv-06332. Securities and Exchange Commission v. Kranz, U., & Balciunas, P. United States District Court, Central District of California. Retrieved September 14, 2024, from https://www.sec.gov/files/litigation/complaints/2023/comp25802.pdf

SEC. (2023, December 19). SEC Charges Tingo Mobile Founder, Three Companies with Massive Fraud and Obtains Emergency Relief. U.S. Securities and Exchange Commission. Retrieved September 14, 2024, from https://www.sec.gov/news/press-release/2023-254

SEC. (2023, September 26). Case No. 23–6553, Hyzon Motors Inc., Knight, C.M., & Holthausen, M.C.B. (Defendants). Securities and Exchange Commission, United States District Court, Western District of New York. Retrieved September 14, 2024, from https://www.sec.gov/files/litigation/complaints/2023/comp-pr2023-200-01.pdf

SEC (2023, September 28). In the Matter of Spruce Power Holding Corporation (Release No. 11247; File No. 3–21748). United States of America. Retrieved September 14, 2024, from https://www.sec.gov/files/litigation/admin/2023/33-11247.pdf

SEC (2024). Fact Sheet Spacs, Shell Companies, and Projections: Final Rules. U.S. Securities and Exchange Commission. Retrieved September 14, 2024, from https://www.sec.gov/files/33-11265-fact-sheet.pdf

SEC. (2024, January 4). Claim #1612, Case No. 23–10831, Lordstown Motors Corp. United States Bankruptcy Court, District of Delaware. U.S. Securities and Exchange Commission. Retrieved September 15, 2024, from https://web.archive.org/web/20240915061918/https://veritaglobal.net/lordstown/document/2310831240104000000000009 https://www.kccllc.net/lordstown/document/2310831240104000000000009

SEC. (2024, February 29). In the Matter of Lordstown Motors Corp. (Release No. 11274). Retrieved September 14, 2024, from https://www.sec.gov/files/litigation/admin/2024/33-11274.pdf

SEC. (2024, September 26). SEC Charges Cassava Sciences, Two Former Executives for Misleading Claims About Alzheimer's Clinical Trial. SEC.gov. Retrieved September 27, 2024 from https://www.sec.gov/newsroom/press-releases/2024-151

Thomas, D. (2022). Theranos Scandal: Who is Elizabeth Holmes and why was she on Trial? BBC News. 2022, November 19, Retrieved September 14, 2024, from https://www.bbc.com/news/business-58336998

Transparency International. (2022). The 2022 Corruption Perception Index. Retrieved September 14, 2024, from https://www.transparency.org/en/cpi/2022

Web Inc. (2021). iWeb Inc, Announced it Will Acquire Tingo Mobile Plc. from Tingo International Holdings, Inc, in a Deal Valuing the Tingo Mobile Plc at $3.7 Billion USD. EX-99.1 3 tm2124018d1_ex99–1.htm EXHIBIT 99.1. Retrieved September 14, 2024, from https://www.sec.gov/Archives/edgar/data/1648365/000110465921099997/tm2124018d1_ex99-1.htm

# 19

# Investigating the Business Model, Products & Services

## 19.1 What Exactly is the Corporation Producing and Selling?

At its core, any company is developing or producing a service or product which it sells. Understanding exactly what and how it is produced and sold is key during the fraud investigation.

A tactic that corporate fraudsters often use is the vanity trap. Especially amongst professional investors, it has been observed that they fear losing face. Corporate fraudsters may abuse this by designing overly complex products or services that nobody understands how actually works. This was touched upon in Sect. 18.3.1 on type of industry and risk of fraud. Out of vanity the professional investor does not want to appear stupid and stops asking questions about how the product or service works too soon. This has been observed with innovative high-tech products and services. Areas like AI, Blockchain, Crypto, Pharma, Biotech and Quantum Mechanics.

It has been observed, if a professional long investor has been trapped by the fraudster, it is subsequently hard to convince that something is wrong with the product and service, despite hard evidence.

In some absurd cases, the investigator might even test the service and find it is not working. Meanwhile, a professional investor that has not tried the service, will still claim it is a fantastic service that thousands of users utilize… according to the fraudster.


J. Sørensen, *Shorting Fraud*, https://doi.org/10.1007/978-3-031-81834-9_19

## 19.2 Too Good to be True Product and Services

One of the first and most common red flags, detecting corporate fraud in an early stage, is the "too good to be true" service or product. It has been observed that if things are too good to be true, in most cases they are.

As reported by e.g., Accardo and Cristoferi (2019), Remondini and Ebhardt (2019), Perry (2023) and S&P Global Intelligence (2019), one may look at the interesting and controversial Italian Bio-On case.

Bio-On ended in suspended trading, bankruptcy, a house arrest and (still ongoing at the time of this writing) investigation/prosecution of the CEO regarding false accounting and market manipulation. The CEO has claimed innocence and that it all was an orchestrated attack by the Hedge Fund behind the initial short report. The case also included a raid on the investment bank, which conducted the IPO of Bio-On.

The case started with a report from the activist short seller, Quintessential Capital Management (QCM) in QCM (2019a) and QCM (2019b). QCM reported that in addition to other red flags, associated with e.g. financial misstatements, Bio-On had put out a long list of claims on e.g. products, production processes and facilities that appeared to be exaggerated or factually incorrect. Here are some of the excerpt examples reported:

- Bio-On announced several production plants and partnerships around the globe that had not materialized.
- Bio-On announced they were state-of-the-art industry leaders, but based on a 100-year-old technology.
- Promoted BIO-on bioplastic as fully biodegradable, which was doubtful. Questionable if bioplastics would fully decompose under real-world conditions.
- Bio-On exaggerated the scalability of production methods, and materially understated the complexity of the production methods.
- The production method could produce unrealistically large volumes of bioplastic from various renewable sources.
- Competitors and industry giants like Zeneca and Monsanto had tried and failed with similar.

Photographic evidence that e.g. production plants had not been completed. In addition, QCM's interviews with scientists, industry participants and former employees were used in the short selling report to sanity check the many public announcements from Bio-On.

According to the reports in the Bio-On case, there appears to have been a steady stream of positive company announcements about product and production development that allegedly never appeared to have materialized in the form initially communicated. The CEO of Bio-On has claimed his innocence in the case as reported by e.g. Teitelbaum (2020). On the 25th of November 2024, the CEO and seven other executives were convicted between 3.5 years and 5 years prison in the Bolgona Court according to Madonia (2024).

Exaggerated claims are a gray zone. From a more general perspective, a pattern of exaggeration and announcements that never materialize is often a red flag, which has been seen in several corporate fraud cases. Therefore, it is advised to sanity check if there is a follow-through and actual execution from a company on corporate announcements.

Some types of exaggerations, also known as puffery, are allowed in some jurisdictions. However, announcing new production plants, multiple joint ventures and new product launches that never happen are unlikely to be accepted as puffery. Since listed companies must publicize all material announcements, they are all publicly available. Therefore, it is often easy to sanity check and see if there are false and fabricated announcements.

When working with deep-dives and sanity checking for exaggerated claims. The investor can always do a make or buy assessment on various inaccessible scientific areas. The investor can hire experts to help assess. On the other hand, with Generative AI, doing initial sanity checking of inaccessible areas has become a lot easier, where the investor may do the initial sanity check herself and consult with specialists if still in doubt.

## 19.3 Patents & Trademarks Sanity Checks

The thing with highly innovative and complex products is that they often build on patents. While it is easy to convince the professional investor about the next big thing, it is harder to convince the meticulous civil servant patent examiner. A person holding a natural science or engineering degree, doing nothing all day long but scrutinizing patent applications and ideas. According to Brown (2023) the average approval rate of a patent application by the United States Patent Office from 2011–2020 was 52.8%.

Therefore, the first place to sanity check a claim is by looking in patent databases. Several times it has been observed that companies claim to have made novel inventions, but never even filed for a single patent, which is a major red flag.

In other cases, there might be patents or patent applications, but the patents or patent applications are unrelated and irrelevant to the product. In the trickiest cases there are patents. The patents might even be related. However, they are merely "token" patent applications, only patented in one jurisdiction, registered for show.

If the fraudster really invented something groundbreaking the fraudster would most likely register the patents in all the main markets. As mentioned above there are a lot of pending patent applications, and patent applications that never turned into patents. Therefore, when investigating, also assess the number of patent applications vs. the number of actual patents issued. A fraudster may file tons of patent applications about bogus patents, waiting to be assessed and of course rejected. This does not stop the fraudster stating a patent is pending and abusing that statement for the fraud.

In the Swedish $500 million Fermenta corporate fraud scandal reported by Lohr (1986, March 3), the CEO Refaat El-Sayed, who amongst other things was exposed as not having a doctorate, was said to hold many patents. However, a simple look up in the Swedish Patent Database, see El-Sayed (1970–2024),the patent applications which are found appear to have been dismissed.

If the patents have been issued or patent documents are available, it is an effective way to get an understanding for the real product.

The investor should also examine branded services or products. Has the company filed for the most logical trademarks, and secured the necessary internet domains, etc. This is easy to verify with a simple lookup on whois.com, domaintools.com and trademark databases.

If one can register trademarks of the service and product under investigation. Or buy "tentpole" internet domains with branded names, it is a red flag that something is wrong. The brand most likely does not exist anywhere else but the fraudster's mind.

## 19.4 Are Permits and Licenses Supporting the Business Model

The business model under investigation might deal with a financial company, a restaurant chain, a transportation company, a pharmaceutical or consumer product. Regardless of business type, in most jurisdictions, by law, it is required that businesses need multiple official licenses, permits, etc. to operate the business model.

If a corporation claims to have a business model, but one fails to find official documentation permitting the corporation to conduct the business model, this is a major red flag.

The more sophisticated fraudsters might operate parts of the business model in foreign jurisdictions. On top of the legitimate token business, they might claim to operate the same business model in foreign jurisdictions, where there is a language barrier or less digitized societies. It makes it harder, but often not impossible, to verify, by e.g. requesting hard copies of permits from the authorities of foreign jurisdictions.

## 19.5 Customer Reviews and Online Presence

Especially if the investor is dealing with a business to consumer company, online presence is important. Therefore, online presence, including Social Media presence and activity of the company online should match the company's size. Discrepancies between the financial size and activity of the company and its counterpart in cyberspace should raise red flags.

Most companies get reviews of their products and services. Also, customer activity related to the company is important. Even the absolute best companies get complaints. So, looking at customer review sites like trustpilot.com, yelp.com, Facebook and Google Reviews, might give you an indication of the true size and activity of the business. It has been observed that corporations claiming to have hundreds of thousands of customers, virtually had no customer activity on any type of social media. Lacking reviews is a major red flag, since it indicates there is no genuine business activity.

In addition, reviews claiming the company to be a scam, or failing to systematically deliver its products and services is also a red flag.

A third kind of red flags are synthetic fake reviews that appear to be doctored and paid for by the company. While some review sites now are employing anti-fraud tactics, "review mills" fabricating fake reviews still exist.

## 19.6 The Reality of Web-Based Services and the Digital Footprint of the Customers

Sanity checking web-based, and phone app-based services is simple. The investor may use tools like https://similarweb.com to sanity check. Does the web traffic statistic correspond with the reported numbers of users / customers supplied by the corporation?

In some cases, it has been observed that companies claim to have hundreds of thousands of customers using their web-based service. However, the unique traffic statistics on the website were only counted in a few hundred or a few thousands.

Similarly, a service based solely on iPhone and Android Apps also claimed to have more than tens of thousands of users—with less than five thousand downloads from the Google Play Store. These numbers simply did not match. In addition, the company claimed to have iPhone users in jurisdictions, where the Apple infrastructure was not even available yet.

## 19.7 Employee Reviews and Corporate Fraud Risks

The investor should look at general Social Media Accounts like Facebook or general recruitment portals that allow rating and employee reviews of the corporations. Dedicated employer review sites like the ones in Table 19.1 is a good place to learn about the company and find inconsistencies and red flags.

From a fraud detection perspective, disgruntled employees or ex-employees might be a really useful source. An investor often does not have access to whistleblower information, so this is the next best thing. Besides these public sites. In the underground forums e.g. on Darknet, employers are also discussed. However, as in the public forums, one should always take everything with a grain of salt.

Again, look for inconsistencies. It could be that the annual report states that the company has a successful gender-neutral diversity policy. However, the ratings from women on the Fairygodboss website tell another story. Focus both on quantitative measures, but also the anecdotes and free-text stories from employees or ex-employees.

## 19.8 Employee Turnover and Growth

The churn rate of top management and C-level staff, dealt with in Sect. 16.2.6 is often stated in public company announcements. Similarly, a high churn rate in lower rungs of employees could be a problem. High employee turnover, low average tenure and specific other skew background demographics may indicate that something is wrong. That could be a disproportionate number of first-time immigrants in the workforce. Immigrants

**Table 19.1** Examples of employer review sites

| Name | Description | Coverage | URL |
|---|---|---|---|
| Glassdoor | A well-known website for employee job reviews. It provides insights into the pros and cons of working for different companies | Global | www.glassdoor.com |
| Fairygodboss | A website, which is dedicated to the female perspective. Helping women find jobs where they are treated fairly, paid comparably | Global | www.fairygodboss.com |
| Vault | The Vault website does employee and internship reviews in addition to academic reviews | Global | www.vault.com |
| Kununu | Austrian startup website, which has expanded and is now considered the "Glassdoor" of Germany | Europe | www.kununu.com |
| CareerBliss | The investor may search millions of company reviews and ratings from real employees | Global | www.careerbliss.com |

highly dependent on the fraudulent company for their stay in the country may be exploited by the fraudster.

These employee statistics of the company may often be analyzed through e.g. a premium account on LinkedIn. Here the investor can see the evolution in total headcount, employee distribution and headcount growth by function, etc. These data all give the investor an alternative impression of the state of the company, which may be compared with the public statements from the company.

If the investor finds that the employee demographics are skewed when doing peer-company comparisons, it might indicate something is off in the company. Other inconsistencies raising red flags could be that revenue is strongly growing, while headcount is plummeting. There could be legitimate reasons for this.

However, what is the likelihood an ordinary company suddenly has a revenue or net income per employee that beats all successful tech companies in history, including Facebook, Google, and Microsoft. Of course, there might be special situations and outliers, like with the pharma companies doing COVID-19 vaccination or Berkshire Hathaway.

Also skim through the employees on e.g. LinkedIn. Do they look like real employees or are there signs of synthetic employees, accounts that are created by management to give an impression of a bigger company?

## 19.9 Frequent or Dramatic Pivots in the Business Model

Another red flag is frequent and/or significant changes in the business model of the company. This was seen in the Enron Corporate Fraud case mentioned in Table 5.1. Enron was initially a gas pipeline company that transformed into a trader of energy derivatives… and much more.

Looking at the Theranos case described in Sect. 18.3.1, Theranos also changed its business model. From selling machines, to partnering with pharmacies. Ironically, even buying competitors machines to conduct the blood sample analysis the old-fashioned way, because Theranos' own wonder-machine was nothing but a sham.

This has also been observed in an undisclosed case. Within a 2.5-year period, the company first offered a medical device. Next it offered strange unspecified software consultancy. Finally becoming an unspecified software development contractor.

For the investor, these frequent or dramatic changes in the business model mean that over time, apples are compared with bananas, which are later compared with bicycles. It makes it hard to grasp the development of the company, which is the whole purpose of these fraud pivots of the business model.

## 19.10 The Corporate Legal Entity Complexity vs. The Business Model

In the search for corporate fraud, the investor should make a holistic assessment of the corporate legal entity setup, and then assess its plausibility.

The investor should analyze the complexity of the corporation's legal entities. Meaning all subsidiaries and associated entities and their relationship. Taking into consideration the number, type, and placement of legal entities, which makes up the corporation. Then compare them with the business model of the corporation. Finally, the investor should assess if this corporate setup is purposeful in supporting the business model, or if the legal setup has been constructed for other purposes than the business model, like corporate fraud or other types of financial crime.

As a rule of thumb, from a profit point of view, any investor wants as lean a corporate structure as possible. The red flag is raised when there are suspicious or unexplainable discrepancies. When there is an above average number of legal entities, spread over many jurisdictions that do not make sense from a business perspective. The investor may do peer—and baseline comparisons to spot these setups.

For instance, a corporation that produces and sells a product in one limited geographical area only, often does not need the corporation spread out on double-digit entities across the world in a network with shell companies in strange places.

To avoid being regulated and complying with standards, laws, and regulations in one jurisdiction, entities are often moved to another jurisdiction. Besides obfuscation of the corporate fraud setup, these complicated setups may be used for e.g., round-tripping, tax evasion, sanctions evasion, and other types of regulatory arbitrage.

Corporations operating legal entities in multiple jurisdictions are often more cumbersome to detect fraud in. Imagine the headquarters, production, operations, and sales department spread over multiple jurisdictions. These, all in different locations, with different rules, standards, and disclosure of activity. Such multidimensional setups make it cumbersome and more challenging to detect and research fraudulent activity in a corporation. Even when reporting potential crime, it is harder for law enforcement to work across different jurisdictions. This is something that the corporate fraudsters know and actively abuse.

## 19.11 Business Models Involving Related Party Transactions

The investor must analyze the financial transactions between the corporate entities. Do they make sense? Are they overly complex in nature? Are they direct or do they go through several layers of subsidiaries before they reach their end point? Are they reasonable?

Often in fraudulent corporate cases, transactions are circled around legal entities with the purpose of temporary propping up, patching, or covering for shortcomings in parts of the corporate structure. It means that without any legitimate reason money and funds are moved around.

A type of financial transaction that is of special interest in fraud detection is related-party transactions. While related party" might be defined legally differently across various jurisdictions, it generally refers to individuals or legal entities, with direct or indirect control over each other's activities or finances. This includes executives, directors, major shareholders (like family members), and any associated subsidiaries or affiliates.

Related party transactions are business dealings between two entities that share a special relationship. This could involve the exchange of goods or services, such as a parent company transacting with its subsidiary. Other examples are asset sales within a corporate group, loans between related entities, employment, leasing, or outsourcing contracts.

The importance of disclosing these transactions lies in the potential conflicts of interest that could arise. It allows investors to understand if any terms are unfairly favoring one party. For instance, a loan agreement with below-market rates between two related companies would affect their financial statements and should be disclosed. If the investor during fraud investigations discovers strange, related party transactions, or even worse, discovers that related party transactions have not been disclosed, these are red flags indicating substantial risk of corporate fraud.

## 19.12 Mergers, Acquisitions, Growth and Expansion of the Fraudulent Corporation

A problem that a fraudulent corporation faces is that the flawed business model setup often cannot support the company in the long run. To expand and grow the fraud, alternative obfuscation tactics might be used by the fraudster. They serve two purposes. First, to make an appearance of growth, second to make it even harder for the investor and other stakeholders to comprehend the fraudulent corporation.

### 19.12.1 Roll-Ups–Organic Growth vs. Inorganic Growth

A Mergers & Acquisitions growth strategy that relies on the method referred to as roll-ups should automatically raise suspicion and be investigated further with regard to corporate fraud. Roll-ups are the perfect fraud-tool for financial engineering and tampering with growth numbers.

In roll-ups, a company buys a string of smaller companies and consolidates them. While this can be done for legitimate reasons, it is also a tactic that has been abused in several corporate fraud cases, like MCI WorldCom, Philip Services, Westar Energy, and Tyco International, according to Carroll and Mui (2008).

It becomes especially interesting when the roll-ups are dispersed over multiple jurisdictions and conducted with the help of multiple different stakeholders, like different Investment Banks, Law firms, Consultancies and Auditors. Following different accounting standards in different languages.

If the data on the acquired target companies in the roll-ups is available, the investor should analyze it. Are these struggling companies, which it makes little sense to acquire from a business model point of view? The reason to buy these is not to support the business model, but to conduct some abusive financial engineering or obfuscation.

### 19.12.2 The Fraud Conglomerate

As with the changes in the business model, one should also raise a red flag when the growth strategy of a corporation turns into a conglomerate style acquisition pattern. Though not common today, the purpose of the traditional legit corporate conglomerate was diversification of risk, through buying unrelated businesses.

The two main purposes of the fraud conglomerate are abusive financial engineering and obfuscation. This is done by acquiring weak and unrelated businesses.

First, the conglomerate will acquire companies that may be used for fraudulent financial engineering. Second, building a fraud conglomerate with multiple different areas makes it hard or impossible to understand the financials at the consolidated level. Furthermore, the investor cannot find peer-companies to compare the fraud conglomerate with. Funds may also be moved between the weakly or unrelated entities in unnatural ways.

Stakeholders, like auditors, will have a challenging time auditing what is going on. Two parts of the conglomerate might also be so different that they need two different auditors for them. Then no single auditor will have an overview of how the fraud conglomerate functions, which may be the aim of the corporate fraudster.

The investor must look at the type of companies that are merged into the conglomerate. If they do not make any sense from a business perspective and are all over the place this is a major red flag of potential corporate fraud.

## References

Accardo, V., & Cristoferi, C. (2019, October 23). Italy's Bio-on CEO Arrested in 'Plastic Bubbles' Probe. *Reuters*. Retrieved September 14, 2024, from https://www.reuters.com/article/us-italy-bio-on-probe-idUSKBN1X21S1

Brown, S. (2023, March 22). Patent Statistics. Patent Experts. Retrieved September 14, 2024, from https://web.archive.org/web/20240207083040/https://patentexperts.org/patent/statistics/

Carroll, P., & Mui, C. (2008). Seven Ways to Fail Big. *Harvard Business Review*, September 2008. Retrieved September 14, 2024, from Harvard Business Review-https://hbr.org/2008/09/seven-ways-to-fail-big

El-Sayed, R. (1970–2024). Patents PRV. Retrieved September 14, 2024, from https://tc.prv.se/spd/search?hits=true&start=0&inventor=el+sayed&lang=en&tab=2

Lohr, S. (1986, March 3). A Fall from Grace in Biotech. *The New York Times*, Section D, p. 1.

Madonia, M. (2024). Bio-on, Marco Astorri condannato a 5 anni e 2 mesi per il crac della start-up che valeva un miliardo in Borsa. *Corriere di Bologna.* Retrieved September 14, 2024, from https://corrieredibologna.corriere.it/notizie/cronaca/24_novembre_25/bio-on-marco-astorri-condannato-a-5-anni-e-2-mesi-per-il-crac-della-start-up-che-valeva-un-miliardo-in-borsa-ba0bc0de-7e8d-45e5-867e-27f8441e2xlk.shtml

Perry, L. (2023, May 24). A Beginner's Guide to Getting Away with Accounting Fraud, Part Two. *Financial Times*. Retrieved September 14, 2024, from https://www.ft.com/content/46803403-2888-459b-80f7-81e57fbd6cfb

QCM. (2019a). Equity Report. Quintessential Capital Management, Retrieved December 7, 2023, from https://www.qcmfunds.com/wp-content/uploads/2019/07/Quintessential-on-Bio-On-English-on-screen-3-v4-compressed.pdf

QCM. (2019b). Bio-on S.p.A.: Trouble in Bologna? Equity Report. Quintessential Capital Management, Retrieved December 7, 2023, from, https://www.qcmfunds.com/wp-content/uploads/2019/07/Quintessential-Bio-on-report-ENG-2-compressed.pdf

Remondini, C., & Ebhardt, T. (2019, October 23). Italy's Unicorn Stumbles as Fund Report Leads to Founder Arrest. *Bloomberg*. Retrieved September 14, 2024, from https://www.bloomberg.com/news/articles/2019-10-23/bio-on-executive-arrested-in-italy-s-plastic-bubbles-probe

S&P Global Intelligence. (2019). Retrieved September 14, 2024, from https://www.spglobal.com/marketintelligence/en/news-insights/trending/zwickfiddjn3eh3dj1fhma2

Teitelbaum, R. (2020). The Managers of These Companies are Corporate Sociopaths. *Institutional Investor*. Retrieved in September 23, 2024 from https://www.institutionalinvestor.com/article/2bsx1z281e38vorxshn9c/portfolio/the-managers-of-these-companies-are-corporate-sociopaths

# 20

# Investigating the CEO and the Executives

## 20.1 Background Checks of the Top Management

Few people wake up one day and decide that today they are major white-collar criminals. There is often a history. Therefore, it is paramount to do extensive background checks and research on C-level executives and top management.

The most obvious is to check in court databases and deep-dive into adverse media investigations. Investigate if there has been any suspicious activity including criminal activity related to any of the top management.

As a practitioner, looking postmortem on missed fraud cases, a missed historic criminal conduct by the executives has often come to light. Therefore, digging up the past of the C-level executives and top management is valuable.

## 20.2 The Picture-perfect CEO Background Narrative

Working with CEOs in corporate fraud, the investor will observe that several fraudsters before their exposure might have been portrayed in the media as successful entrepreneurs or captains of industries. These individuals were getting all kinds of rewards and media exposure. Table 20.1 shows an overview of some of these picture-perfect corporate celebrities that later was involved in corporate fraud cases.


J. Sørensen, *Shorting Fraud*, https://doi.org/10.1007/978-3-031-81834-9_20

**Table 20.1** Media personalities in corporate fraud cases

| Name | Title | Year | Details |
|---|---|---|---|
| Elizabeth Holmes | Several Forbes stories and other media exposure | 2013–2015 | Convicted of fraud linked to Theranos Fraud case and sentenced 11 years in prison |
| Sam Bankman-Fried | Forbes 30 Under 30 | 2021 | Sentenced to 25 years for fraud and money laundering |
| Caroline Ellison | Forbes 30 Under 30 | 2022 | Related to Bankman-Fried. She pleaded guilty to seven criminal charges and sentenced two years in prison |
| Martin Shkreli | Forbes 30 Under 30 | 2012 | Got a seven-year prison sentence for securities fraud in 2018 |
| Trevor Milton | The Forbes 400 richest list | 2020 | Convicted of Securities Fraud Scheme and a four-year prison sentence |
| Charlie Javice | Forbes 30 Under 30 | 2019 | She was the CEO of the startup, Frank. She has been charged with allegedly falsely inflating the number of customers of her company. She has pled not guilty and is awaiting trial at time of writing |

*Source* Forbes (2012–2020) & DOJ (2018–2024)

Three examples of narratives that should raise red flags and be investigated in depth are the "Munchhausen" narrative, the "Fairy-tale Background" and the "Steve Jobs Copycat" narrative.

The "Munchhausen" narrative might be observed with CEOs that fabricate parts or entire backgrounds, often combined with megalomania. In one specific case, reported by Stemann et al. (2023), the founder and CEO was portrayed with a background of a professional football player, successful music artist on Canadian hitlists and finally a Doctor in Neuroscience. If one did a minimal background check, some only taking a few minutes with Google, the investor could reveal that this was an untrue fabricated background. Despite this, the CEO almost pulled off an IPO, but was blocked at the last minute, not because of the board, the underwriters, or the stock exchange. Instead because of the investigative journalists exposing the fabricated background.

Another narrative used by fraudsters is the fairy-tale narrative. This is following the structure of Hans Christian Andersen or Disney movies. E.g. The Ugly Duckling narrative. A rag to riches narrative where an underdog succeeds against all odds. Everybody roots for the underdog, in fairy tales and Disney movies, including the hoodwinked investors.

Even if the fraudster has been brought up in a middle class or affluent family, they may portray themselves as coming from a poor family with little resources, being self-made, to fit the fairy-tale narrative that everybody loves, and have the audience root for them.

In one case, a CEO was portrayed in the media as coming from one of the hardest ghettos, with high unemployment rates, low social status, and high rates of crime. While the fact was, most of the upbringing had taken place six miles away from that specific ghetto, in a nicer neighborhood.

However, the narrative gave the CEO preferential treatment and an image that the CEO had escaped the chains of social inheritance, and was now creating the next Google. The CEO was being celebrated by some of the most high-profile politicians, until the CEO was exposed by the media, ending in bankruptcy and investigations.

The final narrative is the "Steve Jobs Copycat" narrative. The corporate fraudsters tend to follow narratives of the most successful business stories on the planet. More of the fraud cases that have been seen in the tech industry tend to follow that pattern. The CEOs portray themselves as the next Steve Jobs, Mark Zuckerberg, or Jeff Bezos, heading the next big thing in tech.

Red flags should be raised, when the investor starts to wonder if it is the life story of the CEO, or the autobiography of Steve Jobs being read. The problem is that professional investors and investment bankers have read these stories of great entrepreneurs, they resonate with the narrative and are thrilled to think they are the brilliant minds who have found the next Steve Jobs and Apple.

When the fraudster succeeds in selling herself as a Steve Jobs Copycat with the next Apple, the valuation of the company may become exaggerated. Instead of being based on how much cash flow the company and business model generates, they use the FAANG comparison valuation. This despite that the business model might have no similarities or addressable market that resembles a FAANG in any ways. While many cases have been successfully mitigated. Rogue Steve Jobs Copycats are duping even experienced Investment Bankers and investors.

## 20.3 The Too Charismatic CEO

Closely related to the picture-perfect background of the CEO, is the too charismatic CEO. One with high self-promoting tendencies, being confident and charismatic. In the public domain, if the investor watches an interview with CEOs like Elizabeth Holmes (Theranos),, Kenneth Lay (Enron), etc. To most people, these persons may appear charismatic and believable just from appearance, which is why they are so good at defrauding.

In cases of corporate frauds, these charming personality types are often seen. They are extremely good salesmen or women. Confident and ready with an answer on the fly, having rhetorical control and verbal dominance.

Therefore, the investor needs to prepare when meeting and questioning them. Keep them anchored to the facts and drill into the inconsistencies in facts. It is interesting to see how, if they cannot explain, they come up with stranger and stranger explanations.

Also with the too charismatic CEO, there is often a discrepancy, between a low or no educational background relating to what they do. Like no track record that justifies where they are. They might have a cloudy untransparent past. If the investor starts digging, she will often find a track record of dubious or illegal activity. Being pressured, the too charismatic CEO often sells herself with exacerbated claims that cannot be verified, like in the "Munchhausen" narrative. Always ask, scrutinize, look, and verify documentation for any of their claims.

## 20.4 Overexposure and Extensive Self-promotion of the CEO and stock

Closely related to the positive narratives and charismatic CEO is the overexposed CEO. A CEO that delivers on the real bottom line does not need to constantly be in the media, promoting herself and the company. If the CEO or other executives are constantly in the news and features, with positive stories, despite questionable fundamental financial results of the company this is a red flag. The analytic tools of lie detection presented in Sect. 13 can be used to assess the CEO's media participation.

## 20.5 Top Management Behavior and Risk of Corporate Fraud

How the CEO and top management react towards criticism, critical questions and probing is remarkably interesting and sometimes telling in corporate fraud cases and can raise more red flags.

This telling behavior, often indicating fraud, has been observed in several cases. When stakeholders like investors, investigative journalists, and equity analysts, ask critical, clarifying, or probing questions.

A famous public example is in the Enron Case from an Earnings Call on April 17th, 2001, as reported by multiple sources, e.g. Duggan (2019). Investor Richard Grubman from Highfields Capital is skeptical regarding the lack of financial information from Enron. This was also captured on the audio recording of the Earnings Call, which may be listened to in multiple places, e.g. in Gibney (2005), if one is interested in the tone of voice, etc.

| | |
|---|---|
| **Richard Grubman**, Highfields Capital: | *"You're the only financial institution that can't produce a balance sheet or cash flow statement with their earnings,"* |
| **Jeff Skilling, CEO, ENRON:** | *"You … you … you," "Well, uh … thank you very much. We appreciate it. Asshole."* |

Similarly, the various "attacks" and threats in the Wirecard case on Financial Times Journalists and short sellers. Here lawyers and even the German Financial Service Authority BaFin was leveraged to threaten or discredit critical voices. These are also known as Ad Hominem tactics.

### 20.5.1 Attacking or "Killing" the Messenger (Ad Hominem)

Ad hominem attacks, discredits the questioner rather than addressing the question. It is a psychological diversion tactic for deflecting blame and creating distrust in the person(s) that is questioning and probing the person or entity of interest, the fraudster.

The effectiveness of Ad Hominem is supported by academic research. According to an experiment conducted by Barnes et al. (2018), it was found that attacking and discrediting a person may be an effective tactic to disprove empirical evidence.

These personal attacks have been observed directly in corporate fraud cases. Where targets are attacking the messenger and his abilities, instead of addressing the fraud issue. Either directly or by proxy, when the target has obtained the trust of intermediates like pundits. The proxies might also be Law Firms or Public Relation (PR) firms.

Under enough pressure, these Ad Hominem attacks by the top-management might be taken to court in dubious and frivolous lawsuits.

As reported by McCrum (2020, June 25) and Reuters (2020, June 23), in the Wirecard case, to counterattack, Wirecard hired and "abused" the UK Law Firm Schilling and PR specialists like FTI Consulting and PR Company Edelman to manage its external public relations.

While no academic research on the relationship between PR companies, Law Firms, and fraud has been found. Working hands-on with corporate fraud cases, reactions with "lawyer up" threats have been observed.

The fraudulent company and executives might threaten with lawyers for no reason. The fraudulent company fails to produce sound evidence to disprove the information presented by lenders, short sellers, investigative journalists, or other stakeholders. Instead, the fraudulent company responds by hiring Law Firms or PR companies. These Third-party actors tailor threat campaigns or spin campaigns, targeting the sender of the information instead of focusing on the facts.

While attacking the messenger is often highlighted because of its dramatic effect, less dramatic types of responses might also be red flags indicating corporate fraud.

### 20.5.2 Evading the Probing Questions

Direct evasiveness is a tool that has been observed in more corporate fraud cases. This is a common strategy to avoid exposure. It can involve providing misleading partial answers or changing the subject altogether. Emett and Wood (2010) describe these tactics in depth.

Tactics observed in earnings calls may be "will follow up offline" and never do. Others refer to favorable earnings estimates (by own paid sell side analysts) or favorable consensus expectations.

### 20.5.3 Stalling/Not Answering

Like evading, delay tactics have been observed in cases. They have been used for two reasons. One is buying time to formulate a better deception. The other is hoping the person inquiring will lose interest. The ways to stall are often justified with sob-stories like sickness, overwork, or blaming other external reasons for not answering or delivering requested clarifications. These are red flags. A practical example is the CTO of a tech company, who was not able to send simple e-mails with attachments, despite a degree in software development.

### 20.5.4 Bombardment with Irrelevant Data

At the other end of the spectrum of evading and stalling, is the "information overload". Here, top management is willingly providing plentiful, but unconnected and unrelated details. This tactic only seeks to confuse, exhaust, or distract the investors from the core issue. This red flag is raised when the investors ask a specific question but is not provided with the answer or data that could deliver the answer. Instead, tons of often unstructured irrelevant data that the investors must dig through, to in the end realize the question cannot be answered with the data. This is an example of the ambiguity deception mentioned in Sect. 4.2.1.

## 20.6 CEO and Related Parties' Private Finances Entanglement with the Corporation

While in many studies it is proposed that incentive plans are good when they tie the CEO and Executives pay to the performance of the company. There is a flip side of that coin in corporate fraud cases.

### 20.6.1 Executive Remuneration and Corporate Fraud

Assenso-Okofo et al. (2021) found a relationship between CEO remuneration and earnings management. In addition, research by Johnson et al. (2009) found CEOs, which are likely to see their company's stock price drop, might be tempted to lie about the company's financial situation. This is because it could lead to big losses in personal wealth, especially if the CEO owns a significant portion of company stocks. The study also found that this temptation to manipulate finances is even stronger when the CEO holds a lot of unrestricted stocks that can be sold. It means the investor should deep-dive into the following points.

- The remuneration goals related to financial performance are over-ambitious. The executive has an incentive to tamper with the financials to reach the numbers, giving the executive the best payday.
- High CEO remuneration exposure to change in macro-or microenvironment shocks, ending a beneficial growth trend for the company. The reasons could be the general economy, downturn in the industry or superior products or services launched by competitors. Here the investor should look if the surprisingly positive company trend is linked to CEO pay and not actual financial results.
- The company financials work like clockwork, around CEO payment targets. Every quarter the estimates are turned into reality or beaten systematically, giving the CEO a steady positive bonus income stream.

Not only the CEO's pay is interesting. A tournament study conducted by Haß et al. (2015) found the payment gap between the CEO, other CxOs and lower-level management found to be an incentive to commit corporate fraud. An increase in the gap of 100% between the CEO and the mean management pay increased the probability of corporate fraud by 37%. The investor should broaden the scope, look around the executive suite, and investigate further executive payment. Is there a pay gap between the CEO, the rest of the Executive Suite and the next layers of management, which incentivizes them to climb to the top of the corporate ladder by fraudulent behavior?

### 20.6.2 The CEO's, Executives,' or Related Parties' Margin Loans

Not only the remuneration might be tied to the company performance and share price. The investor should deep-dive into ties between executives' private financials and the listed company. How many shares are CEO, executives and related parties owning. Are these shares used as e.g. collateral for margin loans?

A drop in the share price of the corporation will result in margin calls, and personal loans being repaid. This is a conflict of interest that may lead to fraudulent activity to avoid a drop in share price. This pressure might result in temporary short-term earnings manipulation or fraud, to boost results and share price. Buying time for private reasons. This artificial boost means that at some point the earnings will return to an even worse state when the earnings must come back down to the correct level.

## 20.7 Executive International Transplant Risks

Working with this topic, the investor must be cautious not to conduct racial profiling. Models built solely on that basis are bound to fail.

However, as seen in Sect. 18.2, some countries are more prone to risk of corruption than others. Saying that all persons from a high-risk country are criminals is of course not viable. However, it might be hard for a person to entirely detach oneself from the culture, or subculture that a person is raised in, for good or bad.

If an executive grew up and succeeded in a high-corruption country, which relies on bribery and other shortcuts to get ahead, these tools would have been the natural order of the CEO's rise to power. When the CEO moves from a high-risk corruption country to a low-risk country, will these embedded values and moral standards magically disappear on a ten-hour intercontinental flight?

This is a flipside of globalization and an overlooked risk point in low corruption countries, with high general trust. In low corruption countries people in general are less used to fraudulent activity. Hence the corrupt CEO from a high-risk country, sticking to a learnt corruption strategy may have a field day in a low-risk country.

The subject is of course highly controversial and might be considered politically incorrect. However, ignoring the transplant risk entirely has already led to corporate fraud cases. One needs to understand all aspects of the executives' background, which may have an impact on a fraudulent modus operandi of the executive. This includes the origin and lifepath of the CEO.

An interesting high-profile potential example case to study is the Carlos Ghosn case as reported by e.g. Garrahan (2021). Ghosn has a dual background from the moderate-to-high-corruption country, Brazil, and the high-corrupt country Lebanon. Ghosn was working as CEO in the two low corruption countries France & Japan—as the dual CEO of Nissan and Renault.

In 2018, Ghosn was charged with corporate fraud and incarcerated in Japan, but eloped the Japanese justice system during house arrest, by being smuggled out of the country in a box. Ghosn now resides in Lebanon, where he claims his innocence. However, since Japan has no extradition agreement with Lebanon, Ghosn has not faced his trial in Japan at the time of writing.

Also in 2022, reported by White (2022), France issued an international arrest warrant on Ghosn. These related to allegations of misuse of company assets, tied to suspicious payments between the Renault-Nissan alliance and its dealer in Oman. Again, Lebanon has no extradition agreement with France, so Ghosn has not faced any trial in France at the time of writing and Ghosn claims innocence.

The recent example of the still ongoing case of Tingo with founder and CEO Dozy Mmobuosi dealt with in Sect. 18.10.2 is also an interesting example to follow. At the time of this writing Mmobuosi is still considered "at large" by The US DOJ. Meanwhile, the CEO has denied the charges put forward by US authorities.

Other red flags on these transplants are the CEO trying to hide facts on origin. This could be that a person suddenly does not speak her mother tongue anymore according to LinkedIn or is trying to hide that she grew up and worked in a high-corrupt country. Now making it appear her background is tied to low-corruption countries instead.

In addition, hide that her basic education is from a university, known to rely more on bribery than scholastic achievements. Then if she moved to a low corrupt country, married her university professor, and got a degree from the university, where he had a tenure. It is red flags like these, investors should look out for. They may indicate the person, in her basic nature and persona, is fraudulent and corrupt.

## References

Assenso-Okofo, O., Jahangir Ali, M., & Ahmed, K. (2021). The Impact of Corporate Governance on the Relationship Between Earnings Management and CEO Compensation. *Journal of Applied Accounting Research, 22*(3), 436–464. Retrieved September 14, 2024, from https://doi.org/10.1108/JAAR-11-2019-0158

Barnes, R. M., Johnston, H. M., MacKenzie, N., Tobin, S. J., & Taglang, C. M. (2018). The Effect of ad Hominem Attacks on the Evaluation of Claims Promoted by Ccientists. *PLOS ONE*. Retrieved September 14, 2024, from https://doi.org/10.1371/journal.pone.0192025

DOJ. (2018–2024). Sentences from Department of Justice. Retrieved September 14, 2024, from multiple pages on Justice.gov: https://www.justice.gov/usao-sdny/pr/united-states-attorney-announces-extradition-ftx-founder-samuel-bankman-fried-united#:~:text=ELLISON%20and%20WANG%20pled%20guilty,participation%20in%20schemes%20to%20defraud, https://www.justice.gov/usao-edny/pr/martin-shkreli-sentenced-seven-years-imprisonment-multi-million-dollar-fraud-scheme#:~:text=He%20was%20convicted%20by%20a,count%20of%20securities%20fraud%20conspiracy, https://www.justice.gov/usao-ndca/us-v-elizabeth-holmes-et-alhttps://www.justice.gov/usao-sdny/pr/trevor-milton-sentenced-four-years-prison-securities-fraud-scheme, https://www.justice.gov/opa/pr/samuel-bankman-fried-sentenced-25-years-his-orchestration-multiple-fraudulent-schemes

Duggan, W. (2019). Enron CEO Curses Skeptical Analyst on Earnings Call on this Day in Market History. *Benzinga*. Retrieved September 16, 2024, from https://web.archive.org/web/20221207170134/, https://www.benzinga.com/general/education/18/04/11529045/this-day-in-market-history-enron-ceo-curses-skeptical-analyst-on-ea

Emett, S., & Wood, D. A. (2010). Common Question-Evasion Tactics: Identify Ploys and Learn Methods to Get the Specific Answers you Need. *Journal of Accountancy*. Retrieved September 15, 2024, from http://web.archive.org/web/20220324052338/https://www.journalofaccountancy.com/issues/2010/jul/20102545.html

Forbes. (2012–2020). Multiple Forbes.com Profile Webpages, which may be Retrieved Through Following URLs from web.archive.org: http://web.archive.org/web/20240329104446/https://www.forbes.com/profile/sam-bankman-fried/, http://web.archive.org/web/20230528185436/https://www.forbes.com/profile/charlie-javice/, https://web.archive.org/web/20231029212012/https://www.forbes.com/30-under-30/2022/finance?profile=alameda-research, http://web.archive.org/web/20230604185100/https://www.forbes.com/pictures/mdg45jljm/martin-shkreli/, http://web.archive.org/web/20141002032854/https://www.forbes.com/profile/elizabeth-holmes/, http://web.archive.org/web/20230411071148/https://www.forbes.com/sites/giacomotognini/2020/09/08/newcomers-these-18-billionaires-join-the-forbes-400-list-in-2020/?sh=5f883cc45d96

Garrahan, D. (Producer, Director & Editor). (2021, July 26). Carlos Ghosn: The rise and fall of a superstar CEO [Film]. *Financial Times*. Retrieved September 14, 2024, from http://web.archive.org/web/20230321091523/, https://www.ft.com/video/45515fe8-3edc-42b1-8d92-dd5ff28ceeac

Gibney, A. (Director). (2005). Enron: The smartest guys in the room [Film]. Magnolia Home Entertainment.

Haß, L. H., Müller, M. A., & Vergauwe, S. (2015). Tournament incentives and corporate fraud. *Journal of Corporate Finance, 34*, 251–267. Retrieved September 14, 2024, from https://doi.org/10.1016/j.jcorpfin.2015.07.008

Johnson, S. A., Ryan, H. E. Jr., & Tian, Y. S. (2009). *Review of Finance, 13*(1), 115–145. Retrieved September 14, 2024, from https://doi.org/10.1093/rof/rfn014

McCrum, D. (2020, June 25). Wirecard: The timeline | Free to read. *Financial Times*. Retrieved September 14, 2024, from https://www.ft.com/content/284fb1ad-ddc0-45df-a075-0709b36868db

Reuters. (2020, June 23). Wirecard Lenders Mandate FTI Consulting as Financial Adviser in Talks with Company: Sources. Retrieved September 14, 2024, from https://www.reuters.com/article/us-wirecard-accounts-lenders/wirecard-lenders-mandate-fti-consulting-as-financial-adviser-in-talks-with-company-sources-idUSKBN23U2CS/

Stemann, C., Blædel, M., & Jensen, M. (2023). Først blev han afsløret i at være falsk doktor—nu indstilles han til konkurskarantæne for at have ført investorer bag lyset. Frihedsbrevet. Retrieved September 14, 2024, from https://frihedsbrevet.dk/foerst-blev-han-afsloeret-i-at-vaere-falsk-doktor-nu-indstilles-han-til-konkurskarantaene-for-at-have-foert-investorer-bag-lyset/

White, S. (2022). French Prosecutors Issue Arrest Warrant for Carlos Ghosn. *Financial Times*. Retrieved September 14, 2024, from http://web.archive.org/web/20230327102742/, https://www.ft.com/content/46e1dbae-5bd3-4425-b4f2-c5fdc0bc65f3

# 21

# Investigating the Board, Stakeholders & Corporate Governance

## 21.1 The Board of Directors and Corporate Fraud

There is a plentitude of academic research on indicators, like outside directors vs. inside directors, audit committees, the board-CEO relationship, etc. previously touched upon in Sect. 16.1.

With the board and its members, the investor wants to do the same background investigations as with the CEO. What have they been involved in and what else are they currently involved in? In addition to the criminal background check, the investor should do a competencies reality background check.

The CEO might have a major influence on appointing board members. Even in the cases where there is no prior relationship between the CEO and the board member there are multiple risks to be on the lookout for.

**Beware of The Trophy Board Member**, who poses a major risk and is abused by criminals. In several cases there has been observed a tendency that corporate fraudsters use Trophy Board members. These are often highly esteemed, well respected, successful people with public appeal. The only problem is that they have little or no clue about the industry or company of the board they sit on. Instead, the board members are an extended tool of the CEO fairy tale. These Trophy Board members lend credibility to the CEO and help rubberstamp the corporate fraud. In the public domain, this is exemplified by the Theranos case and board. Looking at a list of some of the external directors in Theranos listed by Business Insider (2019, March 14) there appears an interesting pattern from a corporate fraud perspective:



J. Sørensen, *Shorting Fraud*, https://doi.org/10.1007/978-3-031-81834-9_21

- Henry A. Kissinger: Former U.S. Secretary of State.
- George Shultz: Former U.S. Secretary of State
- Jim Mattis: Retired Four-star general—former U.S. Secretary of Defense.
- William J. Perry: Former U.S. Secretary of Defense.
- Gary Roughead: Retired Admiral in the U.S. Navy.
- Riley Bechtel: Former CEO of the Bechtel Group, a large engineering company.
- David Boies: A founder and the chairman of Boies Schiller Flexner, a law firm.
- William Foege: Former director of the Centers for Disease Control and Prevention (CDC).
- Richard Kovacevich: Former CEO & chairman of Wells Fargo, a financial services company.
- Samuel Nunn: Former U.S. Senator from Georgia.

While several of these board members are historical icons and political legends, whose presence will impress most people, many lack the basic skill set to sit on the board of an innovative consumer healthcare company. From the fraudster's point of view a board like this is the perfect match.

- The board members lend invaluable credibility to the fraudster and the fraudulent company.
- At the same time the board members conduct little or no real control of the CEO & executive suite.

As with CEO and executives' entanglement with the company dealt with in Sect. 16.2.5, also members of the board might have similar tie-ins and dependencies. These might have an impact on the control they do on the CEO.

## 21.2 Investors, Financiers and Their Conduct

As already touched upon in Sects. 9.4 to 9.8, the composition of investors, financiers and stakeholders may have an impact on the risk of corporate fraud.

In deep-dive investigations, the investor looks at the specific institutional owners, professional investors, and the banks and other financiers providing the loans. Have any of these stakeholders been involved in dubious transactions and fraudulent companies previously? Looking in legal databases,

**Table 21.1** Court document text snippet from Retten i Roskilde (2023)(*Roskilde Court*)

| English translation | Original court document text |
|---|---|
| *However, it must be stated—supported by the statements made in the criminal case—that the bondholders, the professional investors, did not carry out any form of due diligence at all* | *Imidlertid må konstateres—støttet af forklaringerne afgivet under straffesagen—at obligationsejerne, de professionelle investorer, ret beset ikke foretog nogen form for due dilligence overhovedet* |

litigations etc. This may reveal much about their risk appetite when it comes to fraudulent companies as well as their lack of due diligence.

An example of this is the $100 million Danish corporate fraud case of Hesalight, where the CEO was sentenced seven years in jail for the corporate fraud. In a later case the court documents translated in Table 21.1 reveal that the professional investors, amongst others, one of the biggest Scandinavian banks, the Danske Bank, did not conduct any actual real due diligence into the company, at all.

Therefore, it is always necessary to assess the quality of the institutional investors and financiers involved in the company.

### 21.2.1 Voice or Exit of Traditional Investors—Entry of Untraditional Financiers and Investors

In the case of listed fraudulent corporations, the investors, especially institutional investors with big stakes in the companies have two options—voice or exit.

Voice is investors gaining control and taking actions through the board. E.g. removing directors and the CEO. However, if the institutional investors expect the corporation is going to collapse, they will probably not spend time on proxy fights, extraordinary general meetings or similar. Instead, the investors will dump as much stock as possible, as fast as possible. As described in Sect. 9.7 this is what appeared to have happened in the public OW Bunker fraud case.

In several high-risk cases, it has been observed that some institutional and professional investors dump their holdings and might even start to build up net short positions.

In one suspicious case, a long-term institutional investor, known to hold positions in companies for years, aggressively built up a+10% long position over a couple of months, to suddenly turn around, dump everything again, fast, with a big loss to the investor. Subsequently, allegations of fraud and other problems surfaced, making the share lose even more.

As mentioned in Sect. 9.7, the composition of owners between retail investors and institutional investors is important. Also, holdings by related parties, family ties, dubious trusts and beneficial owners may be problematic. Who is doing the bridge financing? Does it make any logical sense that they are investing or financing this? Investors and financiers operating outside their usual sphere of competence and investment universe are always a red flag with regards to corporate fraud and should be investigated.

In a case it was observed that a company suspected of corporate fraud was in major liquidity problems. They were rejected of traditional financing, but suddenly found a bridge financier in a suspicious foreign country and issued a considerable size of convertible bonds to the financier, to keep afloat.

When investigating this new financier taking on this extreme risk, little information could be found on the financier (and later beneficial owner). The trace ended at a postbox address in a strip-mall, in another part of the world, which was obviously used to obscure who was behind this financing.

These types of post box addresses and office hotels were mentioned in Sect. 18.5 regarding the physical addresses used to create shell companies and fake subsidiaries. These may also be used to hide beneficial owners conducting sanctions evasion, money laundering or other types of criminal activity.

Especially if the past activities of these financiers are related to other dubious companies that collapsed or were taken private. Like financing with convertible debt, then converting them into shares and selling the shares can be used as an advanced form of layering in money laundering or evasion of sanctions.

It will often be seen that institutional investors and traditional financiers will step away from the company where there is a high risk of fraud and they will be replaced by retail investors, and other dubious financiers in the corporate loan shark category.

It may also be a string of different bridge lenders, replacing one after another on extreme terms, for the company to try and stay afloat. Sometimes the endgame for a publicly listed company involved in corporate fraud is delisting, to avoid more public scrutiny of the company and a more lenient control and compliance environment that is related to a private company. If managing to stay alive and carry the fraud forward it may then be re-IPOed a little later in a roundtrip manner, maybe under a new name.

## 21.3 Other Corporate Stakeholders

Another key factor to research is the relationship between the corporations and other stakeholders. Who are the other stakeholders? Have they been involved in other suspicious activities previously?

First, do the stakeholders exist in the real world? Doing fraud investigations on stakeholders, the investor will sometimes find that stakeholders like customers and vendors, might be entirely fabricated. These types often involve document forgery, which is one of the worst red flags encountered in fraud deep-dives.

However, if the stakeholder exists, one should investigate, to see if the stakeholder has been involved in suspicious activity. This includes stakeholders like:

- Customers & Vendors
- Auditors & Corporate Lawyers
- Joint Ventures / Partners
- Consultants
- Corporate Bankers, Banks, and Financiers

It has been observed that the corporations that nobody else wants to audit or service cluster around the same auditors, lawyers, corporate bankers, and banks. Some of these clusters happen deliberately and knowingly because the stakeholder has made a business out of servicing doubtful and fraudulent corporations. Others cluster around the stakeholders because the lack of due diligence and Know Your Customer (KYC) processes are weak compared to the stakeholder's peers. While the former is the worst category, knowingly facilitating, the second category of incompetence may have the same impact, and both should be considered major red flags.

## 21.4 Corporate Governance Maturity and Corporate Fraud

Besides the highly relevant topics regarding composition, competencies and independence of the board members, the investor may also analyze corporate governance maturity more generally.

There are governance best practices, codes of conduct and several standards of Corporate Governance. This could be policies like ICGN Global Governance Principles (2021) dealing with shareholder rights, disclosure and transparency, and the responsibilities of the board. Corporate Reporting like Financial, ESG etc. Internal / external audits, remuneration and risk oversight.

The main problem with some of the softer code of conduct and policy areas is they can be hard to sanity check and verify and are open for interpretation.

A written code of conduct or corporate governance policy is not the same as the policy is actually implemented and embedded in the corporation.

## References

Business Insider. (2019, March 14). Theranos' Former Board Members Included Henry Kissinger, George Shultz, James Mattis, and More. *Business Insider*. Retrieved September 14, 2024, from https://www.businessinsider.com/theranos-former-board-members-henry-kissinger-george-shultz-james-mattis-2019-3

International Corporate Governance Network. (2021). ICGN Global Governance Principles. *ICGN*. Retrieved September 14, 2024, from https://www.icgn.org/sites/default/files/2021-11/ICGN%20Global%20Governance%20Principles%202021.pdf

Retten i Roskilde. (2023). Sag om, hvorvidt de fem sagsøgte, som henholdsvis ledelse i og revisor for sagsøger, Hesalight A/S under konkurs, har pådraget sig erstatningsansvar over for konkursboet (Casenumber BS-9950/2017-ROS). Coutdatabase number 1275/23. Retrieved September 14, 2024, from https://domsdatabasen.dk/#sag/2996/3546

# 22

# Investigating Financial Reports From the Strategic Perspective

## 22.1 Key Areas of Focus in Financial Statement Fraud

The breakdown of the financial reports into the income statement, balance sheet, cash flow statement, MD&A, auditors report, footnotes, etc. was discussed and explained in sect. 10.2. Here the emphasis is on deep-dive investigations related to the areas.

Before diving into the specific parts in sect. 23–27, this section deals with general strategic and contextual clues of the financial statement and company reports—like auditors, general policies and other strategic content and their relevance to reveal the corporate fraud.

What the investor should keep in mind is how these general clues and signals on general policies related to the financial statements and company reports are moving. Especially, if the standard moves from a financial conservative standard to a financial sporadic and open-ended standard the investor should be vigilant.


J. Sørensen, *Shorting Fraud*, https://doi.org/10.1007/978-3-031-81834-9_22

## 22.2 Strategic Changes of Auditor by Management

In several observed fraud cases the change in auditor and the actual conditions around changes in auditor have been observed as a precursor of later revealed fraud. Therefore, deep-dive investigations into the auditor, reason for change, etc. should be conducted.

Timing of the Change:

- A change right before a financial reporting period (end of the quarter or year) could be a way to obscure irregularities. This has been observed in several corporate fraud cases. In one case the auditor even withdrew audited financial report hours after publication.
- A change after a disagreement with the prior auditor about accounting practices raises serious concerns. This has also been observed. The red flag is especially serious. If there has been disagreement and firing of the auditor, when the auditor has made auditor remarks like Qualified Opinion, Adverse Opinion or Disclaimer of Opinion on the reports.
- An auditor change just before the end of the auditing period could also be a tactic to have the new auditor do the audit under extreme time pressure, which might in turn mean fewer deep-dives and sanity checks of the corporation. If the old auditor has partly completed an audit, the management might have an overview of problem areas. Fire the old auditor and try to hand-feed the new auditor with selective material.
- The revolving door auditor. This has also been observed in corporate fraud cases. There is a continuous string of auditors, each making one of two audits then replaced with a new.

Reason for the Change:

- Vague or questionable reasons provided by management for the auditor change.
- If the company claims a desire for lower fees, but the new auditor is equally or more expensive.
- A company replacing seasoned auditor, with auditor that has no companies in the same class.
- Sudden focus on non-audit services with the new audit firm, instead of core audit functions—buying management consulting hours, etc.

## 22.3 The General Accounting Policies and Methods

Cash Accounting is the simplest form of accounting that focuses solely on cash flow. Revenue recognized when cash is received, and expenses recorded when cash is paid out. A concept that is easy to understand and used by small companies.

However, publicly listed companies use Accrual Accounting. Accrual accounting transactions are recognized when they are "on the books," but not necessarily "in the bank": Accruals represent money that is either owed the company, or the company owes to someone else, but the actual cash has not changed hands yet.

Accrual accounting is supposed to give a more accurate picture of the company's financial situation. It does if it is done right. It aims to accurately match expenses with the revenue they helped generate within the same accounting period.

However, at the same time, accrual accounting also opens for interpretations that might lead to creative accounting or outright fraudulent accounting, misleading the investor.

It boils down to two basic questions that have a direct influence on the size of the profits of the company.

- When is revenue recognized?
- When are costs / expenses recognized?

A simple illustrative scenario:

The company, Super Trooper Tech, struggles to meet earnings targets for the quarter ending on September 30th. They want to make things look rosier because they must refinance debt.

**Manipulative Techniques:**

- **Premature Revenue Recognition (Date Manipulation):** On September 28th, Super Trooper Tech records a large sale, even though the delivery of the product and final contract terms are scheduled for October 5th (the following quarter).
- **Delayed Expense Recognition (Date Manipulation):** The company negotiates with a vendor to postpone sending an invoice for significant services rendered in September. They can now avoid recording this expense until October, pushing it a quarter.

**Impact on Financials:**

- Quarter Ending September 30th:
  - Revenue is artificially inflated by including the prematurely recorded sale.
  - Expenses are understated due to the invoice delay, making the company look even more profitable in that quarter.

- **Quarter Ending December 31st:**
  - Revenue might be significantly lower than expected as the premature sale has already been recorded.
  - Expenses spike when the postponed invoice from the previous quarter needs to be paid. Overall, making the quarter appear more negative than it is.

While this example with Super Trooper Tech is a one off, in fraud cases observed, often these are not one offs, but constitute patterns of repetitive manipulative conduct.

The investor should look at this on two levels, the strategic accounting policies level, and at the microlevel in the financial statements treated in sect 23–27.

## 22.4 Frequent or Inconsistent Changes in Accounting Policies and Methods

On the strategic level, companies that switch accounting policies frequently, especially those impacting critical estimates (like inventory costing models, revenue recognition, or asset valuation), might be attempting to manipulate their financial performance. Any change in accounting policies that lead to significant changes in the company's performance is a red flag and should be scrutinized.

The examples of the following changes in general accounting methods or standards should raise red flags.

- Change in inventory costing models.
  - E.g. a change from First-In, First-Out (FIFO) vs Last-In, First-Out (LIFO). In inflationary periods, LIFO results in a higher cost of goods sold (COGS) and lower net income compared to FIFO. Depending on the purpose of the earnings manipulation the inventory costing models might change from LIFO to FIFO or vis-à-vis.
- Change in revenue recognition models.
  - Simple/Immediate Recognition Models
    Sales-basis or Point-of-Sale: Revenue is recognized immediately upon the sale of a product or service, typically when ownership or title transfers to the buyer. This is most common for retail, simple transactions, and goods-based businesses.
  - Contract-Based Recognition Models
    Percentage-of-Completion: Used for long-term projects where revenue and expenses are recognized proportionally to the work completed. Common in construction, software development, and other project-based industries.
    Completed-Contract: Revenue and expenses are not recognized until the entire project/contract is finished. Suited to scenarios where costs or project outcomes are highly uncertain.
  - Specialized Recognition Models
    Installment Method: Revenue is recognized proportionately as the customer makes installment payments over time. Often used for high-value items financed through payment plans.
    Cost Recovery Method: Revenue recognition is delayed until all project costs have been recovered. This is a conservative approach when reliable collection from the customer is in doubt.
    - Special Recognition models abused in fraud cases.
      Enron mark-to-market. Enron used an aggressive revenue recognition method, where they recognized future forecasted (fictitious) unrealistically energy prices, to inflate their books.

## 22.5 Emphasis on Non-GAAP and Alternative Performance Measurement (APM)

Non-GAAP and APM in IFRS might help investors to see beyond one-time events or used to highlight underlying trends that may not be captured, with official GAAP & IFRS numbers in certain special situations.

However, these alternative measures are commonly abused by corporate fraudsters. The investor should understand what is behind this reliance on non-GAAP or APM approaches. Especially if the alternative measures change frequently and in favor of the company's results.

Also, if the alternative measures do not reconcile with standard measures or have misleading definitions. The result of these alternative measures is it makes it harder to compare the company with its peers. Companies like Enron, WorldCom, Valeant Pharmaceuticals all used non-GAAP pro forma measures as part of their corporate fraud.

## 22.6 Analyzing Footnotes in Financial Reports

Footnotes and small print are of prime importance in fraud investigations. While many analysts first read the numbers in financial reports, and (if at all) the footnotes at the end. Some of the most successful fraud analysts do it in reverse order. Starting with the fine print of footnotes. It is often in the footnotes some of the most interesting and often-strategic content regarding corporate fraud is buried. Table 22.1 shows some common observed manipulation techniques in footnotes.

Table 22.1 What to look for in the footnotes from a corporate fraud perspective

| Manipulation | How it works | Red flags |
|---|---|---|
| Changing accounting policies | As noted in sect. 22.4, changing accounting policies may have substantial impact on a company's reported results. Footnotes may be used to minimize the significance of the change or make it seem less self-serving. | Be mindful of any changes in accounting methods, especially when they impact reported results in a positive way. |
| Improper disclosures on complex transactions | Use of technical language or overly brief descriptions can make complex financial instruments, or other transactions look less risky than they are. | If the investor does not understand a transaction described in the footnotes, be careful. Scrutinize more and potentially seek support by expert analysts. |
| Selective emphasis | Fraudsters highlight positive metrics or explanations while downplaying or leaving out unfavorable information in the footnotes. | Heavy reliance on non-standard financial metrics (not in line with industry practices) or an extremely optimistic tone throughout the footnotes. |
| Obscuring liabilities and contingencies | Fraudsters downplay significant debts, legal risks, and potential losses; burying them in complex, lengthy footnotes rather than showing them on core financial statements. | Look for imprecise or excessively technical language in footnotes describing potential liabilities. |

(continued)

**Table 22.1** (continued)

| Manipulation | How it works | Red flags |
|---|---|---|
| Hiding related-party transactions | Companies may conduct transactions with affiliated businesses or individuals (controlled by management) on unfair terms. Footnotes are abused to disclose these relationships in a way that makes them seem ordinary routine and minor problems | Examine footnotes for transactions with entities sharing names with executives or board members, and their relations. In addition to companies operating from unusual locations, like offshore corporate safe havens |
| Inflating revenue | Aggressive or premature revenue recognition practices may be disregarded in footnotes using overly complex accounting language. | Compare the revenue recognition policies described in the footnotes with industry standards and practices. Find sudden policy changes that boost revenue. |
| Misclassifying expenses | Shifting operating expenses to categories like "capital expenditures" may inflate profits in the short term. Footnotes may contain complex and/or bogus rationalizations for these changes. | Investigate sudden or unexplained changes in how expenses are considered year-over-year. |
| Overstating asset values | Companies may overvalue assets like property, inventory, or intangible intellectual property assets. Footnotes may show explanations that display overly optimistic assumptions or subjective valuation models. | Compare the company's asset valuation methods in footnotes to those of its peers. Look for absence of write-downs on assets that may be overvalued. |

(continued)

**Table 22.1** (continued)

| Manipulation | How it works | Red flags |
|---|---|---|
| Deferring costs | Delaying cost recognition into future periods artificially improves current profitability. Footnotes may use creative descriptions to justify deferral. | Look carefully for changes in timing of when costs are recognized. Particularly those changes boosting short-term profits. |
| Manipulating complex estimates | Depreciation, warranty provisions, or bad debt reserves involve estimations. Fraudsters may tamper with these estimates to improve the current financial picture, using justifications in footnotes. | Compare estimation methods described in footnotes with competitors. Look for unexplained deviations from industry norms. |

# 23

# Investigating Balance Sheet, Income Statement and Earnings Manipulation

## 23.1 The Balance Sheet

To give an overview of what the investor should look for, a basic balance sheet with its main categories and fraud risks is illustrated in Table 23.1. Points of interest with regard to fraud are displayed under the different areas in the balance sheet. A 12-month rule of thumb is used to illustrate the difference between current assets and liabilities and non-current assets and liabilities.

## 23.2 Income Statement Manipulation

The purpose of the income statement manipulation is to change the earnings in the direction that aligns with the fraudsters goal as shown in Fig. 23.1.

The direction of the manipulation depends on the fraudster's motivation and goal. While in many fraud cases the goal of income statement manipulation is to inflate earnings, making things look better, this is not always the case. Sometimes (often in more sophisticated cases) the fraudster may also have an incentive to suppress earnings in the corporate fraud scheme, e.g. to avoid taxes or to get government subsidies.

Here are some of the motives for earnings manipulations in each direction. The motives explained in Table 23.2 are paramount to understand, and always keep in mind analyzing earnings and earnings manipulation.


J. Sørensen, *Shorting Fraud*, https://doi.org/10.1007/978-3-031-81834-9_23

**Table 23.1** The balance sheet and where to look for fraud

| Assets | Liabilities & Equity |
|---|---|
| **Current Assets—lifespan less than 12 months** | **Total Liabilities** |
| Cash & equivalents declining relative to total assets. Potential issues with liquidity or the quality of earnings. | "Cookie Jar" reserves. Growth in excessive/unjustified reserves to lower profits in the present period, reversing them in the future periods to boost profits. |
| Accounts Receivable (AR) growing faster than sales | Sudden decline in reserves or payment to reserves |
| AR inflated to boost borrowing capacity | **Current Liabilities—lifespan less than 12 months** |
| Are related party AR included incorrectly | Related parties are on the list of accounts payable |
| Credit sales used to inflate revenues | Unusual growth in accounts payable, not paying vendors |
| Revenue growing much faster than AR, might indicate premature / fictitious revenue recognition to aggressively boost short-term earnings. | Fake accounts payables used to funnel cash out of the company. Usage of fake invoices. |
| Increase in allowances for doubtful accounts (contra-asset account) indicates the company anticipates more uncollectible debts. The allowances are growing as a percentage of overall AR. | Unusual growth in short term debt. May indicate that there are problems with cash flow and liquidity |
| AR Turnover Ratio: (Net Credit Sales / Average AR) A declining ratio over sequential periods is cause for concern | Intentional misclassification of non-current liabilities as current liabilities. This will improve working capital and other financial ratios. |
| Watch for AR (total, long-term, unbilled) growing at a higher percentage rate than sales over multiple periods. Trouble collecting AR | **Non-current Liabilities—lifespan more than 12 months** |
| Inventories growing faster than sales | Usage of off-balance entities to hide debt or toxic assets |
| **Non-current Assets—lifespans more than 12 months** | Are bad debt reserves increasing relative to receivables |
| Are the cost of projects or interest falsely capitalized? | Conspicuous loans from related party |
| Are depreciation & amortization policies used to inflate assets? Changes in Lifetime of assets | Conspicuous convertible debt from related party |
| Loans to executives or related parties. Maybe written off. Provision for bad debt | Tampering with pension fund liabilities |

(continued)

Table 23.1 (continued)

| Assets | Liabilities & Equity |
|---|---|
| Excessive or strange suspicious goodwill. Unusual amounts of goodwill on the balance sheet relative to the company's overall value, could be abused to mask declining performance of acquired assets | "Round-Tripping" loans—Rerecording a loan from a seemingly unrelated entity. However, the money originated from company itself and was routed through intermediaries to create the illusion of new funding |
| Lack of impairment write-downs. | **Shareholders' Equity** |
| All sudden and unexplainable changes on book value of the asset; up or down | Opportunistic share buyback—boosting EPS? Especially interesting in cases of EPS covenants |

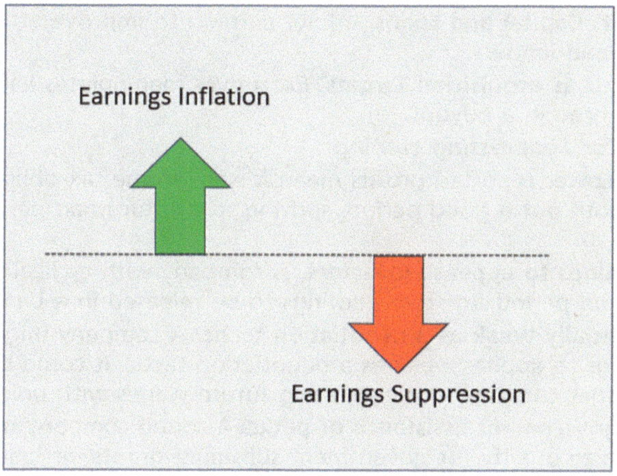


**Fig. 23.1** The two main goals of earnings manipulation

## 23.3 How the Earnings Manipulation is Conducted in Practice

There are many ways to manipulate earnings, with multiple variations. Several of the techniques utilized to manipulate earnings and commit corporate fraud depend on the actual local financial reporting legislation and local implementation of accounting standards. On top of that, the actual enforcement of the regulation in the local setting also has an impact on preferred methods by corporate fraudsters. Rules and regulations that are not enforced are more likely to be exploited by fraudsters.

Table 23.2 Overview of fraud motives for inflating and suppressing earnings

| |
|---|
| ***Fraud Motives for inflating Earnings*** |
| **Executives' Performance.** Inflating Stock Price by earnings manipulation. Direct bonuses, tied to stock price or vanity factor to project image of strong leadership. |
| **Meeting Expectations & Forecasts of equity analysts.** Inflate earnings to hit target numbers, avoiding stock selloffs & negative press. |
| **Avoiding breach of financial covenants on loans.** To protect creditors, financial covenants may have been put in place on loans and other financing. Covenants may focus on the company's financial performance, such as minimum earnings per share (EPS), profitability margins, revenue growth, minimum stock price, etc. If covenants are breached it affects financing and refinancing. This results in increased interest rates, limitations on new loans & re-financing of current debt. In the worst case, immediate repayment of the loan. |
| **New Investments Capital and Loans.** Inflate earning to improve attractiveness to new investors and lenders. |
| **Negotiation Tactic as acquisition Targets.** Executives manipulates earnings to get a lucrative exit through a buyout. |
| ***Fraud Motives for Suppressing earnings*** |
| **Tax Reduction.** Lower reported profits mean lower income tax obligations for a company. Smooth out a good period, shifting to a future bad period to avoid paying. |
| **Smoothing Earnings to appease investors.** A company with cyclical sales numbers deflating a good period, to store earnings to be released in a bad future period. |
| **Appearing financially weak as a negotiation tactic.** A company might artificially deflate earnings to appear weak as a negotiation tactic. It could be when acquiring another company or negotiating future wages with unions. |
| **Qualifying for government assistance or perks.** A sound company may manipulate earnings down to qualify for government subsidies, grants, or loans. This has e.g. been seen in COVID-19 relief packages. |

In addition to accounting rules, one should also have other types of rules like corporate tax, investor protection regulation, corporate governance regulation. Below are some (not all) of the most common globally observed manipulation techniques used by fraudsters.

While financial reports can be overly complicated to read, especially for big corporations, earnings always boil down to two basic simple components—*revenue* and *costs*. Along with the main motives for earnings manipulation outlined in Table 23.2, these two basic components should be in the back of the mind of the investor, when reading financial statements and analyzing them for potential earnings manipulation.

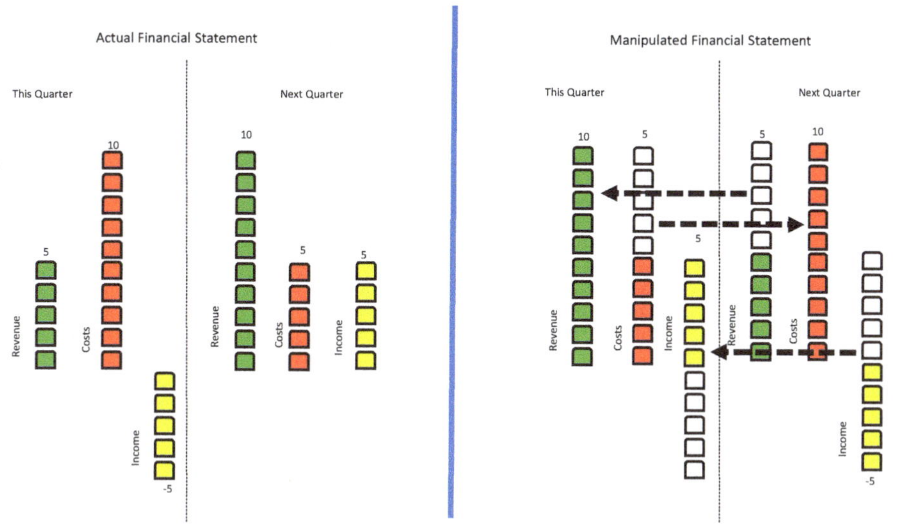


**Fig. 23.2** Illustration of actual earnings vs. Manipulated earnings

Artificially inflating revenue will increase earnings, while artificially deflating revenue will suppress earnings. Conversely, artificially suppressing costs will inflate earnings, and artificially inflating costs will suppress earnings.

In Fig. 23.2, it is illustrated how a financial statement is manipulated by pushing current costs of this quarter into the next quarter and pulling future revenue from the next quarter into the current quarter. Resulting in an actual net loss for this quarter, magically transformed into a net profit this quarter.

The basic red flags the investor must look for are unusual fluctuations in either revenue, costs, or both. This both over time from period to period and compared to peer-companies in the industry. Are they caused by a special situation or created by the management for fraudulent purposes?

# 24

# Investigating Revenue Inflation Techniques to Inflate Earnings

## 24.1 Revenue Inflation

Earnings may be inflated through revenue inflation with various techniques. Some common red flags to look for are unusual favorable swings in revenue which cannot be explained by e.g. seasonal swings or other external induced patterns. The revenue development is inconsistent with peer and competitor companies and the general background economy.

In the below sections are some commonly observed techniques to inflate earnings with revenue inflation. Premature recognition of revenue. Here sales are recognized before products are shipped, services are fully rendered, or all conditions of the sale are met. The exact execution will depend on the industry, products and services that are delivered. The general manipulation technique is to pull future revenues into the present period.

## 24.2 Playing with Calendar Dates and Quarter Length

Playing with calendar dates is a simple inflation tactic, which has been observed in fraud cases. Tampering with calendar dates, moving the sales forward. Simply backdate sales to earlier periods. Either by forgery, changing sales documents and invoices, or collaborating with the customer, agreeing on an earlier date.

A notorious public case on date manipulation is the DOJ (2006)—DOJ vs. Computer Associates' CEO. It includes the "35-day month"-concept.


J. Sørensen, *Shorting Fraud*, https://doi.org/10.1007/978-3-031-81834-9_24

Here the books were systematically kept open for several days beyond a month's end, at the end of each quarter to recognize revenue for the next quarter in the current quarter.

## 24.3 Channel Stuffing

In consumer product industries, excessive inventory may be pushed out to distributors or retailers to inflate sales figures. This even when there is not genuine end-user demand for the product. Channel Stuffing has been observed in multiple fraud cases. In one specific case in combination with foreign related entity. The products were never sold but just shipped to a warehouse in a remote offshore location.

Bristol-Myers Squibb conducted a public example of channel-stuffing. According to SEC (2004, August 4), the pharmaceutical company practiced channel stuffing, offering wholesalers huge incentives to buy more inventory beyond any number of drugs they could realistically sell, hence inflating revenues artificially.

## 24.4 Bill-and-Hold Technique

Bill-and-Hold techniques may be abused in several ways. According to SEC (2001, May 15) one way it was abused was by Sunbeam Corporation, in a variation of channel stuffing. Sunbeam offered deep discounts or extended payment terms to boost short-term revenue without legitimate consumer demand selling a grill out of season. Sunbeam convinced customers who had neither the demand, nor necessarily the storage space for the grill, to buy. This was circumvented by Sunbeam sending its products to their own warehouses and booking the sales immediately, which inflated revenue with sales that would later not materialize.

## 24.5 Mark-to-Market Abuse

In the Enron fraud case, the company abused "mark-to-market" accounting for long-term energy contracts. This allowed Enron to book estimated future profits as current revenue, vastly inflating their earnings as debated in The U.S. House of Representatives, Committee on Energy and Commerce (2002).

## 24.6 Percentage-of-Completion Abuse and Major Project Tampering

In the business-to-business industries where major undertakings are project driven, like construction projects or software projects, the "delivery" may happen gradually over time. Therefore percentage-of-completion accounting is used and may be abused by corporate fraudsters.

The investor should look for recording revenue before the project even begins. Recorded revenue before milestones have been reached. Tampering with milestones, to pull future revenue faster into the present. In the software industry it could be delivery of systems, which are not completed, but in beta or alpha versions.

In other types of industries, like real estate, heavy machinery, or trucks, where long-term leasing is core, or Software-as-a-Service (SaaS) industry, where long-term licensing is core. The investor must look for future revenue streams belonging to future accounting periods, maybe years down the line. When the company starts pulling these future revenues into the present accounting period, this is a major red flag. An example is Xerox that as reported by SEC (2002, April 11) did a settlement for improperly manipulating equipment lease accounting to accelerate revenue recognition. This, among other schemes, created a misleading picture of the company's revenue by pulling future revenue streams into the present.

## 24.7 Products or Services the Customer Will or Cannot Pay For

Another way boosting revenue is falsely recognizing revenue that will never materialize. Items or services the buyer will never accept. The worst examples observed are companies sending subpar quality consumer products or products the customer never acquired in the first place, which are bound to be returned.

Alternatively, if the customer is in a doubtful financial situation, like a delinquent payer, and the company still ships new stuff, e.g. with changes of payment terms or customer collection terms, which pushes payment out into the future.

These tricks can be used to boost the revenue, by recognizing revenues of non-performing sales, doubtful accounts, or uncollectible accounts on the books. The red flags can be observed when the company is relaxing the customer collection and payment terms in suspicious ways at suspicious times. A financial indicator one can use as a red flag is the average number of days for a company to receive payment after a sale, called Days Sales Outstanding (DSO).

$$Days\ Sales\ Outstanding(DSO) = \left(\left(\frac{\text{Average Accounts Receivable}}{\text{Net Credit Sales}}\right) \times \text{Number of Days in Period}\right) \quad (24.1)$$

The DSO is created by the following:

- Average Accounts Receivable is the average amount of money payable to the company by customers for services or goods sold on credit. This is calculated by taking the accounts receivable at the start of the period, adding the balance at the end of the period, then dividing it by two.
- Net Credit Sales is the total credit sales throughout the period, deducted any sales returns or allowances.
- Number of Days in Period is the number of days in the timeframe measured. Common timeframes are monthly (30 days), quarterly (90 days), or annually (365 days).

## 24.8 Extraordinary Side Agreements or Payment Terms

Extraordinary side agreements or payment terms, used as sales incentive to have the customer buy products and services up front that they do not need. Like collection and payment terms that pull future sales into the current period, but risk leaving the company worse off in the future periods. Side agreements on sales might be abused to modify the terms of the sales, which in return can alter the accounting, wrongfully boosting the revenue. A worst-case example could be a side agreement that the customer is allowed to return the product at any time, with a full refund.

## 24.9 Fictitious Revenue Recognition

While the above manipulation are red flags, sometimes they may be in a legal gray zone. However, fictitious sales used to boost revenue that never happened and outright fabrication of revenue are clear-cut corporate fraud.

### 24.9.1 Invoice Forgery

Invoice Forgery has been observed in several variations. One type is where the invoices and the process are entirely fabricated and never sent to customers, but directly to the accounting department. Another where customers are invoiced for materials, they never received or invoiced at overcharged prices they never accepted. The company knowingly conducted fraudulent over-billing of customers. While this is a desperate move and often on borrowed time, it might go on for a while, depending on internal accounting controls at the company and controls at the customers' accounting departments.

### 24.9.2 Revenue Misrepresentation

In revenue misrepresentation, financial transactions are miscategorized as revenue on the books, even though they may have absolutely nothing to do with revenue. This has been observed as wrongfully recording cash received from financiers, vendors, business partners or others. An example in a fraud case observed, was government subsidiaries wrongfully accounted for as sales. It made the company look successful though sales had dropped to nothing.

### 24.9.3 Sales Transactions with Related or Affiliated Parties

While in some jurisdictions under some circumstances this might be legit. Red flags should be raised with transactions involving related parties. Ranging from subsidiaries to entities controlled by executives, including their friends and family, joint ventures and similar. Related party sales transactions are problematic because (if sales are real at all) they might not reflect true market value and be inflated. There is a substantial risk of a lack of independent real negotiation of the sales price between the two parties.

### 24.9.4 Circular Transactions

Another way to artificially boost sales and revenue is circular transactions that might come under different names like round-tripping, boomerang transactions or revenue washing. Boomerang transactions are the simplest way of round-tripping, a two-way circular transaction between two parties.

In more sophisticated cases, a double-digit number of legal entities, spread over a double-digit number of jurisdictions used to round-trip has been observed. The circular transaction might include some real change of assets, products, investments, or be entirely fictitious transactions. Being in control of the whole round-trip architecture, it is the corporate fraudster who decides.

In the public domain the 1999 MicroStrategy—NCR deal published by MyCustomer (1999, October 10) and outlined by Leibovich (2002, January 6) is an example of roundtripping.

This deal was a simple case of roundtripping with two parties. Basically, MicroStrategy signed a large software licensing deal with NCR Corporation. Shortly after, MicroStrategy invested in NCR as part of a partnership. This cyclical pattern was deemed problematic by the SEC (2000, December 14) because money essentially was passed back and forth, raising concerns about the legitimacy and purpose of the transaction. The roundtripping was later negatively restated with an effect on the earnings.

Several more advanced cases of roundtripping have been observed in fraud investigations. In one case it was observed that a distributor of unrelated products did a block investment in a listed company. In parallel, the new shareholder entered into a distributor agreement regarding these products. Products were then shipped to the distributor/owner without any payment and revenue recognized up front. The products were placed in an offshore warehouse and not sold to the end user—the transaction was cross jurisdiction and intermediate banks were used.

### 24.9.5 Abusing Gross Revenue to Inflate Revenue (Not Earnings)

Another way to inflate revenue is to use gross revenue instead of net revenue when it is inappropriate. While this opportunity to manipulate might differ across jurisdictions, the basic concepts can be described the following way.

- Gross Revenue: The company books the total amount of a sale as revenue, without accounting for any related costs or expenses incurred in generating the sales.
- Net Revenue: The company books the revenue after deducting any direct costs associated with that sale (e.g., sales commissions, discounts, returns).

Recently, using gross revenue to boost the impression of revenue has been observed with some "Gig"-economy type of companies. Like hail riding apps, food delivery apps or hotel booking services. Companies that act as agents or matchmakers and take a fee for doing so. These types of companies might boost the revenue significantly by recording gross revenue or parts of gross revenue instead of net revenue.

The gross transaction is the full price paid by the end customer for the hotel stay, food delivered, or ride, including extra tips to the driver etc.

However, the true revenue of the Gig-company is not the full price of the transaction with the customers, but the service fee the gig-company is going to receive from the transaction.

A public example of the difference between gross vs. net revenue recognition may be found in the 2011 S-1 filings from Groupon Inc. During Groupon's pre-IPO period, SEC (2011, September 23) forced Groupon to restate revenue recognition from gross revenue to net revenue.

- Groupon, Inc. (2011, June 2). S-1 Initial version text:
- *"We increased our revenue from $3.3 million in the second quarter of 2009 to $644.7 million in the first quarter of 2011."*
- Groupon, Inc. (2011, September 23). S-1 Third revised version text:
- *"We increased our revenue from $1.2 million in the second quarter of 2009 to $392.6 million in the second quarter of 2011."*

The restatement of Groupon's revenue from gross to net resulted in a significant decrease in the initial reported revenue. The restatement overview text only includes the numbers from the second quarter of 2011. However, looking at the first quarter of 2011 details in the third revised version, the actual revenue was $296 million and not $645 million as first stated. This is a drop of 54% in actual revenue and the difference between net and gross revenue.

### 24.9.6 Inflating Revenue by Utilizing One-time Events and Non-Recurring Income Sources

Converting the one-time income from the sale of a business unit or similar into a recurring revenue stream. On the income statement normally the sale of a business unit will figure as other income. However, such one-time sale of a business unit may also be abused, spreading it out as a revenue stream across several periods—propping up the baseline revenue.

**Example:** Masterpeace Inc. manufactures widgets. The company owns a division that creates specialized software used internally in its manufacturing process. Masterpeace Inc decides to sell this software division as the software has value to similar companies in the industry.

Masterpeace sells the division for $10 million but does not report this $10 million sale as a one-time gain under "other income" on the income statement. Instead, Masterpeace enters into a multi-year support and licensing agreement with the buyer. Under this agreement, Masterpeace Inc recognizes $2 million each year for the next five years as "software support and licensing revenue". For an investor to detect this, she must look at unexplained large accounts receivable of $10 million. Also, on the cash flow statement the yearly $2 million from investing opposed to operations may stand out.

### 24.9.7 Misstatements of Income from Joint Ventures or Similar Investments as Revenue

This depends on jurisdiction, but Joint ventures should in many cases and jurisdictions be treated as investments from an accounting point of view, not as revenue.

**Example:** If Masterpeace Inc. owns a 40% stake in the Joint Venture Holy Grail, and Holy Grail generates a net profit of $100,000, the effect on Masterpeace Inc.'s financial statements would be:

- Income Statement:
  - Investment Income: $40,000 (40% of $100,000)
- Balance Sheet:
  - Assets: Investment in Holy Grail JV increase by $40,000

A way to prop up the revenue is to book the investment income as revenue instead of investment income.

## References

DOJ. (2006). Former Computer Associates CEO Sanjay Kumar and Former Head of World-wide Sales Stephen Richards Plead Guilty to All Charges of Securities Fraud and Admit Lying to Federal Investigators to Cover up the Scheme. US Attorney's Office. Retrieved September 14, 2024, from https://www.justice.gov/archive/usao/nye/pr/2006/2006apr24.html

Groupon, Inc. (2011, June 2). Form S-1 Registration Statement. U.S. Securities and Exchange Commission. Retrieved September 14, 2024, from https://www.sec.gov/Archives/edgar/data/1490281/000104746911005613/a2203913zs-1.htm

Groupon, Inc. (2011, September 23). Amendment No. 3 to Form S-1 Registration Statement. U.S. Securities and Exchange Commission. https://www.sec.gov/Archives/edgar/data/1490281/000104746911008207/a2205238zs-1a.htm

Leibovich, M. (2002, January 6). At the Height of a Joy Ride, MicroStrategy Dives. *The Washington Post*. Retrieved September 14, 2024, from https://www.washingtonpost.com/archive/politics/2002/01/07/at-the-height-of-a-joy-ride-microstrategy-dives/a1c9ac9e-77e6-465a-8ba1-da7187913506/

MyCustomer. (1999, October 10). NCR and MicroStrategy in $52.5m Agreement. My customer.com. Retrieved September 14, 2024, from https://web.archive.org/web/20240217054558/https://www.mycustomer.com/marketing/technology/ncr-and-microstrategy-in-525m-agreement

SEC. (2000, December 14). Administrative Proceedings: Microstrategy, Inc. Securities and Exchange Commission (Release No. 43724; File No. 3-10388).

SEC. (2001, May 15). Sunbeam Corporation, U.S. Securities and Exchange Commission [Administrative Proceedings]. Retrieved September 14, 2024, from https://www.sec.gov/litigation/admin/33-7976#:~:text=Sunbeam's%20Results%20of%20Operations%20Were,the%20four%20quarters%20of%201997

SEC. (2002, April 11). Xerox Corporation: Xerox Settles SEC Enforcement Action Charging Company with Fraud, Agrees to Pay $10 Million Fine, Restate Its Financial Results and Conduct Special Review of Its Accounting Controls [Litigation Release No. 17465/Accounting and Auditing Enforcement Release No. 1542].

SEC. (2004, August 4). Bristol-Myers Squibb Company Agrees to Pay $150 Million to Settle Fraud Charges [Press release]. U.S. Securities and Exchange Commission. Retrieved September 14, 2024, from https://www.sec.gov/news/press/2004-105.htm?mod=article_inline

SEC. (2011, September 23). Letter to Groupon, Inc, from U.S. Securities and Exchange Commission. Retrieved September 14, 2024, from https://www.sec.gov/Archives/edgar/data/1490281/000000000011039811/filename1.pdf

U.S. House of Representatives, Committee on Energy and Commerce. (2002). Lessons Learned from Enron's Collapse: Auditing the Accounting Industry (107th Congress, 2nd session) [Hearing]. U.S. Government Publishing Office. Retrieved September 14, 2024, from https://www.govinfo.gov/content/pkg/CHRG-107hhrg77986/html/CHRG-107hhrg77986.htm

# 25

# Investigating Cost Suppression Techniques to Inflate Earnings

## 25.1 Capitalization of Costs—Pushing Expenses onto the Balance Sheet and into the Future

One way to remove the costs from the income statement is to capitalize the costs and lift them onto the balance sheet. SEC (2002) provides a good example of how WorldCom capitalized the major operational expense called "line costs". A cost which was regular licensing fees, conducting their daily business. However, instead of properly treating them as operational costs, these costs were wrongfully placed in a variety of capital assets accounts on the balance sheet. Capital Assets normally include tangible assets like property and machinery, as well as intangible assets such as intellectual property and goodwill.

While the WorldCom capitalization example may seem obvious, many of today's companies core business models build on some kind of software or technology development elements. Here expenses might be treated as immediate costs or capitalized as capital assets.

These rules are complex, and the implementation of accounting standards might vary across jurisdictions. This makes it even more blurry, dealing with the general GAAP and IFRS standards. Capitalization of costs has been observed being actively abused by fraudulent companies.

Under the GAAP rules there are two accounting standards essential to how software and tech projects should be treated with regards to capitalization of costs.



J. Sørensen, *Shorting Fraud*, https://doi.org/10.1007/978-3-031-81834-9_25

If the software is to be sold externally it should be treated according to ASC-985-20, outlined in FASB (2024, I). If in contrast the software is developed for internal use it should be treated according to ASC-350-40, described in FASB (2024, II). Below the overview of the two standards and their impact on potential fraudulent abuse.

**ASC 985-20: Software—Costs of Software to Be Sold, Leased or Marketed**

- **Scope:** The standard applies to costs incurred to create software that will be sold, leased, or marketed. This may happen either as a separate product or part of a larger offering.
- **Capitalization:** This accounting standard outlines a clear threshold, which can be used to spot red flags of fraudulent capitalization:
  - Costs incurred before technological feasibility (e.g. beta version) is established. This is expensed as research and development.
  - Costs incurred after technological feasibility (e.g. beta version). These are eligible for capitalization.
- **Amortization:** Capitalized costs are amortized over the software's projected lifespan. This begins at the time of the general release of the software.

Some investigative fraud red flags to look for:

- Premature feasibility—project pre-maturely considered feasible, to start capitalization before time.
- Irrelevant expenses—the development project is capitalized with irrelevant expenses.
- Postponing Amortization—the general release is postponed (keep customer on test/pilot). Pushing amortization/depreciation -> pushing the costs into the future. With short-lived software that has a high capitalization this could have a significant impact on the earnings.
- Impairments & lack of adequate write-downs. Gupta et al. (2016) report that 50%-80% of software projects fail. There is a great chance many of these projects are kept on the books and smoothed out over years.
- Intentional misclassified project—is the software project actually a software to be sold, or an internal-use software, which should fall on the stricter ASC 350-40 standard.

### ASC 350-40: Intangibles—Goodwill and Other: Internal-Use Software

- **Scope:** This standard addresses costs associated with developing or obtaining software intended for the company's own internal use.
- **Capitalization:** This standard is more restrictive than ASC 985-20. Capitalization generally occurs in three phases:
  - Preliminary project stage (planning, evaluation)—costs expensed.
  - Application development stage (coding, testing)—capitalize certain costs.
  - Post-implementation/operation stage (maintenance, upgrades)—costs expensed.
- **Amortization:** Capitalized costs are amortized over the software's projected lifespan. Amortization start when the software is fully developed and ready for its intended use.

  Red flags to look for here.

- Costs from the preliminary and operational stages are shifted to the application development stage.
- Irrelevant expenses moved into application development.
- The completion of the software is postponed to avoid depreciation.
- The lifespan of the software is overestimated to spread the cost thinner over future periods.
- Lacking impairments and write-downs of an internal system. The economic impact from the write-down is an assessment of the management.

### IFRS Standard on Capitalization of Software Projects

In contrast to GAAP, the standard IFRS (IAS 38) includes both software development for sale and internal development with regards to capitalization. In addition, IFRS (15) related to capitalization of cloud software.

IAS 38 includes ALL software projects as intangible assets and does not distinctly separate software into the two standards—made for sale and internal projects as with GAAP.

The core principle of IAS 38 is that the software must be identifiable. It means that the software must be a distinct asset, either separable (i.e., it could be sold independently) or arising from specific contractual/legal rights. In addition, the company must have control over the asset's ability to generate future economic benefit. This means usage rights, ownership, or restricting others' access. Third, there must be a likely future economic benefit of the software project to the company. It means either increased revenue, lowered costs, or both.

As with GAAP, IAS 38 distinguishes between the Research and Development stages of a software project. At the research stage the costs incurred when exploring possibilities, conceptualizing, and gathering knowledge are generally expensed immediately.

The project reaches the development stage at the time specific criteria are met. These criteria include Technological feasibility, which is a clear plan with attached resources, making it possible to conduct reliable measurement of development costs. In addition, an intent to complete and sell the software. An ability to complete the software for internal usage or external sale. Be able to demonstrate how the software will generate future economic benefits.

Under IFRS, there is a heavier emphasis on clearly demonstrating how the internal-use software will result in likely future economic benefits to the company, which justifies capitalization of the costs. After that point, some direct costs associated with creating the software might be capitalized.

Another key distinction regarding IFRS is the internal vs. the external market. Software intended for internal use, faces stricter scrutiny, and likely has fewer costs eligible for capitalization than software developed to sell.

Amortization, like GAAP capitalized software costs, are amortized over their projected lifespan.

Like in GAAP, impairment must be written off. If circumstances arise that indicate the software will not deliver expected economic benefits, an impairment review is required. This possibly leads to a write-down of the asset's value.

From a fraud perspective, the IFRS is less strict, and open to interpretation. IFRS does not have the same detailed phases outlined as in ASC 350-40. Accountants and management exercise more judgment about which specific costs might qualify for capitalization at which stage. Also, from a fraud perspective IAS 38 relies more on subjective judgment like:

- Identifying when the software becomes sufficiently 'ready' for capitalization.
- Assessing future economic benefits of the project—especially with internal-use projects.
- Estimating useful life for amortization purposes

Subjective judgements like these may be abused to manipulate costs being capitalized, inflating earnings.

## Should Costs Be Capitalized or Not Capitalized?

Regardless of which jurisdiction and rules a major component which can be abused are the costs that can be capitalized. While there might be variations between the different projects and jurisdictions, the guiding rule of thumb is:

**Typically, Eligible for Capitalization (with Conditions):**

- Direct Labor like the salaries, wages, and benefits for programmers, coders, testers, and project managers, who are directly involved in development of the software.
- External Contractors, like specialized technical consultants or outside developers, when their work is closely and directly related to creating the software.
- Materials & Supplies purchase specifically tied to the specific software (e.g., specific code libraries, specialized hardware).
- Interest Costs (Sometimes). In very specific situations, a portion of the interest cost might be capitalized, if incurred as part of financing a major software project.

**Expensed in Most Cases:**

- Research and Exploratory. The earlier conceptualization, feasibility studies, and general groundwork before a viable project plan exists.
- Training of users in how to operate the software.
- The routine maintenance & upgrades once the software is operational.
- Administrative and general costs, unrelated to the direct development work. Like general office rent, CEOs, or executive salary, etc.
- Marketing and selling costs, getting the software ready for sale and promoted.

What may be observed in fraud cases with regards to costs inclusion and capitalization vary. Most obvious is putting general costs that are not eligible for capitalization on the project, which will reduce and push the costs out in future periods.

Another tactic which may also be abused is when the company runs several major projects that each are distinct assets on the balance sheet.

An example could be two projects developed simultaneously by the company. The first is an internal software development project and the second, an external for sale project. Costs are shifted from one project where it cannot be capitalized onto a project where it may be capitalized. It could be that writing documentation of the software may be capitalized on the for-sale project, while not allowed for the internal software project. Some of these documentation expenses are then moved from the in-house project to the for-sale project and capitalized. The same amount is moved from developers' costs on the for-sale project to the in-house project, where it is also allowed to be capitalized.

While the specific rules and regulations vary amongst jurisdictions. In some fraud cases it has been observed that software development costs wrongfully were lifted off the income statement and placed on intangible assets, to be written off over a longer period. Cost items noticed were unrelated business trips, conference participation, general manager salary. Things that had absolutely nothing to do with the development of the software project.

## 25.2 Overstatement of Asset Useful Lives

As seen in Sect. 25.1, amortization and depreciation and asset lifespan may be abused to capitalize costs. Moving costs away from the income statement to the balance sheet.

Capital assets including buildings, machinery and vehicles are all on the balance sheet. These assets have an expected lifetime that will be amortized/depreciated over time and incurred as costs on the income statement. A way to lower these deprecation costs is to tamper with the lifetime of the capital assets.

A particularly good example of this tampering with capital assets lifetime is seen in the 1998 Waste Management Inc. accounting scandal and litigation reported by SEC (2005).

On its balance sheet, Waste Management had a fleet of several thousands of garbage trucks, which were capital assets. The executives of Waste Management extended the estimated useful life of the garbage trucks several times in the accounting records. By extending the lifespan of these garbage trucks they at the same time reduced the yearly depreciation expense, lowering yearly costs, and artificially inflating earnings.

The red flags to look for are unusual changes in lifespan of assets, especially lifespan extensions.

## 25.3 Failure to Write Down or Write Off Impaired Assets

Major industry changes or economic disruptions should sometimes lead to impairment and shorter lifespan of capital assets. The impaired asset might be kept too long on the balance sheet. Even though that assets should be written off if they have no value.

The importance of writing down impaired assets is clear from the famous case of Lehman Brothers as reported by Valukas (2010). Lehman failed to write down impaired assets on their balance sheet in the form of mortgage-backed securities. These investment assets were not written down, making the investment bank look much healthier than it was.

Management might have impaired assets linger on the balance sheet to avoid the write-down turning into a cost on the income statement. This might happen with tangible, intangible and investment assets. However, it is often easier to keep intangibles lingering, since they are related to more subjective assessments in comparison to tangible assets like e.g., real estate, machinery, or investments in listed securities.

Write-down and write-offs of impaired assets is especially important in industries and companies facing creative destruction mentioned in Sect. 2.2, rendering their technology and assets worthless.

The traditional home movie industry with DVDs, the traditional Music Industry with CDs, and traditional film photography industry all experienced seismic shifts. This happened when the MP3 player, digital streaming, digital cameras, and smartphones were introduced as better alternatives. It meant that within a few years, those capital assets in the industries producing traditional DVD and CD players and analog cameras, as well as the CDs, DVDs, and physical film media itself became obsolete over a relatively brief time.

Any type of company facing major disruptions, regardless of the cause, but which is not reflected in write downs or asset write-offs should raise red flags and are interesting from a corporate fraud perspective.

## 25.4 Regular Operating Expenses Are Reclassified as Non-Recurring and Non-Operating Items

Moving normal recurring operating expenses like employee salaries, rent, supplies, etc. "below the line" will categorize them as extraordinary events. It does not change the final net income, but it does make the ordinary operation of the business look in better shape than it is, by boosting operating income.

## 25.5 Isolating Losses in Discontinued or Divested "Black Sheep" Entities

Sometimes operational costs and losses might be carved out from the corporation and placed in operational legal entities that are discontinued or divested. Instead of being operational losses they are now below-the-line non-operational extraordinary losses.

Red flags to look after is if "too much" is carved out from other parts of the corporation and dumped on the discontinued legal entity. It has a short-term boost to operational income that is short-lived since the costs will return to operations the next period when the black sheep entity has been offloaded, but the recurring operational costs are still there.

## 25.6 Not Recognizing Appropriate Losses with Accounts Receivable

Not all customers are going to pay their bills. Not writing down these doubtful accounts in a proper manner is another way the company can keep costs off the income statement and have it linger on the balance sheet to boost earnings.

Allowance for doubtful accounts is a contra-asset (value adjustment) account on the balance sheet—directly below Accounts Receivable (AR). Allowance for doubtful accounts represents the total estimated amount of AR that the company is not to collect. The bad debt expense is found on the income statement under the category of operating expenses. This is the estimated amount of AR that the company believes it will not be able to collect.

Red flags to watch out for is if suddenly there are significant changes in allowance for doubtful accounts, leading to less write-off of bad debt, and boosting earnings. Another red flag is how allowance for doubtful accounts evolves as a percentage of overall receivables. Sudden decline in the allowance or unusually low level of allowance.

Note that in the case of banks or other financial institutions these will be called something else like inadequate or lending reserves. The names are different, but the concept is the same—loans are not written off appropriately.

## 25.7 Other Types of Reserves That May Be Abused to Inflate Earnings

In accrual accounting, it is often needed to estimate and recognize potential future costs associated with the current period's business activities and expenses.

This may be done through creating reserves or accruing liabilities. These are related to partly subjective risks, which leaves room for assessment, manipulation, and fraud. Depending on the industry and company situation these reserves might be:

- Warranty Reserves for future expected warranty claims or repairs.
- Litigation Reserves for potential losses from lawsuits or other legal action.
- Environmental Remediation Reserves are funds set aside for potential future cleanup costs.
- Inventory Obsolescence Reserves are provisions for inventory unlikely to be sold at intended price.
- Self-insurance reserves are funds set aside for e.g. product liability and work injury incidents.
- Sales Return Reserves are funds set aside for customer returning products.
- Restructuring Reserves are money set aside for planned reorganizations or downsizing.

Reserve accounts might be used to boost earnings in two ways:

- Wrongly releasing accumulated reserves onto the income statement when needed.
- Underestimate reserves needed in the future keeping the costs down.

The red flags to look for are sudden changes in reserves, which cannot be explained by changes in operations or some external event.

## 25.8 Failing to Record an Expense from a Transaction

This simple omittance is something that has been observed in fraud cases. Simply not recording the expense appropriately in the bookkeeping before the end of the period. From the inside this is easy to detect by analyzing bank payment patterns that do not reconcile with the expenses. From the outside this might be hard to detect for the investors or only happen with some lag.

A red flag to look for is strange evolvement in expense ratios. Expense ratios drop since the denominator (revenue) remains the same while the numerator the expenses Cost of Goods Sold (COGS) shrinks.

$$ExpenseRatio = \left(\frac{\text{COGS}}{\text{Total Revenues}}\right) \tag{25.1}$$

In the longer run, the investor might observe the red flags of growing discrepancies between cash flow from operations and net-income.

## 25.9 Reversing Expenses

Normally salary or semi-finished goods are costs. If they suddenly are reversed, lowering costs, there is something wrong. With salary it could be bonus reversal or employee expense outlay reversal. With other costs it could be discounts from the vendor. These reversals might not be obvious from the financial statements, but sometimes hidden in footnotes.

## 25.10 Hiding Obligations and Costs by Moving Them Off the Balance Sheet

Another way to hide expenses, losses and debt is to simply move them off the balance sheet and hide them. If and how this can be done depends on the regulations in the different jurisdictions. Regulation regarding off-balance sheet activity is generally being tightened. However, some common tricks to unload obligations from the balance sheet include:

- Special Purpose Entities (SPEs) are legal entities designed to hold debt or risky assets. The sponsoring company may be able to avoid consolidating the SPE's financials with their own. Hiding liabilities. In the Enron case SPEs were used to extensively hide massive debt.
- Also, non-consolidated Joint Ventures may be abused when financial results are not completely merged into the main company's statements. This may conceal losses or postpone reporting obligations.
- Operating Leases. Historically this could be abused. However, recently FASB (ASC 842) under GAAP and IFRS (16) have introduced limitations in this off-balance activity. There are still some gray areas with regards to judgment calls such as defining lease term lengths. With short term and low-value leases that still qualify as off balance-sheet.

The red flags to look for are the footnotes in the financial report, that state or hint if off-balance activity exists and could impact on the costs and net-income. Also, if the footnotes try to hide off balance activity, with minimal disclosure, overly technical language, or inconsistent explanation over time.

## 25.11 Abusing Corporate Administered Pension Schemes

In the case that the company is administering their employees' pension scheme, there are cases of abuse using this scheme to manipulate earnings as touched upon by Bergstresser et al. (2004). With regards to cost suppression, this is done by simply setting less aside for the pension scheme. The justification could be tampering with the conditions for the overall pension scheme.

Red Flags to look for are repeated changes in actuarial assumptions like e.g. lifespan of the workers. Other red flags could be overly optimistic return on investment in the pension scheme funds or significant sudden changes in the return on investment.

## References


Bergstresser, D., Rauh, J. D., & Desai, M. A. (2004). Earnings Manipulation, Pension Assumptions and Managerial Investment Decisions. Brandeis International Business School, Stanford Graduate School of Business, Hoover Institution, National Bureau of Economic Research (NBER), and Harvard Business School—Finance Unit. Retrieved September 14, 2024, from https://papers.ssrn.com/sol3/papers.cfm?abstract_id=551681

FASB. (2024, I). FASB (ASC-985-20) may be Retrieved September 14, 2024, from https://asc.fasb.org/1943274/2147481457

FASB. (2024, II). FASB (ASC-350-40). Retrieved September 14, 2024, from https://asc.fasb.org/1943274/2147482532

FASB. (ASC 842) Retrieved September 14, 2024, from https://asc.fasb.org/842-10/tableOfContent

Gupta, S., Mishra, A., & Chawla, M. (2016). Analysis and Recommendation of Common Fault and Failure in Software Development Systems. In 2016 International Conference on Signal Processing, Communication, Power and Embedded System (SCOPES) (pp. 1730–1734). Paralakhemundi, India. Retrieved September 14, 2024, from https://doi.org/10.1109/SCOPES.2016.7955739

IFRS (15) Retrieved September 14, 2024, from https://www.ifrs.org/issued-standards/list-of-standards/ifrs-15-revenue-from-contracts-with-customers/

IFRS (16) Retrieved September 14, 2024, from https://www.ifrs.org/issued-standards/list-of-standards/ifrs-16-leases/

IFRS (IAS 38) Retrieved September 14, 2024, from https://www.ifrs.org/issued-standards/list-of-standards/ias-38-intangible-assets/

SEC. (2002). Complaint: SEC v. WorldCom, Inc. U.S. Securities and Exchange Commission, 2002, November 5 Retrieved February 15, 2024, from https://www.sec.gov/litigation/complaints/comp17829.htm

SEC. (2005, August 29). Dean L. Buntrock, Phillip B. Rooney, James E. Koenig, Thomas C. Hau, Herbert A. Getz, and Bruce D. Tobecksen—U.S. Securities and Exchange Commission [Press release]. Retrieved September 14, 2024, from https://www.sec.gov/litigation/litreleases/lr-19351

Valukas, A. R. (2010). Report of the Examiner in the Chapter 11 Proceedings of Lehman Brothers Holdings Inc. Jenner & Block. Retrieved September 14, 2024, from https://web.archive.org/web/20240000000000; https://web.stanford.edu/~jbulow/Lehmandocs/menu.html

# 26

# Investigating Revenue Recognition & Cost Inflation Techniques to Suppress Earnings

## 26.1 Earnings Suppression

In contrast to earnings inflation, earnings suppression is less used in fraud cases. In most cases the fraudsters try to make the company look as good as possible. Several of the techniques in earnings inflations might also be used in earnings suppression, just in the opposite direction.

Therefore, the focus and examples in this book are limited. However, as previously stated in Table 23.2 there are motives when suppression may be used. Investigating all types of potential fraud, the investor should always be aware of the risk, especially in very advanced fraud schemes.

When pushing revenue into the future it may be done in several ways with revenue recognition. While pulling future revenue into the present will often raise red flags of both auditors and investors, pushing them into the future might not have the same attention. It is often sold and looked upon as a more conservative revenue recognition policy. However, as was seen in Table 23.2, the motive might be another.

## 26.2 Intentional Postponing Recognition of Delivery or Milestones to Delay Revenue Recognition

An example used in Sect. 24.6 was the percentage-of-completion method abused to pull revenue for non-completed future revenue into the current. In contrast, now actual completed parts of the revenue are pushed into the


J. Sørensen, *Shorting Fraud*, https://doi.org/10.1007/978-3-031-81834-9_26

future by tampering with progress and completion estimates in the opposite direction.

Percentage-of-completion accounting can be abused both ways. Instead of boosting revenue by saying uncompleted parts of projects are delivered, the company pushes revenue into the future, by artificially postponing the delivery of products or services. The postponement may be done by e.g. re-negotiation of contracts with extended terms or complex side agreements.

In contrast to when future earnings are pulled into the present, where the customer normally would be reluctant to have the cash flow follow the revenue back in time. In the case of delaying recognition of the revenue, the customer might have an incentive to collaborate with the company to postpone the revenue recognition. The cash flow may follow the delayed revenue recognition, and the customer would be in a better cash position.

These red flags may be hard to find, since the interest of the customer is often aligned with the seller.

## 26.3 Bundling Sales with Company-Controlled Sub-Delivery

Bundling a sale with future services is a way to change the completion definition of what is completed work, delaying recognition. This might be done by bundling a sale with a future service that the company has control over when it is delivered, thereby deferring revenue as it suits the company.

## 26.4 Artificial or Unrealistic Sales Contingencies

Artificial or unrealistic contingencies in contracts to make the revenue dependent on highly specific conditions, which are unlikely to be met in the current period. It could be that for an IT-system, unless an uptime rate of 99.999% of the newly introduced system is reached, the revenue is not fully recognized until the next period. In a case of a more realistic uptime of 90%, if the vendor has control over the uptime metric, it could also intentionally pull the plug on the system for a few hours making sure the condition is not met, and revenue is postponed.

## 26.5 Delaying Deferred Revenue Recognition

The deferred (unearned) revenue is money a company receives in advance for goods or services it has not yet provided. On the balance sheet it is recorded as a liability since the company has an obligation to deliver or fulfill the service at some point in the future.

As the company performs the service or delivers the goods to the customer, gradually over time, deferred revenue should be taken off the balance and moved to earned revenue on the income statement.

Delaying the deferred revenue recognition, the revenue stays on the balance sheet as a liability longer than it is supposed to, suppressing current earnings, for later to be released onto the income statement, boosting earnings, when it suits management. Some red flags to look out for is, if deferred revenue suddenly grows. Especially compared to ordinary sales/revenue. In addition, if the cash flow from operations grows at a faster pace than revenue.

## 26.6 Bill-and-Hold(ing)... Too Long

This trick is used when the agreement has been signed, the products are in stock. When the revenue is acknowledged at delivery. The company might keep the products in their warehouse and delay the delivery into the next period. Postponing the delivery, resulting in delaying the revenue recognition. These red flags might be found analyzing order book data, inventory evolvement and sales. Like if inventory turnover suddenly drops, the products might sit in warehouses longer than expected.

## 26.7 Cost Inflation Techniques to Suppress Earnings

In general, the investor should look for sudden large one-time costs, happening out of the blue. Also look at collapsing gross margins (revenue minus cost of goods sold). If it suddenly collapses, compared to historic trends and competitors, it could be a sign that the company is in trouble. It may also be a sign that costs are overstated with the motive of lowering earnings.

### 26.7.1 Artificially Inflating Costs by Accumulating too Much Reserves

The reserve accounts were touched upon in Sect. 25.7. In this contrasting scenario, the company builds excessive reserves—setting too much aside for a rainy day. This happens by overstating the risks of e.g., warranty, litigation, etc. building reserves that may later be released and abused by management to boost or smooth earnings.

Again, the red flag is sudden and significant changes in the reserves. Especially, if all over the board accumulation happens in Warranty Reserves, Litigation Reserves, Environmental Remediation Reserves, Inventory Obsolescence Reserves, Self-insurance Reserves, Sales Return Reserves, Restructuring Reserves, Accounts Receivable reserves, etc. Either a cataclysmic event is confronting the company in the future, or earnings suppression is taking place.

### 26.7.2 Fast Growing Impairment Charges and Subsequent Impairment Reversals

Avoiding impairment write-downs used at the discretion of the management to boost earnings was described in Sect. 23.1. This may also happen in the other direction. Sudden large impairment write-offs should be investigated for fraud, since they may suppress earnings artificially. Especially if they may later be reversed somehow and reappear with higher values on the balance sheet once again.

# 27

# Investigating Cash Flow Statements & Fraud Manipulation

## 27.1 How to Spot Red Flags in the Cash Flow Statement

In addition to the balance sheet and income statement, the cash flow statement is the third main part of the financial report.

In a normal functioning company, the cash flow is supposed to show the net amount of cash and cash equivalents being transferred in and out of the company. The investor, scrutinizing the specifics of the cash flow statement and its relationship to the income statement and balance sheet might reveal indicators of fraud.

In the long run cash is king in all successful businesses. However, cash may come from different sources that have absolutely nothing to do with the operation and success of the business.

The cash flow consists of three principal areas:

- Cash Flow from Operations (CFFO) is the cash inflow which is generated from the core business operations, like selling the company's services or products minus the cash outflow of money used to generate these products and services.
- Cash Flow from Investing (CFFI) is the cash used for investing in assets as well as the proceeds from the sale of businesses, equipment, financial or other long-term assets.


J. Sørensen, *Shorting Fraud*, https://doi.org/10.1007/978-3-031-81834-9_27

- Cash Flow from Financing (CFFF): This includes all cash inflows from banks and shareholders, in the form of share capital and loans. In addition to outflows to shareholders as dividends, debt repayment to lenders, stock repurchase, etc.

A basic fraud indicator to look for is if earnings are growing, while free cash flow is lacking or lagging behind the net income. This basically shows there is a profit (on paper), while there is no actual money in the bank to support it.

The other indicators of fraud are if cash flow from e.g. financing or investing is shifted to operations. This gives the impression that operations are more successful than they are. However, lending money and pretending to be part of products sales or sold services is trickery. There are multiple ways to move the cash around. Below are some of the indicators of this happening. The main emphasis is on the motive of inflating cash flow from operations. However, bear in mind cash flow, like earnings suppression might also go in the opposite direction.

## 27.2 Shifting Financing Cash Flow to Operating Cash flow

Cash related to loans, Accounts Receivable, or inventory that is treated as operating cash flow, making operations look healthy.
Red flags to look for:

- A loan might be recorded as revenue or other income, inflating cash flow from operations.
- Selling Accounts Receivable before the collection date, boosting cash flow from operations.
- Selling receivables with recourse, if third-party cannot collect, the company is still responsible.
- Faking the sale of Accounts Receivable that did not occur.
- Write off inventory, then record large profits when selling that inventory.

## 27.3 Shifting Operating Cash Outflows to the Investing Cash Outflow

Here operating cash outflows are moved to the investing cash outflows, to lower the operating net cash flow, making operations look healthier than they are.

Red flags to look for:

- Recording normal operating costs as capital expenditures.
- Creating new unusual asset accounts to obscure certain transactions related to operations.
- The capital expenditures experience unexpected increase.
- Recording the purchase of inventory as an investment.
- Purchase working capital assets and record the costs as investing outflows not operating cash flow.

## 27.4 Inflating Operating Cash Flow Using Acquisitions or divestitures

Acquiring or divesting corporate entities in creative ways might inflate the cash flow from operations.

Red flags to look for:

- Company acquires another company and records the acquired company's cash flows as its own.
- Serial acquisitions (roll-ups) used to inflate its cash flow from operations.
- Strong cash flow from operations, but the free cash flow (CFFO—capital expenditures) is declining.
- Acquire contracts or customers, inflating its cash flow from operations.
- Sell a business or asset in a way that inflates its cash flow from operations.
- Sell a business unit but keep the Accounts Receivable.

## 27.5 Boosting Operating Cash Flow Using Unsustainable Activities

Activities like paying vendors or other creditors slower or obtaining more pre-payments from customers might boost cash flow from operations, temporarily.

Red flags to look for:

- A company might systematically delay paying its vendors, paying them late.
- Increase in accounts payable without a corresponding increase in cost of goods sold.
- Increase in other payables accounts.
- Large positive development on operating cash flows that are not supported by actual operations.
- Financing accounts payable instead of paying them.
- A company might record a one-time item that inflates its cash flow from operations.
- Offering incentives for customers to pay pre-maturely.
- Inventory purchase halt/slowdown/timing tampering.

# 28

# Link and Network Investigation—Connecting the Dots of the Fraud

## 28.1 Introduction to Link and Network Investigation

Any classic whodunit crime movie has a physical investigation board with victims and mugshots of suspects, multicolor sticky notes - all tied together with yarn and linking the pushpins in the board.

In corporate frauds, it is often not enough only to see the red flags, clues, and pieces of evidence on the investigation board, the investor also needs to group and tie it all together. This is analyzing the content in a context, which was mentioned in Sect. 17.5.2.

Criminals in many corporate fraud cases create a complex setup of legal entities, cross holdings, obscure ownership, and relations to dubious persons in safe haven jurisdictions. A setup, which might not make any sense to the investor, e.g. looking at a list of the fragmented legal entities and related persons.

Understanding and detecting corporate fraud, the investor needs to understand the actors and how they relate to the surrounding environment. Network (Graph) analytics are tools used by law enforcement, intelligence units and other types of investigators trying to understand and detect advanced financial criminal activity.

The digitalization of the physical investigation board combined with the research in Network analytics, on criminal networks deliver super potent analytics and investigation tools. Especially if the investor integrates these tools directly with Open-Source Intelligence (OSINT) data sources like company registrars, social media networks like LinkedIn, media monitoring


J. Sørensen, *Shorting Fraud*, https://doi.org/10.1007/978-3-031-81834-9_28

services, the ICIJ Offshore Leaks database, etc. Literally in seconds, the investor may have an initial overview of complex international corporate setups, and natural persons relationships that would take days or weeks to create manually.

In addition to a swift overview, working with these complex corporate fraud cases the investor will also start to recognize certain suspicious patterns of criminal setups. Some indicate corporate fraud like round-tripping, or other types of financial crime like tax evasion, sanctions evasion, money laundering, etc.

Working with link and network analysis, the investor will also start seeing hidden connections and "usual" suspects or auditors and corporate lawyers facilitating multiple of these criminal setups. In the below let us look deeper into networks and link analysis, with emphasis on white-collar crime and corporate fraud.

## 28.2 Points and Links of the Network

**Networks** (formally called graphs) consist of two fundamental parts. One part is the **point** of interest (also called a node). The point represents an individual entity within the network. This could be a natural person, a legal entity, a computer, a bank account, etc. In Fig. 28.1, the points are the circles in the form of two natural persons called Adam and Beth and the two legal entities called Good-Corp and Bad Corp.

The other part is the **link** (formally called an edge) between points. The link represents a relationship, connection, or interaction between two points. This could be a relation between two people, ownership between two legal entities, data transfer between computers, or a transaction between bank accounts. In Fig. 28.1, the multiple links are the lines illustrating that Adam and Beth are CEOs and Chairmen of the two interrelated Good-Corp and Bad-Corp respectively. While at the same time Adam and Beth are cousins.

All types of points and links are of interest when detecting corporate fraud. However, in our investment use cases there are some practical limitations, which law enforcement agencies, intelligence units and financial institutions might not have. We are outsiders, analyzing points and links only publicly available as OSINT. Therefore, some points, links and networks are more interesting than others. Let us refer to them as focal points, links, and networks.

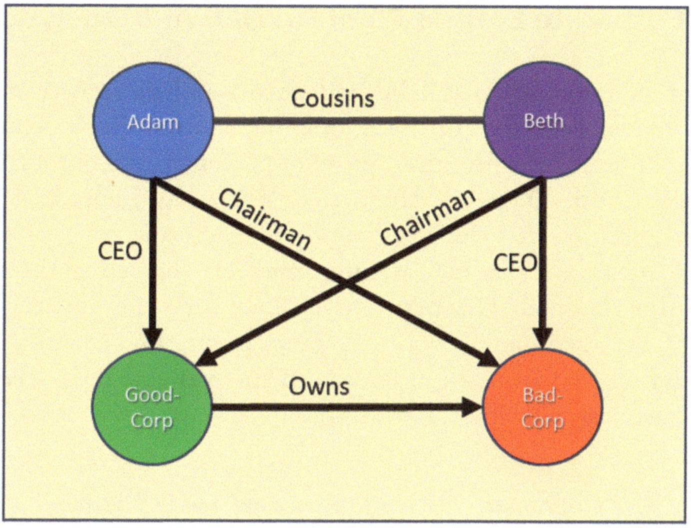


**Fig. 28.1** A simple network

### 28.2.1 Focal Points, Links, and Networks in Corporate Fraud

In corporate fraud detection, two types of intertwined networks are of particular interest. First, the **Corporate Network** that depicts the corporate entities and relations to other entities. Second, the **Social Networks** that are related to the natural persons of the Corporate Network.

Basically, we are interested in who is controlling which entities. What relations do these natural persons have to other natural persons of interest, or legal entities of interest?

- Corporate Entities are the corporations and legal entities, which can be focal points if they are involved or used as tools in fraudulent activities.
- Key Individuals are typically high-ranking executives or employees who could commit, prevent, or assist in conducting material corporate fraud. C-level staff, board of directors. Strawmen directors with relations too many other legal entities.
- Third-Party Facilitators are external auditors, consultants, or other entities that may knowingly or unknowingly facilitate the fraudulent activities.

### 28.2.2 Corporate Entities Points in Network Analytics

A company or corporation can be understood and illustrated in different ways. E.g. like a traditional organizational hierarchy, with the CEO on the top, or as a value chain with input, primary processes, and output.

Corporate Entities Network Analytics offers a unique approach in corporate fraud detection. It views the corporate landscape of legal entities as points and their interrelations as links, thereby enhancing the ability to identify corporate fraud. This perspective allows for a comprehensive understanding of the intricate network of corporations. In detecting corporate fraud, analyzing the corporate networks themselves and their relations and interconnectedness with social networks.

#### 28.2.2.1 *The Corporate Entity Points and their Feature Attributes*

Feature Attributes of the legal entities like the location of the company, industry, type of legal entity, number of employees, street address and similar are characteristics that will help define the corporate point. For instance, a legal entity that is in a tax haven, with no employees and a mailbox or office hotel as a street address will be a red flag.

#### 28.2.2.2 *The Corporate Entity Links*

How many points and links are there in the corporate setup? As discussed in Sect. 19.10, one typical way to discover a fraudulent company is that it is overly complex in its setup. The corporation has too many points in the form of legal entities and links between those corporate entities compared to what is the norm in the industry.

An example to illustrate. In the furniture production industry, the path from sourcing raw materials to delivering the finished product is straightforward. However, within the FurnitureCorp conglomerate, the landscape is a complex network of subsidiaries, each operating semi-independently across different jurisdictions worldwide. This global presence, while allegedly a strategy for market diversification, also provides a potential cover for financial irregularities.

The differing regulatory standards and legal frameworks across these jurisdictions can create loopholes that may be exploited for fraudulent activities. The complexity of tracing transactions and operations across borders can make it difficult for authorities to detect and investigate potential financial crimes. This setup, while seemingly a business strategy, could potentially be used to conceal illicit activities, making FurnitureCorp not just an overly complex entity in a simple industry, but also a potential vehicle for financial crime.

#### 28.2.2.3 *Investigating the Relationship Between the Corporation and Its Stakeholders*

In addition to the background investigations on the stakeholders. The investor should analyze the links and relationships between the corporation and its stakeholders, to better understand the context the company is operating within.

To get a deeper understanding of the context, the investor may include other types of stakeholders in the network analytics like suppliers, customers, financiers, shareholders, beneficiary owners, auditors, lawyers, or other specific corporate advisors, government entities and individuals.

First the investor should sanity check if the corporation actually has entered a claimed relationship with a stakeholder. It has been observed in multiple cases that a corporation claims to have relations with high-profile stakeholders, like selling products and services to well-known brands, which they have never done.

If the relationships exist, the next step is to analyze the type of relationship and the evolvement of the relationship over time between the corporation and its stakeholders, since red flags might be found here.

Some examples could include:

**Customers and vendors**—are the customers and vendors closely related to the corporation. E.g. subsidiary or sister company. When researching a corporate network structure, one might find that customers are not independent, but part of, or under the umbrella of the same general corporate entity. These close relationships in the value chain should raise red flags. Especially clandestine relationships. These close and obscure relationships could be abused to conduct round-tripping, channel stuffing and similar fraud tactics to manipulate earnings, as discussed in Sect. 24.

**Auditors.** Who are the auditors, who else do they serve? Also, the evolvement of auditors, what is the tenure of the auditor. Is there a high churn rate of auditors, or multiple auditors? A major red flag can be a corporation that shifts auditors frequently. Especially if the auditor replacements come subsequently to auditor remarks like Qualified Opinion, Adverse Opinion, Disclaimer of Opinion on the reports as discussed in Sect. 22.2.

**Banks and Financiers.** A risk which may be seen from network analysis is when the corporation does not have a primary main bank, but instead multiple bank relations, especially spread over multiple jurisdictions. This spreading tactic might be to avoid giving a primary bank or financial institution an overview of transactions of the company. Also, relations to dubious types of financiers might appear in the network analysis.

From a dynamic network analysis point of view, also frequent shifts in banks relations and other lenders might be a red flag. Anti Money Laundering Controls will often mean that if the bank does not understand (read: the bank understands but does not want the risk of money laundering) the bank will offboard the corporation. The detection of suspicious activity by a bank might take as long as 2–3 years. This means that the fraudulent company might change banks every 2–3 years.

**Name throwing** relationships to popular "branded" entities and natural persons to create a fake impressive high-profile network. Claimed, weak or non-existing relationships with popular and successful entities used for self-promotion is a red flag. This is related to the too-good-to-be-true business fairy tales mentioned in Sect. 8.5.

This will often stand out in network analysis. For example, the prominent ownership or relations to business world superstars does not appear from company registrars or any public records. Another red flag is the network is littered with too many recognizable household names and brands as all types of stakeholders, compared to the state and nature of the corporation.

Name throwing might be related to all kinds of stakeholders. The claims might be delivered informally or even on the fraudulent company's website as references. Sometimes these are quite easy to sanity check, by a single e-mail or phone call to the entity or representatives of the natural person in question. In many cases, simply by looking up the partnership references on the stakeholder's website.

More advanced tactics could be claims that Goldman Sachs or JP Morgan is investing or working with the company. While these names immediately give some kind of credibility in the financial world, one should always understand in what context they are working with the company in question, if at all.

In addition, most financial institutions will often deny commenting on a potential relationship with clients, even if there is no relationship at all. The corporate fraudsters know this "no comment" policy of financial institutions and actively abuse them.

In addition to the direct financial involvement, companies might also name throw other successful stakeholders like important customers, partnerships, joint ventures, suppliers and vendors.

In the worst case the successful stakeholder might never even have had a relationship with the fraudulent company, and it is totally fabricated. In the trickier cases it has been observed that they might have had:

- A minor relationship (maybe years back), that is blown out of proportion.
- A pilot or test project that never amounted to anything real.
- One type of stakeholder is re-purposed and leveraged as another type of stakeholder.
  - Most companies on the planet have Microsoft as vendors using their Office Products. However, this simple customer relationship might be repurposed as Microsoft being partners, business associates, collaborators, business affiliates or similar.
  - Buying a few billable hours from McKinsey or Boston Consulting Group could be wrongfully repurposed as partnerships with these top management consultancies.
- The stakeholder is real, like a customer. However, e.g. the testimonial from the stakeholder is fabricated in corporate material. Say Microsoft bought a one-time service, and the corporate fraudster puts up a testimonial that Microsoft had a positive experience. These fabricated testimonials are common in corporate fraud cases.

If during network investigations, the investor finds that instead of focusing on the core of the business, there is focus on name dropping network relations and other artificial tactics, this is a major red flag.

### 28.2.3 Social Network Analytics

Social Network Analytics provides an alternative perspective in corporate fraud detection by viewing points as natural persons and the links as relationships and connections among those persons, thereby enhancing the ability to detect and prevent corporate fraud.

#### 28.2.3.1 *Natural Persons and their Relationships*

When natural persons are points in a social network, they have some characteristics, which could include e.g., age, gender, location, occupation, education level, nationality, etc. Both current and historic properties.

Feature attributes specifically interesting concerning corporate fraud are if the natural person has been involved in rule violations or criminal activity. Because of the way that white-collar crime works, they might not even need to have been involved themselves. Network relations to other natural persons involved in financial crime may also be a red flag. Of course, a person is not guilty by association, but when more criminals appear in the network this is a red flag. In white-collar crime the abuse of strawmen directors or similar with relations too many other legal entities are common. This may hide and obscure ownership and direct relations to the crimes. Looking at this from a network analytics perspective will often reveal these types of organized white-collar crime risks.

Also do the natural person's connections and relationships make sense? For example, if a person working in the furniture production industry has an abnormally high rate of business relations with persons in the food truck industry, with no prior working relations to that industry. This skewed network setup could be an indicator that something is wrong.

### 28.2.4 Designing Criminal Network Visualizations

In the former Fig. 28.1 example of the Good Corp & Bad Corp, we had only two corporations, two natural persons and six relationships between these points. This is an easy network to visualize and understand. Unfortunately, as criminal networks grow, they often do not grow in a linear fashion, but in an exponential fashion. Figure 28.2 shows how a more realistic minor network looks. Think of that as a minimum of what the investor might expect, when analyzing networks exposing corporate fraud. Natural persons and corporate entities have been anonymized.

It is not abnormal in corporate network cases to see hundreds of points, thousands or ten thousand of different types of connections and relations. Here the right software tools helping the investor get an overview is important.

Analyzing small networks, the investor might utilize tools like Visio, manually constructing the networks. This is one step up from the physical evidence board. However, this is a very cumbersome and time-consuming task. The

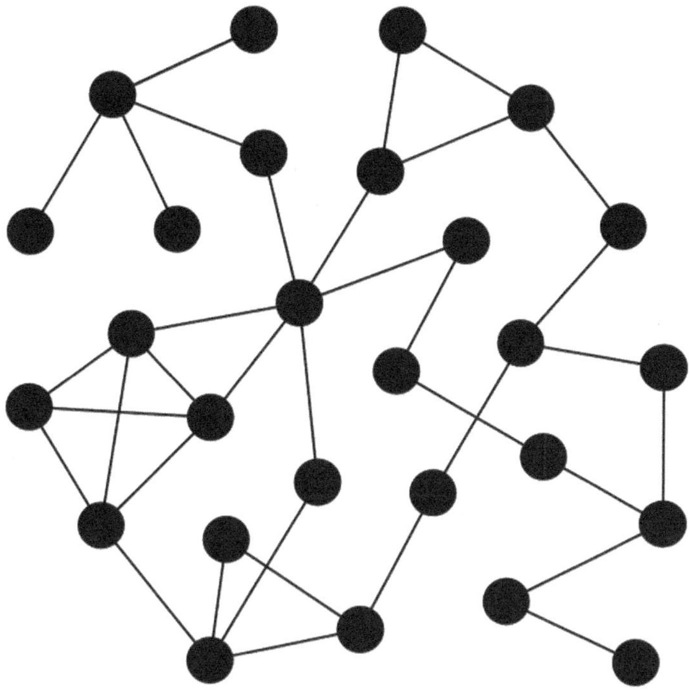

Fig. 28.2 An example illustration of an anonymized minor network to illustrate a relatively simple corporate setup

benefit of semi-automatic professional specialized tools is that they integrate with most types of open-source databases, like corporate registrars, and other financial databases that the investor already works with. This helps the investor immensely. The time is not spent on manual collection of data but studying and finding the relations between them. These tools also offer a way to see the networks from different perspectives, focusing on specific links, by zooming in and out of interesting parts of the network. These tools are touched upon in Sect. 28.2.11.

### 28.2.5 Where to Start, When Constructing the Network Visualization

There are several ways to start when constructing network visualization. The investor may start with a suspect like e.g. the CEO and work the way out or the investor can start with the main legal entity of the suspect. Then gradually expand along two dimensions of the corporate entity network and the social network. Analyzing directors, sister companies, subsidiaries, majority investors, insiders, etc.

The more times an investor has analyzed corporate criminal networks, the faster she will detect if something is abnormal with the setup and in which direction to expand the network analysis. The investor will start to see patterns that resemble elevated risk of criminal activity.

### 28.2.6 When to Stop Expanding the Network Visualization

It is said that everybody on the globe is connected to each other by six degrees of separation. Studying Facebook, Edunov et al. (2016) found 3.5 degrees amongst its users. This also means that a network analysis can become big amazingly fast. Especially when using automatic or semi-automatic tools.

It means the investor must learn to make choices in which directions to go when constructing the network visualizations to detect corporate fraud. Also, when to stop expanding the network. These are judgment call skills that may be hard to teach in a book but can be obtained working on cases. However, studies and research of criminal networks described in Sects. 28.2.7–28.2.10 may serve as pointers.

### 28.2.7 Detecting Criminal Networks

As a practitioner, the investor will gradually learn what to look for after having seen a few financial crime networks. Based on general network theory, described in foundational books by e.g. Newman (2010) and Barabási (2016) let us first focus on four main areas and their impact on corporate fraud.

- **Centrality Measures** will help identify the key players in the criminal networks. In a corporate fraud context, there are more examples. It could be a natural person with a high degree centrality, orchestrating fraudulent activities - the archcriminal. For instance, a CEO who has direct connections with many subsidiaries might be manipulating financial statements across the network of legal entities. Another example could be a street address, shared by many questionable companies. This might be an indication of a shell- or front company.
- **Paths and Traversal**: Paths represent the connections between entities. Detecting cyclical patterns can uncover complex fraud schemes. For example, in a network of companies, a circular ownership structure.

Company A owns Company B, Company B owns Company C and Company C owns Company A. The circular network design could be a sign of round-tripping fraud, a tactic used to e.g. inflate revenues.

- **Points/Entity Link Analysis** are techniques predicting the likelihood of a relationship between two entities. In corporate fraud detection, it could reveal undisclosed relationships that are legally or ethically problematic. For instance, two companies might appear unrelated, but link prediction could reveal a common director, suggesting conflict of interest or fraudulent collusion. Another example is when actors try to hide links by using secrecy. Some examples also include the usage of anonymous trusts or informal nominees and straw men- and women. This is looking for the missing links that might connect partial networks into bigger ones.

  In a major international pyramid scheme case, the setup consisted of hundreds of legal entities with almost hundreds of different corporate officers. The missing link between two major parts of the network boiled down to one single person controlling and abusing an educational trust in the Middle East.
- **Cluster Analysis** identifies groups of entities with similar characteristics on Feature attributes. An example observed in a corporate setting could be clusters of related competing companies with similar financial feature attributes in an industry. This pattern might indicate coordinated fraud. For example, if several companies in the same industry report remarkably similar and unusually high profits, it could suggest a wider cartel operation to fix prices, divide the market and deceive consumers. While the direct victim is the consumer, not the shareholder. The shareholder will suffer when exposed.

### 28.2.8 Hands-on Working with Incomplete Networks

As a practitioner one will often encounter the question; what percentage of the picture we have captured, and what is still in the dark, unknown to us.

From a practical point of view, it has been observed that it is paramount to have an overview of the points in the network, like the legal entities and natural persons involved. While still important, the type and strength of the links between the points has been found to be of secondary nature. Even a very weak link, like members of the same club, can turn out to be very profound for understanding the network. Also, the investor will most likely not discover each and every link between the points.

This practical observation is supported by Ficara et al. (2021) that in a study of criminal networks found that even removing 10% of the links the investor still has a good overview of the criminal network. However, moving only 2% of the points like natural persons and legal entities, the general understanding of the network may significantly change.

### 28.2.9 Static Networks vs. Dynamic Networks—The Temporal Aspect

Often, the investor sees a static view of the potential criminal network. A snapshot of a setup, frozen at a specific point in time. In many cases corporate fraud networks evolve over time and sometimes so fast that even company registrars and data aggregators lag way behind. The graph the investor is looking at might be a month or more old. The investor is one step behind, looking at a historic network. While the investor might be one step behind and cannot look into the future, the investor might be able to "re-wind" and investigate the past. Here the investor might discover networks including repeat offenders, unindicted or simply overlooked connections that now make sense from a criminal point of view. Think of it as looking at a single photo of a criminal network vs. a movie of how the criminal network evolves over time.

The investor might discover that the same group of transitory financiers or investors are only temporarily related to a fraudulent corporate entity that later is exposed. If the investor analyzes the network from a static point of view the investor will miss this. If the investor analyzes from a dynamic point of view, the investor might find that the same actors have been financiers in a string of historic dubious companies. Like supplying bridge loans or similar transitory financing to criminals. These types of corporate loan sharks and their temporary lending stints might seem insignificant at first glance. However, analyzing evolving networks over time, these specific stakeholders' involvement may become leading indicators of future fraudulent activity.

An example of the dynamic time aspect in fraudulent networks is the tenure and entrenchment risk, touched upon as a potential, but complex red flag in Sect. 16.2.5. Not only the time a CEO has spent in the company is important. The context is also important, which must be investigated in depth.

For example, in a case where the CEO is also the original founder of the company. Many of the executives and board members owe their position to the CEO. From a practical point of view, it has been observed that frauds will go undetected longer if the CEO is socially entrenched by having appointed or had heavy influence on appointing the people around her. Both other executives in the top management, and directors on the board. These practical observations are supported by studies by Khanna et al. (2015) that found appointment-based CEO connections with the executive suites and boardrooms pose a risk of not detecting the fraud. Also, in cases where fraud is detected, it is more likely that fraud is covered up, and less likely to face any enforcement or consequences regarding the corporate fraud conducted. This resembles what one might experience in other types of organized crime networks.

### 28.2.10 Criminal Network Commonalities and Archetype Crime Networks

Practitioners in the field of network analytics within law enforcement and intelligence work with different forms of archetype criminal network structures for distinct types of organized and complex crime. These models are mostly confidential and will often be localized with different law enforcement agencies.

Besides local variations these criminal network archetypes vary across the different types of crime. Street Gangs, Mafia Style, Terrorist networks, etc. Inspiration on how criminal networks look, may be drawn from publicly available research by e.g. Arquilla and Ronfeldt (2001) or more recent studies by Cavallaro et al. (2021) that studied the network of two Sicilian Mafia networks, trying to construct artificial networks that mirrored criminal behavior. While these types of criminal networks do not resemble networks in white-collar crime one-to-one, investors may take cues from them as to what to look for.

Focusing on white-collar crime, Hardy and Bell (2020) studied the Social Networks related to one of the biggest fraud cases in history. The Bernie Madoff Ponzi Scheme. The research found four main social groups related to the fraud.

- **The Core Group** consisting of individuals, who had leadership over both the legitimate part of the operation and the criminal part of the network.
- **The Compliance Group**, containing natural persons / legal entities, which goal was to comply with SEC oversight regulations. This group played a role in rubber-stamping audit documents to meet regulatory requirements.
- **The Capital group** included numerous funds that gave Madoff complete control over trading decisions in their accounts. These funds enabled Madoff to impose exorbitant fees while evading due diligence probes.

- **The Facilitator Group** with accountants, banks, and financial services companies that provided numerous services to both Madoff's companies and victims. This group played a crucial role in providing flexibility and resilience to the Madoff network collapse by holding accounts, facilitating transactions, and providing loans.

Sophisticated network models and archetype networks in the public domain are limited. However, as the investor specializes in corporate fraud, a library of network archetypes and patterns associated with corporate fraud may be gradually constructed. These baseline criminal networks, the investor can use for training or reference. On top of training humans to understand these criminal networks, they may also be used as inspiration for working with new ML models.

## 28.2.11 Tools Used to Analyze Criminal Networks

There are two main types of tools that are used by analysts and investigators to analyze criminal networks.

The first type of tools is driven mainly by human analysts but have semi-automatic and advanced automatic features to support the analysts in the work. Like collection of data, and visualization of the criminal networks.

The second type are tools mainly driven by Machine Learning and AI, with minimal intervention by humans during the analytics phase. Humans might design the models behind and interpret the results, but the analytics often on multifaceted big data sets are conducted by machines.

### 28.2.11.1 *Network Analytical Tools Used by Analysts*

There are several of these first type of OSINT tools where human analysts is in the driver's seat. Two of the most common tools used by professionals are Maltego and Blackdot Videris. Both tools have many automatic and semi-automatic features that may reduce many hours of collecting data, constructing, and illustrating networks down to sometimes a few seconds.

Instead of using the bulk of time designing the network visualization, the analyst will spend the time on analyzing and trying to understand the criminal networks.

These tools have integrations and tie-ins with open-source databases, like e.g. Bureau Van Dijk Orbis, Dow Jones, Factiva and OCCRP. This makes it easier to analyze both Legal Entities and natural persons in social networks.

#### 28.2.11.2 *The Human Limitation Understanding Complex Networks & Machine Learning support*

Some humans excel in analyzing complex networks and may be aided vastly by professional network tools. However, in a practical setting most humans start to lose track and overview when the networks steadily grow along multiple dimensions, with hundreds of points and thousands of links. That said, there are special individuals with special talents that might be able to see patterns across many dimensions.

In the real world, few excel in analyzing these types of networks when they grow beyond a certain complexity. While tools add support for pruning and re-focusing on parts of networks, many people are lost when it comes to complex networks.

Therefore, ML are tools that may be used to support the human analyst trying to find complex patterns or clues that suggest corporate fraud. With e.g. archetype criminal networks as baseline and inspiration, the investor might build ML models that can help detect fraud.

Inspiration and foundation on what to build future ML models on, may be found in Wills and Meyer (2020) that gives a general introduction to how the investor from a more pragmatic angle can use metrics like e.g. spectral distances & matrix distances to compare different networks to each other.

Spectral distances are used to compare networks. These distances are based on the 'spectrum' or the set of different values that come from the network's structure.

Matrix distances are represented by a 'distance matrix', which is a table that illustrates the shortest number of steps to get from one point in the criminal network to another.

When screening and analyzing new potential criminal networks, the investor could use these distance measures to compare with criminal archetype networks. Finding similarities and distances between archetype criminal networks and other networks, might be an indication that the networks are structurally similar.

## References

Arquilla, J., & Ronfeldt, D. (2001). Networks and Netwars: The Future of Terror, Crime, and Militancy. RAND Corporation.

Barabási, A. L. (2016). *Network Science*. Cambridge University Press.

Cavallaro, L., Bagdasar, O., De Meo, P., Fiumara, G., & Liotta, A. (2021). Graph and Network Theory for the analysis of Criminal Networks. In Data Science and Internet of Things. Springer. Retrieved September 14, 2024, from https://doi.org/10.48550/arXiv.2103.02504

Edunov, S., Bhagat, S., Burke, M., Diuk, C., & Filiz, I. O. (2016, February 4). Three and A Half Degrees of Separation. Meta Research. Retrieved September 14, 2024, from https://research.fb.com/blog/2016/02/three-and-a-half-degrees-of-separation/

Ficara, A., Cavallaro, L., Curreri, F., Fiumara, G., De Meo, P., Bagdasar, O., Song, W., & Liotta, A. (2021). Criminal Networks Analysis in Missing Data Scenarios through Graph Distances. *Plos One, 16*(8), e0255067. Retrieved September 14, 2024, from https://doi.org/10.1371/journal.pone.0255067

Hardy, J., & Bell, P. (2020). Resilience in Sophisticated Financial Crime Networks: A Social Network Analysis of the Madoff Investment Scheme. *Crime Prevention and Community Safety, 22*, 223–247. Retrieved September 14, 2024, from https://doi.org/10.1057/s41300-020-00094-7

Khanna, V., Kim, E. H., & Lu, Y. (2015). CEO Connectedness and Corporate Frauds. *Journal of Finance, 70*(3), 1203–1252.

Newman, M. (2010). Networks: An Introduction. Oxford University Press.

Wills, P., & Meyer, F. G. (2020). Metrics for Graph Comparison: A Practitioner's Guide. *Plos One, 15*(2), e0228728. Retrieved September 14, 2024, from https://doi.org/10.1371/journal.pone.0228728

# Part V

## Executing the Fraud Short Investment

# 29

# Execution of the Fraud Short Investment Strategy

## 29.1 The Overview of the Fraud Short Investment Execution Process

Below is a simplified overview of the fraud short investment execution process:

- Do a risk, reward & cost assessment if the fraud targets are worthwhile.
- Choose financial instruments and conduct roll–out plan.
- Build investment positions.
- Release the fraud report.
- Monitor share price development.
- Close profitable positions… or stop losses.
- Follow up reporting, rebuttals handling and investment repositioning.

### 29.1.1 The Risks Related to a Fraud Short Investment

Each case should include a thorough risk assessment before eventually executing on the fraud short investment, consisting at least assessment of:

- Market risks
  - Timing—according to Keynes (1923)"*…in the long run we are all dead.*" This may also be true in a fraud short investment strategy. In the days, weeks, months, years, or decades up to the market acknowledges the



J. Sørensen, *Shorting Fraud*, https://doi.org/10.1007/978-3-031-81834-9_29

fraud, the contrarian view is wrong, and the market (falsely) right. This can be seen in the Wirecard walkthrough in Sect. 29.1.3.
  - Various financial instruments come with different risks—temporary fluctuations may wipe out the short seller, as e.g. seen in Sect. 29.1.2 on fraud squeezes.
  - Share buyback—the fraudulent company start buying up own shares to support price.
  - White knight risk—a related party buys up or takes over supporting the price despite fraud.
  - Retail investors will flock to the fraud in hope of a quick buck supporting the share price.
  - Fraud Short Seller is plain wrong—in some cases the investor might have misread or misunderstood the situation of the company. Especially if research is not solid enough.

- Non—market risks
  - Rules of engagement change - short banning on markets, industries, or single companies.
  - Litigations—the investor might be accused, litigated, or charged with market manipulations and need to involve professional legal, assessment, advice, and support in each case.

### 29.1.2 The Threat of the Short Squeeze

While different fraud short strategies come with different risks, one basic risk to understand, which shows how risky it is to invest in expected company collapse, is the short squeeze. The short squeeze underpins the substantial risk in investing short with the threat of an abrupt, immediate and significant loss.

A short squeeze is triggered when the price of a stock rises sharply, causing short sellers (who had bet on the stock's decline) to reconsider their positions. The short sellers exit their short positions by covering the position (buying the stock) and returning it to the lender they borrowed the stock from. The short seller buying the stock might further drive up the price of the stock fast.

It is a sudden surge of demand, having the share price rise several hundred or even thousands of percent in a flash. Li (2021) gives an overview of the historic VW 2008 short Squeeze (NOT related to the VW US fraud case).

- Early 2008, VW trades around €150–€170.
- Mid–2008 Porsche started intensified buy up of VW shares.

- Oct. 26th, 2008: Porsche announces majority stake and takeover intentions. Share price: ~ €200.
- Oct. 27th, 2008: Short sellers begin to panic, driving the price up. Share price: ~ €400.
- Oct. 28th, 2008: The squeeze reaches its peak. Share price: ~ €1,000.

So, in a few days the short sellers lost 500% and VW became the most valuable company on the planet. When the panic faded, so did the share price. However, according to Rao (2021) it was reported that the short sellers in VW lost $30 billion, while short sellers in the 2021 GameStop Squeeze, described below, lost $10 billion.

The GameStop squeeze played out in Dec. 2020–Jan. 2021, which can be seen in Fig. 29.1. The fading video game retailer GameStop was heavily shorted by hedge funds. The short sellers expected GameStop to go out of business due to Creative Destruction and be replaced by online delivery channels. Like Blockbuster and the DVD scenario.

However, some retail investors, aware of the short squeeze mechanisms, saw this as an opportunity. These retail investors began buying GameStop shares, in a coordinated effort, using Social Media Platforms like Reddit. This pushed the price of GameStop upwards. A short squeeze, forcing the hedge funds to cover their short positions, and driving the price up even further.

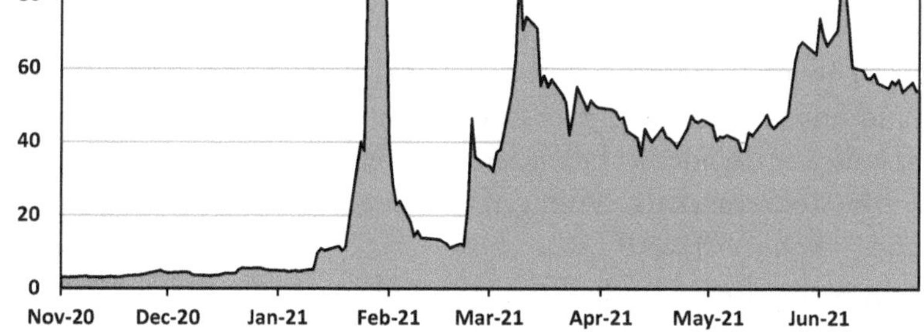


**Fig. 29.1** Short squeeze gamestop share price USD 2020–21 (*Source* NASDAQ)

Using the closing price of November 30$^{th}$, 2020, of \$16.56 and the peak price of +\$500 in the pre-market of January 28$^{th}$, 2021, the share price exploded by 3,000%, without any fundamental changes in the actual business of GameStop.

Focusing on Fraud Short Squeezes, one of the biggest known single losses was estimated to \$760 million and taken by Bill Ackman and Pershing Square capital according to Orol (2018).

During a five-year campaign, Bill Ackman and Pershing Square Capital Management made a big, short bet against the global Multi-Level-Marketing company Herbalife. A company that in some jurisdictions were accused of being as a pyramid scheme.

In public interviews like David (2012), Ackman publicly called Herbalife a pyramid scheme, expecting the share price to drop. Meanwhile another activist investor Carl Ichan, took the opposite long position. The battle between the two played out in the media. While the stock initially dropped, the involvement of Ichan meant it rebounded and eventually Ackman covered Pershing Square's short position.

The three examples show that even when the short seller is right, temporary, or other external factors, might initiate a surge in the stock. As can be seen from the following description of the Wirecard case, the market can be wrong for decades in fraud cases, in which case the fraud short investment strategy might not be profitable, all though the investor is 100% right about the corporate fraud.

### 29.1.3 The Wirecard Case and the Timing Factor of Profiting From Fraud Shorting

Sections 2.2–3 described the academic supported evidence that revealing fraudulent companies on average may result in potential corrections of corporate valuations, which may be realized as Corporate Fraud Exposure Capital Gains for the fraud short investor. However, the actual valuation correction and timing will vary from case to case.

From an investment practitioner's point of view, reactions are far from perfect and logical after corporate fraud exposure. These fraud cases may take months, years, or decades to be understood by auditors, authorities, and most importantly stock markets. This can be observed from timelines and share price charts in the Wirecard case.

Starting with a look at Fig. 29.2, which displays the price chart for Wirecard's full life as a publicly listed company from reverse merger "IPO" until

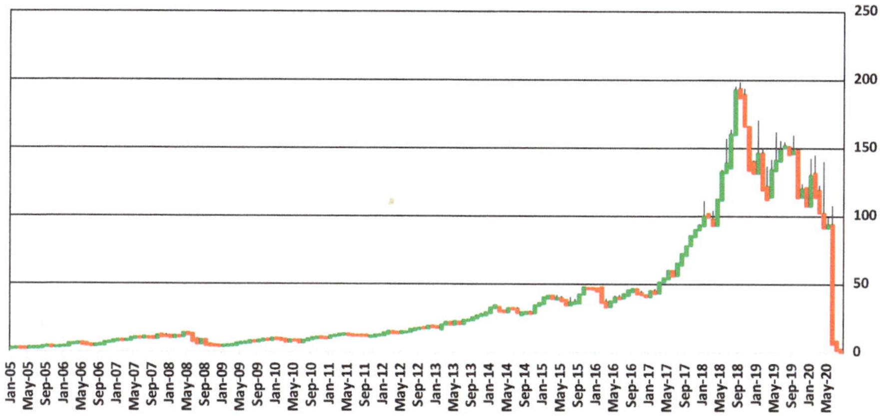


**Fig. 29.2** Wirecard share price EUR from reverse merger (IPO) until corporate fraud collapse (*Source* Frankfurter Börse)

collapse. The share price development tells the story of a "successful" and not a fraudulent company for most of its 15 years history as a public company.

Despite early major red flags, much of the time a fraud short strategy would have incurred a loss.

#### 29.1.3.1 The First Wave

In the timeline Fig. 29.3, we see that red flags were present as early as at the introduction of the company into the Frankfurt Stock Exchange. The introduction happened by a reverse merger (see Sect. 18.10.2 for description) according to the German press release by Wirecard AG. (2004, December 15) on 1$^{st}$ January 2005. Hence, Wirecard introduced a red flag 15 years before the CEO Markus Braun is arrested and Wirecard files for insolvency.

Later other red flags came along with the acquisition of XCOM in 2006, where Wirecard introduced adjusted alternative financial statements, a concept explained in Sect. 22.5. These adjusted statements made it opaque for investors to understand what was going on in the company.

Two years later, in 2008, the first irregularities were voiced by the head of the German shareholder association, SdK, Klaus Schneider. Rumors were also circulating that Wirecard was cooking the books.

Wirecard aggressively rebut and according to Reuters (2008, July 18), Wirecard filed a lawsuit with the Munich prosecutors against SdK, with accusations of insider trading and market manipulation. In addition, Wirecard also reported a complaint to German stock market watchdog BaFin. These

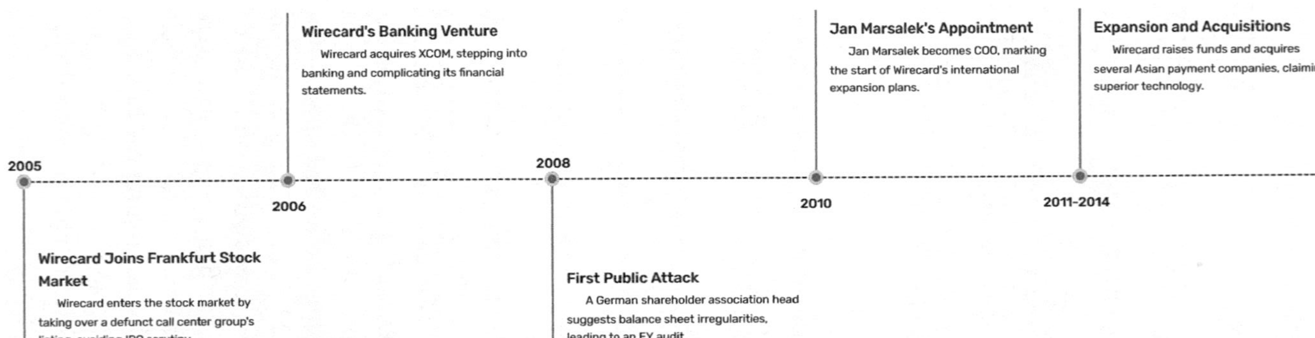


**Fig. 29.3** The first wave the beginning and initial red flags. (*Sources* Wirecard AG public disclosures, McCrum [2020, 25 June] & Reuters [2021, March 16])

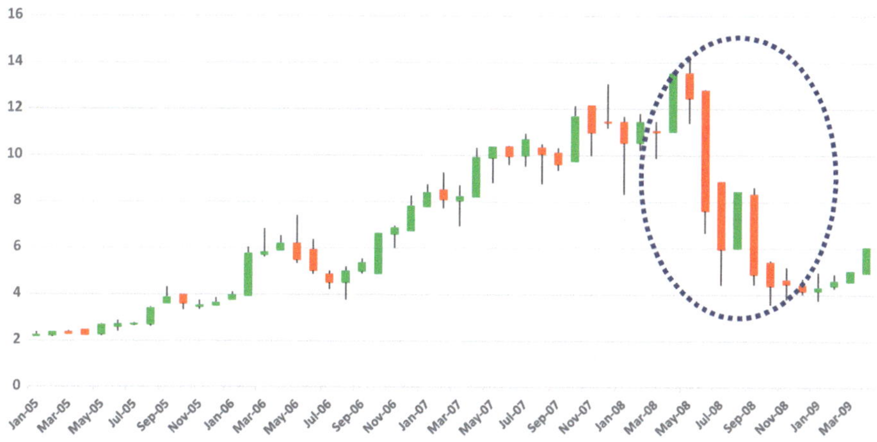


**Fig. 29.4** The first questions (*Source* Frankfurter Börse)

were the beginning of Ad hominem attacks described in Sect. 20.5.1, trying to scare or "kill the messenger."

Subsequently, EY does an audit but does not find anything. The next five years, Wirecard raised funds and acquired several Asian payment service providers.

Despite the early red flags, as can be seen from Fig. 29.4 it mostly would be a bad idea to short Wirecard from its stock market introduction in January 2005 until Klaus Schneider from the German shareholder association SdK, first questioned Wirecard in the summer of 2008.

For a period in the summer and fall of 2008, the shares fell. However, after Wirecard came out with the aggressive rebuttals, the price decline stabilized, rebounded, and the stock price generally followed a growing trend for the next 7 years seen from Fig. 29.5. Continuously, the company posted solid, while fraudulent earnings.

#### 29.1.3.2 The Second Wave

As can be seen from the timeline in Fig. 29.6, the second wave started when Financial Times were tipped and investigative journalists published a series of articles questioning Wirecard in 2015, and fraud short sellers started targeting Wirecard in 2016.

Despite the critical articles from Financial Times at the end of April 2015 questioning Wirecard (with a share price drop around 10%) and the anonymous Zatara Short seller report in February 2016 (share price drop of 25%), the drops were temporary. Once again Wirecard was acquitted by EY. The

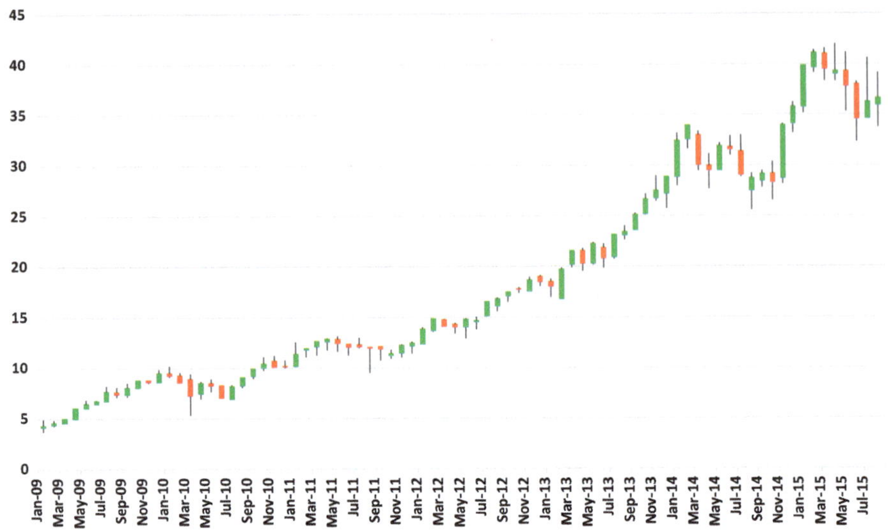


**Fig. 29.5** Share price supported by fraudulent earnings (*Source* Frankfurter Börse)

Wirecard stock rebounded and skyrocketed from a price hovering around 40 in 2015–16, quintupling to top around 200 on Tuesday September 04, 2018.

### 29.1.3.3 The Third wave

In the third wave, illustrated by the timeline in Fig. 29.7, near the 2019 peak, the institutional investor, SoftBank, injected EUR 900 million into Wirecard. Furthermore, later EUR 500 million of corporate bonds (rated investment grade by Moody's) were issued by Deutsche Bank, Crédit Agricole and ING as global coordinators. In addition to Credit Suisse, Citigroup, ABN AMRO and Lloyds Bank as joint bookrunners according to Wirecard AG (2019, September 12).

Meanwhile Financial times continued questioning the Wirecard setup and an independent KPMG audit is conducted. The KPMG-audit is first delayed, then inconclusive and cannot verify profits in Wirecard. As can be seen from Fig. 29.8 the major financial institutions involvement helped prop up the share price right up till the endgame.

On January 30$^{th}$, 2019, Financial Times published another story on potential fraud problems in Singapore and the Singaporean police raided Wirecard on February 8$^{th}$, 2019. With an opening price of 166.20 on January 30, 2019, and trading as low as 86.50 on February 8 the share price is almost halved in little over a week, which would be very profitable for a fraud

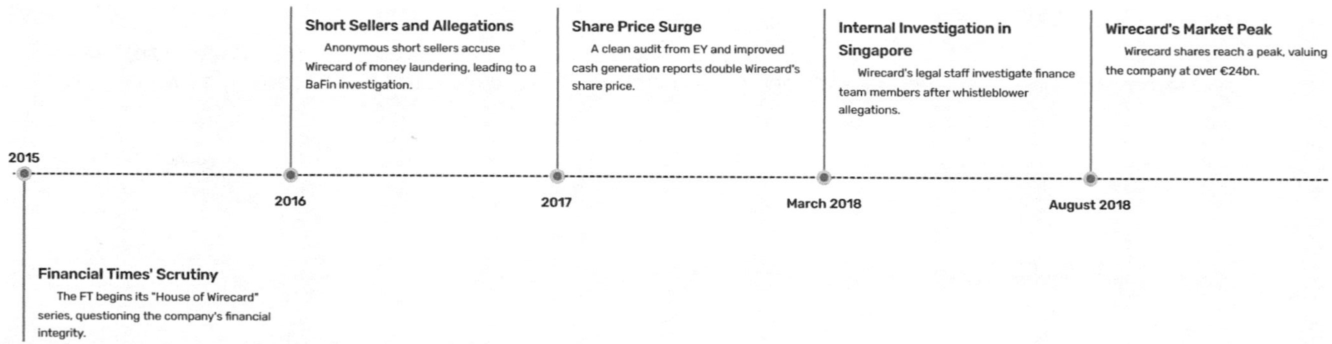


**Fig. 29.6** The second wave Financial Times and fraud short sellers. (*Sources* Wirecard AG public disclosures, McCrum [2020, 25 June] & Reuters [2021, March 16])

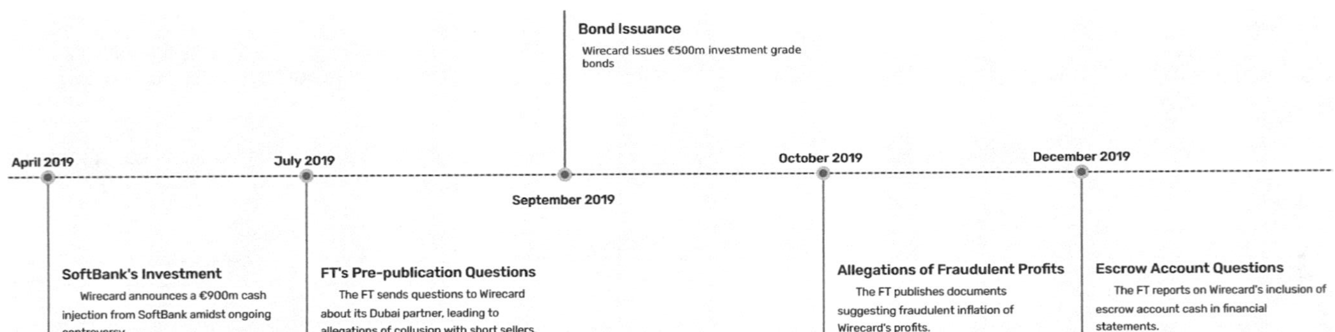


**Fig. 29.7** The third wave institutional investors and beginning of the end. (*Sources* wirecard AG public disclosures, McCrum [2020, 25 June] & Reuters [2021, March 16])

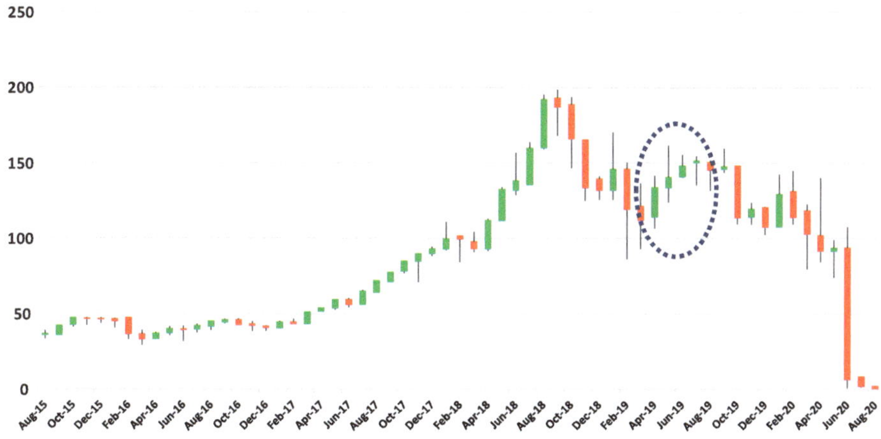


**Fig. 29.8** Major institutional investors propping up the company just before the endgame. (*Source* Frankfurter Börse)

short position. However, the German Financial Service Authority (BaFin) introduced a two-month short ban on February 18, 2019, which supported Wirecard. The share price rose again, also supported by an injection of EUR 900 million by SoftBank in April and the investment grade bond issue in September. However, in October Financial times revealed potential fraudulent documents. Then KPMG is brought onboard finding irregularities in the spring 2020, illustrated in Fig. 29.9. Hereafter the share price goes southwards, finally ending in a collapse in summer 2020.

In June 2020 everything fell apart in only 20 days. Starting with the Munich prosecutor launching an investigation on June 5th, it is later revealed that EUR 2 billion is missing.

As can be seen in Fig. 29.10 in the last days, the CEO resigned and was subsequently arrested. Then it is revealed that the EUR 2 billion is missing due to suspected fraud - the company files for insolvency on June 25th.

The Wirecard case illustrates several important things regarding the time factor in a Fraud Short Investment strategy.

Although the share price eventually came to zero when the company collapsed, it took 15 years. If we sum the case up. Despite there being red flags indicating corporate fraud from the very beginning, most of the time it was not profitable or viable being in a short position. The investor had to time movements in and out of the short position very carefully.

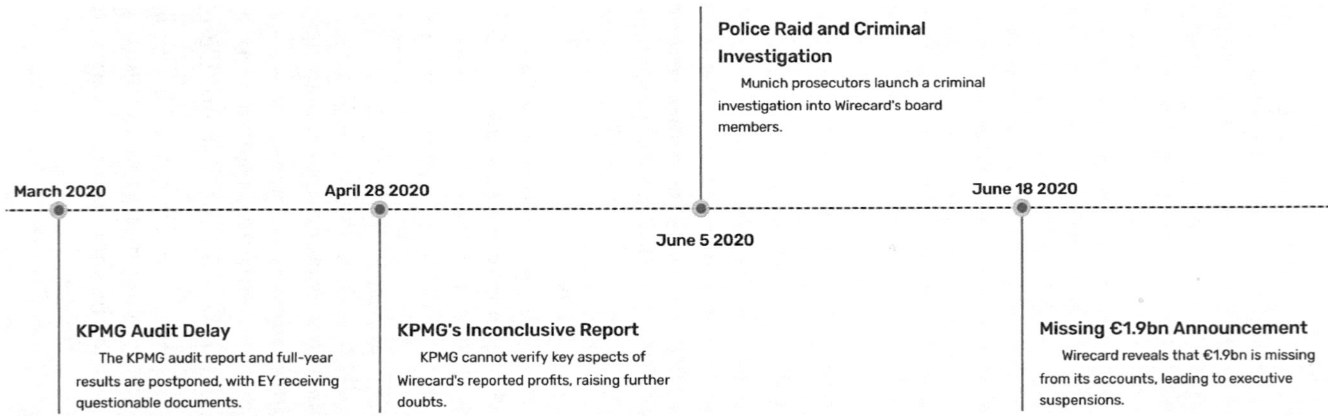


**Fig. 29.9** The downfall of wirecard. (*Sources* Wirecard AG public disclosures, McCrum [2020, 25 June] & Reuters [2021, March 16])

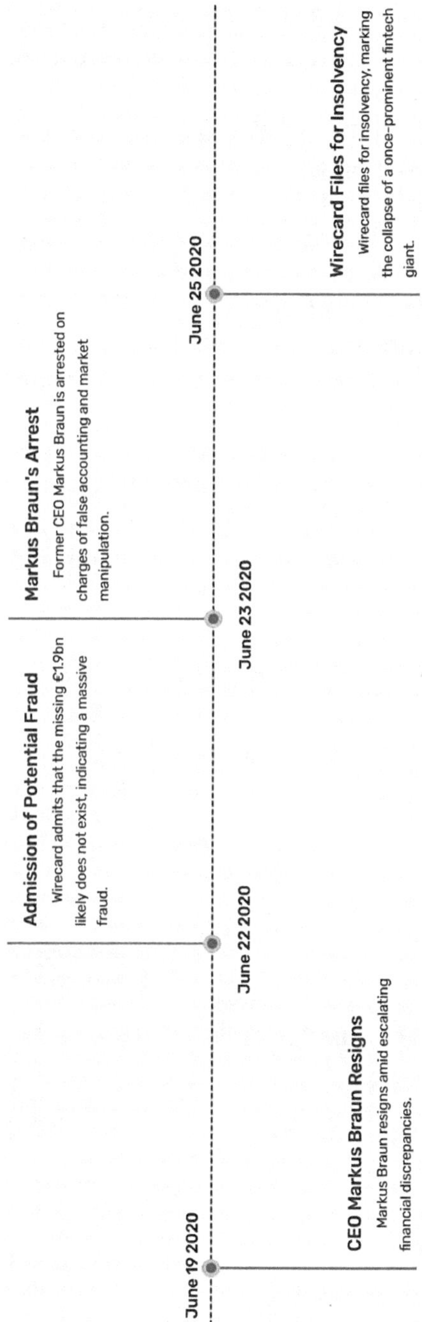


**Fig. 29.10** The last days (*Source* Wirecard AG public disclosures, McCrum [2020, 25 June] & Reuters [2021, March 16])

## 29.2 Timing of the Fraud Short Investments

The specific timing of the Fraud short investments will of course vary from case to case with regards to the expected and actual playout of the fraud shorting investment case.

From a more general point of view, Chen (2022) has defined two types of hedge fund activity interesting in relations to activist short seller campaigns. Some of the central insight from the research is shown in Table 29.1.

From this it appears that the general strategy for activist short sellers is a quick hit'n run strategy. With a lot of preparation, and then main execution within a week. From a practical point of view, this general picture does not depict the entire truth. Generally monitoring twitter announcements, newsletters, and follow-up announcements from undisclosed fraud short sellers indicate something else.

In fraud shorts some announcers appear to be lingering in short positions for much longer periods than 3–4 days. Announcers might also be utilizing alternative financial instruments as explained in Sect. 31, where there could be less public oversight in some jurisdictions, compared to the traditional short sale.

**Table 29.1** The two types of shorting hedge Funds. (*Source* Chen [2022])

| Type | Fund | Strategy |
|---|---|---|
| Announcers | Younger Funds; AUM $3.04 bn | Announcers build up short positions before the release of the short report. Especially, increasing the short positions 3–4 days before the release of the report, peaking at 1.4%. After the release of the report, announcers cover positions and take profit within 2–3 trading days |
| Followers | Older Funds; AUM $28.43 bn | Followers are hedge funds that keep silent, adding short positions after announcers have released their reports. Followers continue to add and hold positions long after announcers have exited, remaining at 1.4%, even a year (250 trading days) after the initial release |

## 29.3 Financial Instruments Used to Realize Corporate Fraud Exposure Capital Gains

To actively extract profit from an investment in a fraudulent company, the investor needs to use financial instruments. There are several types of advanced financial instruments, which may be used. The actual availability of these instruments depends on the jurisdictions and investor class. These instruments will vary with regards to risk, liquidity, taxation, potential return, and losses. All these factors should be taken into consideration and understood to the full before engaging in any investments.

It is highly recommended to take professional advice, including special legal and tax advice sought before conducting any investment. Below is a basic primer giving an overview from a fraud short investment perspective. Before eventually using these instruments, the investor should familiarize herself with and understand these instruments in more detail than given in the primer. Some of the instruments come with extreme risks of losses.

Section 30 explains traditional short selling. Sect. 31 explains alternative financial instruments to realize the Corporate Fraud Exposure Capital Gains. Finally, Sect. 32 describes instruments to capture fraud induced volatility around the fraud short campaign.

## References

Chen, J. (2022). See it, Say it, Shorted: Strategic Announcements in Short-Selling Campaigns. Retrieved September 14, 2024, from https://ssrn.com/abstract=4491506 or https://doi.org/10.2139/ssrn.4491506

David, J. E. (2012, December 20). Ackman Defends Calling Herbalife a 'Pyramid Scheme'. CNBC. Retrieved February 26, 2024.

Keynes, J. M. (1923). *Tract on Monetary Reform.* Macmillan and Co., Limited.

Li, Y. (2021, February 2). As GameStop Plunges, Volkswagen's 2008 Short Squeeze Gives an Idea of How Painful It Will Get. CNBC. Retrieved September 14, 2024, from https://www.cnbc.com/2021/02/02/as-gamestop-plunges-volkswagens-2008-short-squeeze-gives-an-idea-of-how-painful-it-will-get.html

McCrum, D. (2020, June 25). Wirecard: the timeline. Financial Times. Retrieved September 14, 2024, from https://www.ft.com/content/284fb1ad-ddc0-45df-a075-0709b36868db

Orol, R. (2018, February 28). It's Over: Icahn Beats Ackman in Battle Over Herbalife. TheStreet. Retrieved September 14, 2024, from https://web.archive.org/web/20200606142556/https://www.thestreet.com/markets/mergers-and-acquisitions/it-s-over-icahn-beats-ackman-in-battle-over-herbalife-14505289

Rao, S. (2021, February 2). Factbox: The Long and Short of It: GameStop and Other Market Squeezes. Reuters

Reuters. (2008, July 18). Wirecard Accuses Shareholder Group of Wrongdoing. Retrieved September 14, 2024, from https://www.reuters.com/article/germany-wirecard-idINL1891001820080718/

Reuters. (2021, March 16). Timeline: The Rise and Fall of Wirecard, a German Tech Champion. Reuters. Retrieved September 14, 2024, from https://www.reuters.com/article/technology/timeline-the-rise-and-fall-of-wirecard-a-german-tech-champion-idUSKBN2B811J/

Wirecard AG. (2004, December 15). Börsengang der Wire Card AG. Retrieved September 14, 2024, from https://www.pressebox.de/inaktiv/wirecard-ag-aschheim/Boersengang-der-Wire-Card-AG/boxid/28593

Wirecard AG. (2019, September 12). Corporate News. Retrieved September 14, 2024, from- https://www.wirecard.com/wp-content/uploads/2021/01/120919-Wirecard-AG-successfully_EN.pdf

# 30

# Using Short Selling to Realize Corporate Fraud Exposure Capital Gains

## 30.1 Understanding the Mechanics of Short Selling

Short selling is basically borrowing stocks, and selling them at a high price, with the intention of acquiring them later, at an (anticipated) lower price, returning the stock to the lender and profiting from the price difference. Short selling is often conducted on margin, where the investor only puts up collateral for part of the value in the transaction.

Short selling is associated with major risks that are not present in long positions and involves additional costs not existing in long positions. Risks and costs can be both volatile and substantial and eat away the proceeds of the short if not conducted in a thorough manner.

Here is a basic example of short selling the fictitious Fraudco Inc. company.

### 30.1.1 Profit Scenario:

- **Borrow the shares**: Investor borrows 1000 shares of Fraudco Inc. from her broker.
- **Sell Fraudco Inc.** Investor sells shares on the stock market, at $5 and receives $5000 (1000 shares*$5/share).
- **Wait for the price to drop**: When the fraud is exposed, the price of Fraudco Inc. drops to $0.001 per share.
- **Buy the shares back**: Investor buys 1000 shares of Fraudco Inc. on the market for $1 (1000 shares*$0.001/share).



J. Sørensen, *Shorting Fraud*, https://doi.org/10.1007/978-3-031-81834-9_30

- **Return the shares**: Investor returns the borrowed 1000 shares of Fraudco Inc. to her broker.
- **Profit**: Investor initially received $5000 from selling the borrowed shares and then spent $1 to buy them back. So, the profit is **$4999** ($5000–$1), minus any fees or interest paid to the broker for borrowing the shares.

**The potential risks of profit and losses in short selling**
A share price cannot be negative; therefore, the investor's gain is always capped at maximum 100% or in the above example $5000 if the price of the share hit $0. On the other hand, if the share price moves the other way, there are no limitations to the investor's losses. If instead the share price rallied to $15 per share, the loss would be.

## 30.1.2 Short sale loss Scenario:

- **Borrow the shares**: Investor borrows 1000 shares of Fraudco Inc. from the broker.
- **Sell Fraudco Inc. shares on the stock market**: Investor sells the borrowed shares on the stock market and receives $5000 (1000 shares*$5/share).
- **Wait for the price to drop**: Contrary to investor predictions, the price of Fraudco Inc. increases to $15 per share, instead of dropping. The investor is forced to close the position.
- **Buy the shares back**: Investor buys 1000 shares of Fraudco Inc. on the open market for $15,000 (1000 shares*$15/share).
- **Return the shares**: Investor returns the 1000 shares of Fraudco Inc. to the broker.
- **Loss**: Investor initially received $5000 from selling the borrowed shares and then spent $15,000 to buy them back. So, the loss is $10,000 ($15,000–$5000), plus any fees or interest paid to the broker for borrowing the shares.

As seen from below this is a percentage loss of 200%.

$$\text{Percentage Loss} = \frac{(\text{Buyback Price} - \text{Initial Selling Price})}{\text{Initial Selling Price}} \times 100,$$

$$\frac{(15-5)}{5} \times 100 = 200\% \qquad (30.1)$$

## 30.2 Risks Associated with Fraud Shorting

In addition to the threat of a short squeeze discussed in Sect. 29.1.2. Also, just an ordinary general market rally might be a risk to the short strategy. Depending on the individual strategy a sharp rise, trading on margin, could lead to margin calls, and if investors cannot put up collateral, they must close positions at a most inconvenient time leading to losses.

There are some general risks. Takeover of the fraudulent company. If the corporate fraud is not considered devastating, another company or related (dubious) party might want to take over. This means a potential rebound in the price, which theoretically could end up higher.

In addition, there could be liquidity risks (few sellers), day gaps (major price jumps), bad bid-offer spreads (costly to close) and inconsistent volume (hard to exit), all jeopardizing the profitability of the short position.

The short position could already be overcrowded if the investor is a late-comer to the "party." This increases the risk of a potential squeeze. E.g. cheap penny stocks have a risk of retail-investor driven sudden wild price spikes.

Depending on the jurisdiction there might also be rules limiting the usage of short sales, which might come into effect suddenly, for a briefer or longer period.

There could also be special situations, with e.g. corporate actions or regulatory actions that require a premature buy-in, where the lender is forced to recall the stock at a most inconvenient time for the short seller.

Minimizing risks with stop-out orders. Like stop loss orders in long positions. A short seller could place a stop-out order. If the share price rises and reaches the stop-out price, the broker automatically repurchases the shares and closes the short position. This will limit the losses. However, with fast-moving prices and in cases of short squeezes the execution price can be much higher than the stop-out.

## 30.3 Revisit risks in Wirecard Fraud

Revisiting the Wirecard Fraud case in Sect. 29.1.3. Imagine an investor had shorted Wirecard around May 2008, along with the first major red flag from the investor association. At a share price of about 10. The investor had taken the short position, expecting the fraud to be revealed, the CEO arrested, and the company to go bankrupt, resulting in the share price dropping to zero. Stubbornly, the investor, knowing this was an obvious fraud, held onto the short position. Time passes, nothing happens. The next ten years the share price grew to 200, topping in September 2018. If we look at the return on this Fraud Short Strategy at the top in 2018, the return would be negative 1900% of the initial investment as seen in equation.

$$\text{Percentage Loss} = \left(\frac{\text{Loss}}{\text{Short Price}}\right) \times 100, \left(\frac{190}{10}\right) \times 100 = 1900\% \tag{30.2}$$

So, while the investor fifteen years down the line would be right, in the short and medium term it would not have been a sensible strategy to short and "hold." The investor would have had to move in and out of the short position until the endgame in 2020—or time the investment for the end game.

Now let us imagine that the German authorities and auditors looked through the fraud already in 2008, and Wirecard had gone bankrupt in 2008, sending the price to zero in the Summer of 2008 and the investor would have pocketed a 100% profit from the investment in a few months.

From a percentage return point of view that would have been:

$$\text{Percentage Profit} = \left(\frac{\text{Profit}}{\text{Short Price}} \times 100\right) = \left(\frac{10}{10} \times 100\right) = 100\% \tag{30.3}$$

## 30.4 The Costs of Short Selling—Negative Carry

Besides the risks, the factor of costs related to short selling should also be considered. Sometimes referred to as negative carry. When a short seller borrows a share to sell, they are charged a borrowing fee by the lender of the stock. Borrowing fees compensate the lender for lending out their shares. The longer time the short position is held, the higher these borrowing costs. Borrowing fees will vary between the stocks borrowed. The fee typically ranges between 0.5% to 3% of the borrowed amount on an annualized basis but can be much higher. The size of the fee will vary with the availability of the borrowed share. In other words, how many short sellers want the stock, how liquid is it, etc.

D'Avolio (2002) found shares can be divided in three categories with regards to Cost to Borrow (CTB).

- *General collateral shares,* which make up 91% of shares. These General shares cost less than 1% per annum in borrowing fees.
- *Special shares* consist *of less than* 9% of shares. They have a cost above 1% per annum to borrow, with a median of 4.5% p.a.
- *Extremely Special shares*: A very small fraction of less than 1% of shares on loan, has fees exceeding the risk-free rate by far, with examples as high as 50% & 35% for Krispy Kreme & Palm Inc.

From Table 30.1 more recent examples of high cost to borrow can be seen. Note that the Fraud Shorting of Nikola (NKLA), the fraudulent EV company described in Sect. 18.10.1 had a 33% cost to borrow rate.

A recent paper by Daniel et al. (2024) highlights the importance of costs related to short selling. While the study found that over 60% of U.S. common stocks had an annualized indicative borrowing fee of less than 1%, the average indicative lending fee for small-cap stocks increased from 2.8% in 2010 to near 40% in 2023. Also, for the most extreme "special" shares, the annualized fee may exceed 1000%. This is more than 80% monthly. In such high-cost cases the holding periods should be brief, and the price decline significant to even cover these costs.

If the share pays dividends, the short seller is responsible for covering those dividends payments. When dividends are distributed, the short seller must compensate the lender for the missed dividends income. Dividends vary by factors as country, industry, and company. In Table 30.2 one can see dividends examples by industry.

If we look globally there are outliers with much higher dividends yields, illustrated in Table 30.3.

In the case that the investor invests borrowed funds, the investor must also pay interest expenses or margin interests. These costs will vary with the investor type, broker, and financial situation.

**Table 30.1** High cost to borrow examples December 2022. (*Source* Business Insider [2022, 17 Dec])

| Ticker | MMAT | BYND | MSTR | DWAC | NKLA | GOEV | BLNK | UPST | FSR | AMC |
|---|---|---|---|---|---|---|---|---|---|---|
| Cost % | 117.1% | 97.8% | 54.6% | 49.6% | 33.1% | 29.1% | 25.6% | 24.3% | 22.1% | 21.8% |

**Table 30.2** The average S&P 500 dividends yields. (*Source* O'brien [2020])

| Sector | Materials | Goods | Financial | Healthcare | Industrial | Technology | Utilities |
|---|---|---|---|---|---|---|---|
| Dividends | 2.50% | 2.50% | 2.50% | 1.75% | 2.00% | 1.50% | 3.70% |

**Table 30.3** Top 5 dividends yields in the World—08–31-2023. (*Source* Dividends ranking [2023, Aug 31])

| Company | Dividend | Country | Sector |
|---|---|---|---|
| Evergreen Marine | 65.73% | Taiwan | Industrial Transportation |
| Sud Americana Vapore | 48.96% | Colombia | Industrial Transportation |
| Yang Ming Marine Tra | 47.34% | Taiwan | Industrial Transportation |
| China COSCO Holdings | 45.43% | China | Industrial Transportation |
| Tambang Batubara Buk | 38.25% | Indonesia | Mining |

Just like any other stock trade, short selling incurs transaction costs, including brokerage commissions and transaction fees. A fee when the short position is taken and once again when the short position is covered.

Summing up, the investor needs to understand the total costs behind the short sale strategy before engaging. The breakeven for the barebone financial costs may vary considerably between the different cases. In some cases, the trading costs of the short sale campaign might cannibalize all the capital gains from even the most successful short campaign.

## References

Business Insider. (2022, December 17). Top 10 Highest Short Interest Stocks And 10 With Highest Cost To Borrow: Where Do Carvana, MicroStrategy, Fisker And AMC Rank? Retrieved September 14, 2024, from https://markets.businessinsider.com/news/stocks/top-10-highest-short-interest-stocks-and-10-with-highest-cost-to-borrow-where-do-carvana-microstrategy-fisker-and-amc-rank-1031978494

D'Avolio, G. (2002). The Market for Borrowing Stock. *Journal of Financial Economics, 66*(2–3), 271–306. Retrieved September 14, 2024, from https://papers.ssrn.com/sol3/papers.cfm?abstract_id=305479

Daniel, K. D., Klos, A., & Rottke, S. (2024). Optimists, Pessimists and Stock Prices. *Annual Review of Financial Economics*. Retrieved September 14, 2024, from https://doi.org/10.2139/ssrn.4700311

Dividends Ranking. (2023, August 31). Highest World Dividend Stocks. Retrieved September 14, 2024, from http://www.dividendsranking.com/highest-world-dividends.php

O'Brien, S. (2020). Comparing Average Dividend Yield by Sector. Retrieved September 14, 2024, from https://www.dividend.com/how-to-invest/comparing-dividend-stock-sectors-by-yield/

# 31

# Using Other Financial Instruments to Realize Corporate Fraud Exposure Capital Gains

## 31.1 Choosing a Fraud Short Strategy

The investor might utilize other financial instruments as an alternative to short selling. While these are more complicated to understand, they can also be tailored to the investor's individual expectations and risk profile. Using e.g. options the investor might not have to stop out, in the case of a temporary short squeeze, before eventual corporate collapse.

The availability of these alternative financial instruments will vary with several factors. Including the jurisdiction and type of investor. Some may only be available to highly professional and institutional investors. This has an impact on which tailored strategies the investor can make, and the costs of the strategies.

When choosing a fraud short strategy, the investor should consider two basic factors regarding the collapse of the share price, and the potential collapse of the company.

- How much will the share price drop—total wipeout or only a significant drop?
- How fast will the price drop—hours, days, weeks, months, years, or decades?

As we saw in the Wirecard example, it took decades of rising share prices before the swift collapse over a couple of days in June 2020. Looking at other corporate fraud examples in Table 31.1, it shows that the corporate fraud


J. Sørensen, *Shorting Fraud*, https://doi.org/10.1007/978-3-031-81834-9_31

**Table 31.1** Different share price collapses in different fraudulent companies. (*Sources* NYSE, NASDAQ & TSX)

| Company name | Year | Description |
|---|---|---|
| Luckin Coffee | 2020 | Share price collapsed from over $50 to below $1 within **months** |
| Nikola Corporation | 2020 | Stock price dropped from over $80 to around $20 within **weeks** |
| Valeant Pharmaceuticals | 2015 | Stock price fell from over $250 to around $10 within a **year** |
| Sino-Forest Corporation | 2011 | Shares collapsed from over $25 to near zero within **months** |
| Satyam Computer Services | 2009 | Share price collapsed nearly 94% within **days** |

collapse might play out differently, at different paces and, ending at different price levels.

The investor needs to understand the path the collapse may take, how much leverage and risk of being temporarily wrong to take. An effective way to have it all come together is by putting up "playout" scenarios. With different actions taken as the collapse unfolds in different directions, at different paces. Then adapt the strategy as the collapse unfolds.

In the below sections are outlined some of the financial instruments that might be used in the connection of fraud short investments. Financial Instruments to capture the capital gains of the collapsing share price. Usage of each of the instruments depends on the expected situation of the collapse and the risk /reward profile of the individual investor.

## 31.2 Short Selling with a Call Option Protection

This strategy is a combination of a short sale and a hedge with a call option. Even in cases where the short seller is 100% right about the fraud, there is a risk that an abrupt stock market rally or short squeeze imposes a sudden, substantial loss to the shorting strategy. Fraud shorts are not only about being right, but the market must also realize the investor is right, as we saw with Wirecard.

A call option is a basic right, not the obligation, to acquire the reference share at an agreed price (the strike price) on or before a specific expiration date. This may be used to stop losses by hedging a fraud short selling strategy that goes the wrong way.

- The investor first shorts the stock with a normal short sale.

- At the same time the investor buys a call option for the same stock.
- This option gives the investor the right to buy the shorted stock at a predetermined price.
- If the stock unexpectedly soars, the short seller, might have to buy the stock back with a loss, to cover his position, but will be offset by the call option on the same stock.
- This strategy helps mitigating the potentially unlimited losses that comes with short selling.

Let us re-do our loss scenario.

- A fraud short seller believes the share of Fraudco Inc., trading at $5, is overvalued and will decrease in price. The investor decides to short sell 1000 shares of Fraudco Inc. This means the investor borrows 1000 shares from a broker and sells them on the market for a total of $5000.
- At the same time, the investor buys a call option for Fraudco Inc. at a strike price of $10, which expires a month from now. The call option costs the investor a premium of $0.5 per share, so for 1000 shares, the total cost is $500.
- If the stock price of Fraudco Inc. unexpectedly soars to $15, the short seller would have to buy the stock back at this higher price to cover his position. This would cost $15,000 (1000 shares*$15/share), resulting in a loss of $10,000 ($15,000–$5000).
- However, because the investor bought a call option, they have the right to buy the stock at the predetermined price of $10. So, instead of buying the stock at the market price of $15, the investor may exercise the call option and acquire the stock at $10. This would cost $10,000 (1000 shares*$10/share).
- Therefore, by using this strategy, the investor's loss is limited to $5500 ($10,000–$5000+$500 premium for the call option), instead of $10,000. This strategy helps mitigate the potentially unlimited losses that come with short selling, capping it at $5500.

## 31.3 Long Put Options

Put options offer another way to invest in a collapsing share price, in a long put strategy. A put option is a financial instrument, which gives the investor a right, but not the obligation, to sell a specific stock at a prearranged strike price within a specified period. This is a less risky way to invest in a short strategy expecting the company to collapse. In the put option strategy the investor can maximum lose the premium paid for the options. Short selling offers higher profit potential with unlimited risk, while put options provide limited risk but potentially lower profits.

### 31.3.1 Long Put Option Profit Scenario

Let us redo the short sale profit scenario where Fraudco. Inc. is exposed and the share price collapses. In this example we pay a put option premium of $0.50 per share. The scenario would play out the following way.

- The investor buys a put option for 1000 shares of Fraudco Inc. with a strike price of $5 per share. The premium for this option is $0.50 per share, so the total cost for the option is $500 (1000 shares*$0.50/share).
- When the fraud is exposed, the price of Fraudco Inc. drops to $0 per share. The investor exercises the put option. The investor gets $5000 from exercising the put option. After subtracting the $500 premium, the net profit is $4500.

The risk is limited to the premium paid if the stock price does not drop as expected which the next put loss scenario illustrates.

### 31.3.2 Long Put Option Loss Scenario

In this scenario, which is comparable to the short selling loss scenario, instead of collapsing, the price of the company rises to $15.

- The investor buys a put option on 1000 shares of Fraudco Inc. with a strike price of $5 per share. The cost of the option (the premium) is $0.5 per share paying $500 (1000 shares*$0.5/share).
- Contrary to the investor's prediction, the price of Fraudco Inc. increases to $15 per share.
- Since the market price is higher than the strike price, the put option expires worthless. The investor does not exercise the option.
- The total loss is the premium the investor paid for the option, which is $500.

The loss when this short strategy fails is $500, which is significantly less than the $10,000 loss in the short selling scenario we initially saw in Sect. 30.1.2.

### 31.3.3 Long Put Option Out of the Money

In the case of an expected collapse, the investor also has the opportunity to use the Out-of-the-Money (OTM) put option, which is a put option with a strike price that is lower than the current market price of the underlying stock. If the investor exercises it now, it would not be profitable, because the share price is higher than the strike. However, the OTM would become profitable if the share plummets below the strike price in a fraud collapse before the option expires.

So, the value of the OTM is decided by theta (time decay). How deep the put option should be OTM, depends on the investor's specific expectations and risk tolerance. A put option just OTM will have a higher premium than one that is more deeply OTM. However, the just OTM also has a higher probability of becoming In-the-Money and profitable if the share price decreases. A put option more deeply OTM will be cheaper, but it will require a larger decrease in the stock price to become profitable.

## 31.4 A Bear Put Spread Option Strategy

This short position strategy might be used if moderate price declines are expected, but not a total wipeout of the share. For example, in the case it is not expected that the fraud will make the company totally collapse, the company may continue in some form, e.g. with new top management, restructured.

In a bear put spread strategy, the investor simultaneously buys and sells put options on the same stock. The options have the same expiration date, but at different strike prices. The investor acquires the put with the higher strike price and sells the put with the lower strike price. The strategy caps both potential loss and profit. The maximum profit is the difference in strike prices, adjusted for the cost of the options, while the maximum loss is the cost of the options.

Here is a breakdown of an example:

- The Fraudco Inc. share currently trades at $5.

- The investor buys a put option at a strike price of $6 with a premium of $0.50, giving a right to sell the stock at $6.
- Simultaneously, the investor sells a put option at a strike price of $4 and receives a premium of $0.25. This obliges the investor to buy the stock at $4 if the option is exercised.

If the share price falls to $2.50:

- The bought put option allows the investor to sell the stock at $6, generating a profit of $3.00 per share ($6–$2.50–$0.50).
- The sold put option obligates the investor to buy the stock at $4, resulting in a loss of $1.25 per share ($4–$2.50–$0.25).
- The net profit from this strategy is $1.75 per share ($3.00–$1.25).

If the stock price drops to $0.5:

- The investor exercises the right to sell the stock at $6, even though its market value is now $0.5. This generates a profit of $6–$0.5 (stock price)-$0.50 (premium)=$5.00 per share.
- The investor is required to acquire the share at $4. Since the current market price is $0.5, this results in a loss of $4–$0.5 (stock price)-$0.25 (premium)=$3.25 per share.
- The profit on bought put ($5.00) outweighs the loss on the sold put ($3.25), for a net profit of $1.75 per share.

If stock price rises to $10

- The investor has the right to sell the stock at $6. However, since the market price is $10, this option is "out of the money" and it would not make sense for the investor to exercise it. Therefore, the investor loses the premium paid for this option, which is $0.50 per share.
- The investor is required to acquire the share at $4 if the option is exercised. However, since the market price is $10, it is not profitable for the option holder to exercise the option. Therefore, the option is not exercised, and the investor retains the premium for selling this option, which is $0.25 per share.
- Net loss for the investor is the difference in premiums-$0.50-$0.25=$ 0.25 per share

**The bear put spread example in summary**
The bear put spread strategy starts making money when the stock price of Fraudco Inc. drops below the acquired put option's strike price, after accounting for the net premium paid. It starts losing money when the price of the stock is above the strike price of the bought put option, up to the point of the net premium paid.

In this case:

- The strike price of the bought Fraudco Inc. put option is $6 and the net premium paid is $0.25 ($0.50–$0.25).
- So, the strategy starts making money when the stock price falls below $6–$0.25=$5.75.
- The maximum profit of $1.75 is achieved when the stock price is at or below the strike price of the sold put option, which is $4.
- If the stock price is above $6, the options expire worthless and the loss is the net premium costs, which is $0.25.

## 31.5 Other Option Strategies

The investor might tailor and execute various other options strategies related to profiting from the corporate collapse, depending on how the collapse is expected to play out. A few others are:

- **Put Backspreads**—It profits from significant declines in the share price, compared to the bear put spread.
- **Put Spread Collars**—right when the investor anticipates a significant decline but wants well-defined risk. The investor believes the price will drop considerably but wants to limit potential losses if the investor is wrong.
- **Synthetic Short Stock**—right when the investor is unsure about the timing of the collapse and is expecting low volatility in the share price.

## 31.6 Single Stock Futures

A single stock future (SSF) is a financial instrument tied to the underlying stock. It is a leveraged instrument conducted on margin. With a margin requirement ranging from 10 to 20%, and $100,000 in investment account, investors could short SSFs equivalent to a value ranging from about \$500,000 (at 20% margin) to about \$1,000,000 (at 10% margin). This means, depending on the margin requirement, the investor is controlling a stock value that is approximately 5 to 10 times more than the capital invested.

SSFs have some similarities to options, but also some differences. Both types of instruments derive their value from the underlying stock and may be used to hedge or speculate. Main differences are that the SSF is a contract that obligates the buyer to purchase the underlying stock at a specific set price by the expiration date. Whereas the option holder has the right, but not the contractual obligation to do the same.

SSFs are more directly tied to the underlying stock, whereas the options have other factors like time to expiration, volatility, etc. The exercise and settlement are also different—as are availability and liquidity of the instrument. Options tend to be more available in more shares and the option instrument is generally more liquid than SSF.

A single stock future theoretically has unlimited loss potential. However, it is a contract settled daily and stopped out if margin calls are not met. Therefore, they do not compare directly to the short sale since the investor does not "physically" need to return the share.

Once again, the investor is sure that shares of Fraudco Inc. are overvalued, due to indications of fraudulent activities, facing a collapse. However, the investor is worried about the unlimited risk potential of traditional short selling, since the company has a charismatic CEO that several times has been able to inflate the share price (at least temporarily) with mere pep talk. Below, the realization of the Corporate Fraud Exposure Capital Gain is generated with the help of the SSF.

Example of Single Stock Futures strategy

- The investor has \$100,000 in the margin account with a margin requirement of 20%.
- The investor shorts a Single Stock Future (SSF) on Fraudco. Inc, which is currently trading at \$5.
- The investor may buy \$500,000 worth of SSFs (5 times leverage).

Scenario 1—The company collapses
The investor prediction is correct and the price of Fraudco Inc. drops to \$0.10 by the contract's expiration date. The investor can now buy 100,000 shares at the new market price of \$0.10 per share, costing \$10,000.

The investor delivers these shares as per the futures contract and receives \$500,000 (100,000 shares*\$5/share), resulting in a gross profit of \$490,000 (\$500,000–\$10,000).

Scenario 2—The company value rises

The price of Fraudco Inc. rises to \$7 by the expiration date, then the investor must deliver 100,000 shares at the agreed price of \$5 per share. They will have to buy 100,000 shares at the new market price of \$7 per share, costing them \$700,000. They then deliver these shares as per the futures contract and receive \$500,000, resulting in a gross loss of \$200,000 (\$500,000–\$700,000).

However, the position would be stopped out (i.e., automatically closed by the broker) if the stock price rises to \$6.25, as investors would need \$125,000 (20% of \$625,000) to maintain the position, exceeding account balance. The stop out loss at \$6.25. The loss is the gap between the price at which the investor shorted the SSFs and the price at which the broker bought them back to close the position. In this case, the loss would be \$1.25 per share (\$6.25–\$5.00), or \$125,000 for 100,000 shares.

## 31.7 Forwards

Forwards are sharing some similarities with futures. A forward is a contract between two private parties to sell or buy an asset at a specified price in the future. In contrast to futures, they are not traded on an exchange.

If there is no traded future or other suitable derivatives available, the investor might use a forward contract for shorting.

In the short case, the investor may sell the stock at a future date at today's price. If the price drops the investor can acquire the share at the lesser price and sell at today's price and pocket the difference.

They share some of the same risks as futures. However, there are also other risks. They are over-the-counter, so there is little or no liquidity, which means they may be hard or impossible to get out of if things go in the opposite direction. Futures are settled daily, and forwards are settled on the specific future date.

Also, the counterparty risks if the counterparty cannot honor the agreement. Because of the counterparty risk, short forwards are limited to a narrow group of investors.

## 31.8 Contracts for Difference (CFDs)

Contract for Difference (CFDs) are contracts which allow the investor to speculate the future price of the asset (in this case a stock), while the investor does not have to own the underlying stock. They are leveraged products, and illegal in some jurisdictions. Only 10% or less may be required as margin.

- The investor basically bets on if the stock goes up or down.
- In the case of a fraudulent company, the investor would open a short CFD and bet on a price fall.
- When investor closes the CFD trade she makes a profit if price fell or takes a loss if the price rose.

The general accessibility (in some jurisdictions), the liquidity and potential of highly leveraged bets, might make them suitable for some investors. Especially investors who speculate in the short-term or ultra short-term. This could be market reactions to the publication fraud reports in the minutes and hours following the release of the report. The investor may profit fast, but also lose as fast if the trade goes even temporarily against the investor.

## 31.9 Spread Betting

Spread betting is a tool normally used by retail investors but may be used by the professional investor if there are limitations on other potential instruments conducting a fraud short investment. Spread betting is a variation of derivatives trading that allows the investor to speculate on the price movements in assets. This financial instrument is available in a limited number of jurisdictions.

When the investor shorts a share using spread betting, the investor bets that the price of a share will fall. The capital gain or loss is determined by how *accurate* the investor's prediction is.

The investor does not acquire the underlying share. Instead, the investor determines a stake per point of movement in the share. Where the point is the unit used to determine the price movement of the share. For simplicity let us assume $1. The investor then places a stake for each price point movement. Let us say the investor's stake is $1000. This means that each time the share moves $1 up or down, the investor either loses or gains $1000, depending on the direction of the bet.

A spread consists of two prices. First, the buy or bid price. The higher price at which the investor can buy (go long) on the market. Second, the sell or ask price. The lower price at which the investor can sell (go short) on the market. For simplicity let us say the current price is $5, the bid price is $6 and the ask price is $4. The investor opens a sell (short) position at 4$. Here is a simplified example of how the investor might short Fraudco Inc. using spread betting:

- Fraudco Inc. is currently trading at a share price of $5. The investor found that Fraudco Inc. is fraudulent, which will be exposed, expecting the share price to plummet.
- The investor decides to place a spread bet before the exposure, shorting Fraudco Inc. The investor decides to risk $1000 per point (in this case, a point is $1 movement in the share price).
- Fraudco Inc. is exposed as a fraud, and its share price drops from $5 to $0.
- The investor went short, so for every point the price dropped, the investor gains $1000. The price dropped 4 points (from $4 to $0), so the investor would make a profit of $1000*4=$4000.

## 31.10 Inverse Single Stock ETFs

Inverse Single Stock exchange-traded funds (ETFs) are a special type of ETFs that are designed to profit from the opposite direction of the underlying stock. This means when the underlying stock falls, the Inverse ETF rises in value. These ETFs may be leveraged by a factor, are daily reset and hence short term in focus. Currently very few listed companies are offered as inverse Single Stock ETFs. Only major ones like Alphabet, Tesla and Nvidia. These are highly liquid, but then again only useful if the investor has found a major fraudulent company as a fraud target.

## 31.11 Credit Default Swaps (CDS)

Credit default swaps (CDS) are a type of derivative that resembles an insurance contract that protects the buyer from the risk of default on a debt obligation.

The seller of a CDS agrees to make payments to the buyer if the issuer of the debt (the company) defaults. This can be used to profit from an expected decline in the creditworthiness of a company or bankruptcy, subsequently to the release of a fraud report.

In the case of a fraudulent company collapsing there is a high likelihood it will not be able to repay its debt. For instance, when balance sheet manipulation has inflated assets far beyond reality, and cash flow from operations is not there, there is no collateral or cash to service the outstanding debt.

Engaging in a "naked" CDS (not holding debt in the company) from a short fraud perspective is betting that the company will default partly on debt or go entirely bankrupt.

Here is a basic example of how the investor might use a CDS to bet on Fraudco Inc. going down due to fraud:

- Let us assume face value of the corporate bonds are $10 million.
- Investor buys CDS from a seller, which is essentially an insurance policy on the bonds issued by Fraudco Inc. The investor pays a regular premium to the seller for this coverage. Like annually 2% of $10,000,000=$200,000 per year. The coverage paid semi-annually in this example.
- When Fraudco Inc. is exposed a quarter later for fraud it goes bankrupt and defaults on the debt
- The seller of the CDS is obligated to compensate the investor for the loss in value of the bonds, which is $10,000,000.
- The compensation received from the CDS due to the default is $10,000,000. The cost is the semi-annually premium of $100,000. The net profit is $9,900,000.

## 31.12 Equity Swaps

An equity swap is a derivative contract that lets the investor trade the performance of a stock without having to own the underlying equity.

The swap involves an agreement between two parties, swapping the risk and return on e.g. a specific share. Here is how to mimic short selling using equity swaps.

- Investor A, who wants the short exposure, pays a variable total return based on the performance of the specific stock to Investor B. This includes the dividend and capital gains.
- Investor B pays fixed/floating interest rate to Investor A and share price losses.

Investor A, holding the "short leg" of the swap benefits if the underlying stock goes down in value, as the variable payments will decrease. This mirrors a short position's profit. This strategy can be used in cases where there are shorting restrictions, to avoid bottlenecks or costs in stock borrowing. Below is a practical simplified example of the collapse of Fraudco Inc.

Initial Conditions:

- Fraudco Inc. Share Price: $5.
- The Equity Swap Notional Amount represents the equivalent of 1000 shares of Fraudco for a total value of $5000.
- Fixed/Floating Rate: Investor B agrees to pay Investor A a fixed interest rate of 2% per year.

Scenario (1)—Fraudco Inc. collapses to a price of $0.

- Investor A (Short Seller):
  1. Investor A no longer needs to make variable payments based on Fraudco's performance, since the stock is worthless.
  2. Investor A still earns the fixed interest rate of 2% from Investor B on the $5000 notional amount, which is $100 for the year).
  3. Assuming no transaction costs, Investor A has a net profit of $5100 ($5000 from the stock decline and $100 in interest).

- Investor B (Long Investor):
  1. Investor B no longer receives any variable return based on the stock's price.
  2. Investor B must continue to pay the fixed interest rate of 2% to Investor A.
  3. Investor B incurs a net loss of $5100 ($5000 from the stock decline and $100 in interest payments.

## 31.13 Binary Options

Binary options are financial instruments often associated with retail investors. Binary options are banned in multiple jurisdictions because of the high risk and similarities to gambling with the all or nothing nature of the instrument. Like betting on black or red at the roulette table—you win or lose.

A binary option is a bet on a price movement in a simple yes or no way. Has the asset passed a certain strike price (threshold) at a specific point in time (expiry time)—a simple yes or no question. If yes, the investor won the binary bet and is paid out the fixed return. If not, the investor lost the bet and all the money at stake. Binary options have a substantial risk, but also a high return rate of 70%–95%.

If other financial instruments are not possible, binary options might be considered, since the fraud short investor from a risk point of view has an advantage, compared to the average binary options investor. The fraud short investor knows it is more likely that the ball will land on "red" or "black", when the research report is published.

Here is an example.

- Fraudco Inc. currently trades at $5. However, the investor has found that the company is fraudulent in nature and will expose this to the world. Before, the investor places a bet of $5000 buying a binary put option with a strike price of $4, expiring by the end of the day.
- The fraud is exposed during the day and the share price of Fraudco Inc. drops to $2.75 at close.
- This is below the strike price of $4 and the investor payout is $9250, corresponding to a return rate of 85%.

## 31.14 Pairs Trading

Normally pairs trading is a market neutral strategy. Pairs trading is conducted by taking offsetting long and short positions in two stocks that are historically correlated.

The goal is to profit from temporary divergences in the price relationship between the pairs, regardless of overall market direction.

In pairs trading, the investor can invest in competitive companies, which are correlated historically. Examples could be Coca Cola / Pepsi Cola or Visa / Mastercard.

In the case of the fraud short the investor expects that these patterns between e.g. competitors to the fraudulent company will diverge after the release of the fraud report. The investor constructs a pair trade taking benefit of this divergent assumption. The investor knows one company is fraudulent, while its competitors are supposed to be legitimate. The investor could construct a pairs trade assuming the fraud exposure will hurt the fraudulent company's stock, meanwhile the competitors might benefit due to less competition, increased market share, general re-balancing of investors' portfolios, etc.

Example:

- Short the fraudulent company
- Long the competitor, which the investor expects to perform better in comparison.
- If the investor expectations play out, the spread between the two stocks would widen (fraudulent company's stock declines, competitors may rise), resulting in a profit on the investor pairs trade.

This risk is of course related to the divergence. If investors generally think the entire industry is fraudulent, subsequent to the fraud report, the competitors' shares will also tank.

## 31.15 Spillover Effect on Market Environment

The exposure of the fraud might not be limited to the fraudulent company itself. If the company is a significant player, and e.g. part of an index, it might also have an impact on the return of other financial instruments like ETFs. This was seen by the broader impact of the released Hindenburg Research (2023, January 24) fraud report, on companies in the Adani Group.

After the release of the Hindenburg report with allegations of material corporate fraud in the Adani Group, the companies suffered substantial share price drops. But not only the Adani Group companies suffered major price drops. Also, it was observed by Agarwal (2023) that the Indian benchmark indices, like the BSE Sensex and NIFTY 50 experienced significant declines in the immediate aftermath of the Hindenburg report.

The exposure of a fraud might have some complex impacts on returns, which impacts financially broader on the market than just the fraudulent target company.

On the one hand, the wipeout of a fraudulent competitor can mean that other competitors were undervalued. On the other hand, depending on the fraud, it might also have a negative impact that the investors start questioning other similar companies in the industry, or the broader economy.

Depending on which broader outcome the investor expects from the fraud, the investor may invest accordingly. If the investor expects the industry or broader indexes are getting hit, the investor could potentially short these too.

## References

Agarwal, N. (2023, January 27). Hindenburg Effect! Sensex Loses Over 870 Points: 8 Key Factors Behind the Selloff. *ETMarkets.com*. Retrieved September 14, 2024, from https://www.etmarkets.com

Hindenburg Research. (2023, January 24). Adani Group: How The World's 3rd Richest Man Is Pulling the Largest Con in Corporate History. Retrieved September 14, 2024, from https://web.archive.org/web/20240816174205/https://hindenburgresearch.com/adani/

# 32

# Financial Instruments to Capture Fraud Induced Volatility

## 32.1 Capturing Fraud-Induced Volatility

The financial instruments in Chapters 30 and 31 were used to try and realize the Corporate Fraud Exposure Capital Gain from the downward price correction or price implosion of a fraudulent company. However, there are more ways to extract capital gains from exposing corporate fraud.

In a perfect world, after the activist investor has revealed the fraud, everybody will agree and the price will correct to the underlying real value of the company, which might be close to zero in the total wipeout corporate fraud case. The world is not perfect. Some of the biggest fraud cases like Enron and Wirecard show that.

Releasing a fraud short report may play out in several ways over the time horizon. Even in the case where the company eventually collapses entirely, the final swan song may linger.

Top management is desperate to avoid having the fraud exposed. At the same time investors, regulators, and the public in general may have a tough time accepting their perception of reality as a fabricated mirage. This type of denial is commonly observed when working hands-on with corporate fraud.

On top of this, investors on the sidelines might be betting that the price implosion is an overreaction from the market, buying the dip, propping up the share price for shorter or longer periods.

Therefore, the tune of the company's swan song might be volatility. With fraudulent companies one might experience some sharp and extreme swings in the share price of the fraudulent company.



J. Sørensen, *Shorting Fraud*, https://doi.org/10.1007/978-3-031-81834-9_32

This volatility might not only be isolated to the fraudulent company share but have spillover effects. The spillover effect could be to other listed companies in the industry. If the fraudulent company has significant weight in e.g. share indexes and broader ETFs, it might even impact broader volatility instruments transiently.

## 32.2 Volatility Options Strategies on the Fraudulent Company

Focusing on making a return on volatility, in relation to the unmasking of the deceitful corporation, volatility options strategies may be used.

**A Long straddle strategy** involves simultaneously buying a call and put option. The two options both have the same strike price and expiration time. This way the investor benefits from significant share price swings in either direction, related to the fraud exposure. This investor is covered for both a potential selloff and chaotic rebounds typical of a collapsing stock. A basic example is below.

Before releasing the fraud report, the investor purchases a call and put option on Fraudco Inc. stock, both with a strike price of $5 and an expiration date in a month. The call option costs $0.50, and the put option costs $0.75, so the total premium is $1.25.

The fraud report is published, and Fraudco Inc. is exposed of the fraud, causing a massive stir in the market. The stock price becomes highly volatile.

- **Scenario 1**—Stock price drops: The stock price plummets to $2 due to the fraud news. The investor's call option expires worthless, but her put option is worth $3 ($5 strike price–$2 stock price). Subtracting the premium, she has made a profit of $1.75 ($3–$1.25).
- **Scenario 2**—Stock price rises: After an initial drop, surprisingly, the stock price jumps to $8, perhaps due to speculators or a takeover bid. The investor's put option expires worthless, but her call option is now worth $3 ($8 stock price - $5 strike price). Again, subtracting the premiums, she has made a profit of $1.75 ($3 - $1.25).

**A long strangle strategy** is somewhat like the long straddle strategy. The difference is that the investor purchases a put option with a lower strike price and simultaneously a call option with a higher strike price. This reduces the upfront premium cost but still benefits from sharp swings that are related to the exposure and aftermath of the fraud revelation.

Before releasing the fraud report: the investor purchases a put option with a strike price of $4 and a call option with a strike price of $6 on Fraudco Inc. The options both have an expiration date one month from now. The call option costs $0.40, and the put option costs $0.60, so the total premium is $1.

The fraud report is published and Fraudco Inc. is exposed of the fraud, causing a massive stir in the market. The stock price becomes highly volatile.

- **Scenario 1**—Stock price drops: The stock price plummets to $2 due to the fraud news. The investor's call option expires worthless, but her put option is now worth $2 ($4 strike price–$2 stock price). Subtracting her total premium, she made a profit of $1 ($2–$1).
- **Scenario 2**—Stock price rises: After an initial drop, surprisingly, the price jumps to $8, perhaps due to speculators or a takeover bid. The investor's put option expires worthless, but her call option is now worth $2 ($8 stock price–$6 strike price). Again, subtracting her total premium, she has made a profit of $1 ($2–$1).

Whether to choose straddle or strangle in relation to the fraud scenarios depends on the investor's expectations, how much volatility the fraud exposure will cause.

In addition to straddle and strangle strategies, other options strategies, which will not be treated in this book may be used depending on the expectation and circumstances around the individual fraud cases. These include, e.g. Long Call Butterfly Spread, Long Put Butterfly Spread, Long Guts, Short Iron Butterfly.

## 32.3 Volatility & Variance Swaps

Using volatility or variance swap strategies could be especially beneficial if the company has had a stable (fictitious) predictable growth and low share price volatility up to the fraud exposure.

Depending on the circumstances the investor might expect to see a much higher share price volatility after the fraud exposure, due to the uncertainty about the underlying stock, caused by the exposure of the corporate fraud. This new development in volatility might be captured by the investor using volatility or variance swaps.

**Volatility swaps** is betting on the volatility of the fraudulent share. The investor agrees on a fixed volatility strike. If the actual volatility of the fraudulent share turns out to be higher than the strike, the swap will be profitable for the investor.

The payoff is linear in volatility swaps. This means that if the realized volatility is higher than the strike volatility, the payoff increases proportionally to the share price fluctuations of the fraudulent share.

**Variance swaps** are similar derivatives directly betting on price fluctuations of the fraudulent share over a specified period. In the case of fraudulent companies, they might be used to make a return on the share price fluctuations after the fraud is exposed. Also, here before releasing the fraud report, the investor enters into a variance swap contract on the fraudulent share.

In basic terms the payoff in a variance swap is the difference between the actual realized variance of the share during the lifespan of the variance swap and a pre-settled fixed variance, also called the strike variance.

The payoff in variance swaps is quadratic. This means that the payoff of variance swaps accelerates as volatility grows.

The detailed, complex calculations of volatility and variance swaps may be found in e.g. (Bossu et al., 2005; Demeterfi et al., 1999).

Whether to use volatility or variance swaps depends on the investors risk profile and the expectancy of the fraudulent company's share price volatility. Due to the quadratic nature of variance swaps, if the investor expects large wild swings in fraudulent share price, variance swaps might be the choice. If the investor expects more gradual changes in the fraudulent share price, volatility swaps might be the choice.

## 32.4 Calendar Spreads in Fraud Shorting Cases

A calendar spread is a bet that a stock price will change volatility in the future, compared to today. One may profit from this strategy if the implied (market expected) volatility increases after the investor has entered the position.

This strategy is conducted by trading options in the fraudulent share. The investor simultaneously sells and buys options with same strike price but different expiration dates.

This strategy may be profitable with sudden volatility spikes, that in turn impact the pricing of options. These calendar spreads can take advantage of sudden volatility spikes caused by company-specific factors like corporate fraud exposure, which may have this shock effect on the volatility.

An example could be that an investor uncovers evidence of fraud within Fraudco Inc. and plans to publish a research report in the near future. The investor believes this will cause significant immediate uncertainty, a surge in implied volatility and a drop in Fraudco share price, leading to higher options prices.

In this scenario, a short calendar spread strategy might be profitable since the investor knows about the fraud before the market.

Before the publication of the fraud report, the investor might sell a longer dated put option on Fraudco Inc. Let us say a 3-month put option with a strike price near the current stock price. The investor receives a premium for selling this option.

The investor will also buy a shorter dated put option on Fraudco Inc. For example, a 1-month put option with the same strike price as the other option. The investor pays a premium for buying this option.

Then the investor publishes the fraud report, other investors panic and sell off shares in Fraudco Inc. The share price of Fraudco Inc. drops and volatility spikes. The value of both options increases, due to the higher implied volatility. The short-dated option increases in value more significantly, since it has a higher sensitivity to changes in volatility (gamma) due to its shorter time to expiration.

The investor closes the positions by buying back the long-dated option, and selling the short-dated option, securing a net gain.

In this case, the investor bets that the initial spike in volatility caused by the fraud announcement will eventually subside.

The timing of the fraud report, choice between the length of the spread, taking and closing positions is contingent on the investor's investment purposes, market expectations, and risk tolerance in the individual fraud case. This depends on what impact the investor expects the fraud revelation to have on the market participants in each case, over the time horizon.

## 32.5 Spillover to Other Volatility Instruments

As seen in the Adani Group case in Sect. 31.15, if the target company is big enough it might have an impact on the return of an index or ETF. Similarly, it might have impact or cascading effects on more broader volatility instruments like volatility ETFs or other exchange-traded notes (ETNs): VXX or UVXY, which track VIX futures. These instruments could spike if the investors' fraud report induces broader market volatility. The collapse of a major target company could contribute to a surge in these volatility instruments in a short or ultra short term.

## 32.6 Other Tailored Customized Derivatives

Customized derivatives in all shapes and forms allow investors to create all kinds of synthetic short positions on specific stocks, which are only limited by human imagination.

## References

Bossu, S., Strasser, E., & Guichard, R. (2005). Just what you need to know about variance swaps. JPMorgan Equity Derivatives Report. Retrieved December 7, 2023, from https://doi.org/10.13140/RG.2.2.30958.33609

Demeterfi, K., Derman, E., Kamal, M., & Zou, J. (1999). More than you ever wanted to know about volatility swaps. Goldman Sachs Quantitative Strategies Research Notes. Retrieved December 7, 2023, from https://www.researchgate.net/publication/246869706_More_Than_You_Ever_Wanted_to_Know_About_Volatility_Swaps

# 33

# Publication of the Fraud Short Report—Maximizing the Impact

## 33.1 Legal and Ethical Considerations

The results of the investor's general analysis, deep-dive investigations and collected evidence are all presented in a fraud short report also called a research report, outlining the corporate fraud thesis to the public.

The report must demonstrate that the investor understands the company and its current situation as well as (preferably better) than the management, the auditors, and other stakeholders of the company.

Before publication of the report there are several factors to consider. These should all help maximize the impact and minimize the risk of legal or other negative blowback against the short seller and the campaign. These factors include target audience, timing, ethical and legal considerations. The one general advice on these reports, is always stick to the facts that can be backed up by evidence and do not present falsehoods.

Short selling is a legal trading strategy in most jurisdictions, but there are several ways it can become illegal and legal advice should always be obtained before engaging. This is because the legal boundaries on this type of free speech in short reports might vary between jurisdictions.

Here are some of the major, but not all, examples of what to avoid conducting an activist fraud short campaign.

- **Insider Trading**: Using non-public material information to make trading decisions is illegal in most jurisdictions globally.


J. Sørensen, *Shorting Fraud*, https://doi.org/10.1007/978-3-031-81834-9_33

- **Coordination**: Short sellers should not coordinate their trades with one another since this might be considered market manipulation in some jurisdictions.
- **Do not promote fallacies**: Short sellers cannot mislead the public about the independence of their research. This could involve concealing relationships with other parties who stand to benefit from the stock price falling. Also means short sellers cannot conceal compensation they receive from other parties for publishing research. This is a conflict of interest that must be disclosed.
- **Do not publish falsehoods** about a public company to manipulate its stock price. That is not activist fraud shorting but an illegal "short and distort" scheme.

## 33.2 The Target Audience

Identify who would be most interested in the fraud report. These are mainly financial journalists and investors. Investors include both human investors and machines investing in the form of trading and investment algorithms.

## 33.3 The Content of the Report—Ethos, Logos and Pathos

Credibility (Ethos), Logic (Logos), and Emotion (Pathos) are the three main modes of persuasion described by Aristotle (350 BC, 1991), which may be used to influence an audience's perspective by the fraud report.

While Aristotle wrote solely for humans, the investor writes the fraud report for humans as well as machines. Hedge funds use alternative data streams in combination with traditional news sources feeding ML models that turn it into trading signals. This happens either in fully automatic algorithmic trading, human trading, or hybrid man/machine trading.

While humans may be influenced by emotions, ML models tend to focus mainly on logic and credibility and ignore the emotions. Therefore, focus on facts first. Since humans are still involved in the investment process emotional language may also be used, but only as support.

Highlight the mismanagement in severity order. While machines read everything, humans need the most telling and serious problems up front in bold. This could include discrepancies in financial reports, evidence of unethical practices and outright fraud.

Leverage informational advantages. These are the key findings on discrepancies in financial statements that nobody else found. The interviews conducted with industry experts undermining the actual state and potential of the corporation's products and services. The photos of the empty land plot where a factory should be.

Also, put up questions to the management on the inconsistencies and red flags found. In a format that may be easily answered by the management. At the same time, these questions may have other investors analyze and reassess the state of the company themselves.

Also put in questions or statements about both the loose ends and dead ends. This induces the investors or investigative journalists to do their own follow-up investigations. This way the fraud report is only the ignition point of a potential crowdsourced investigation and reporting effort. An effort that might grow into a wider investigative journalistic story, where the public is activated and more people may come forward, with facts supporting the original report.

These reports may vary considerably in length, style, language and content. Examples of how actual Research Reports look can be seen for informational purposes by reading Block (2024), Hindenburg Research (2024) and Scorpion Capital (2024). Note that these reports are illustrative examples for informational and educational purposes only and they are not a validation of the claims and content in the individual reports.

## 33.4 Publication Platforms

The fraud short campaign can utilize various media channels to distribute the report.

- Traditional media like newspapers, TV, and reputable websites with press releases tailored for journalists.
- Social media, with general investment forums and specific forums on short selling. Tailored campaigns using relevant hashtags, target influential accounts, etc.

The investor might hire professional media relations specialists to help with press releases, media advisories, and direct contact with journalists and media outlets. However, the basic advantage of a fraud research report is that its content is perfect for fast news diffusion. Besides the general urgency related to dealing with a short report—the research report also:

- Impacts the wealth of thousands of investors, employees, and stakeholders of the company.
- May have thousands of potential investors seeing an opportunity to profit from a corporate collapse.
- Is negative news, which spread faster than positive according to Fang and Ben-Miled (2017) & Bellovary et al. (2021).
- Is a scandal with a wow effect, catching the attention of the general public.

## 33.5 Report Teasers and Pre-Reads

Some short sellers use teasers to announce a big thing is going to be released at a specific point in time, to have maximum focus, without giving away the target.

Depending on the jurisdiction, pre-reads by credible journalists under embargo may also be an option. However, pre-reads should be handled with extreme care, since it may be considered a market violation of selective publication. Finally, some short sellers, in some jurisdictions may notify authorities before the publication.

## 33.6 Timing of the Release of the Short Report

There are several timing issues to consider with regards to the release of the report. Most importantly the investor needs to coordinate with the short investment strategy, align it with the general news cycle, and other firm-specific events coming up. Consider the following in relation to the release:

- Is there a specific event or news cycle that the fraud report could align with for peak relevance? Can the fraud report piggyback on upcoming focus and attention on the company?
- Financial instrument timing. If the investor e.g. uses a calendar spread, the investor might have the report release as close to the options expiry as possible.
- Corporate Events – earnings calls, quarterly releases. If an investor sees a pattern of hype around the quarterly results where the stock price pops, the investor could drop the fraud report here to get the most out of the short.

- Other events not related to the company. This is harder to predict. However, the investor might try to find sweet spots with less expected relevant news, avoiding the report drown in a sea of news.

## 33.7 The Rebuttals by the Target

As described in Sect. 20.5.1, in many cases the target company of the short will rebut the report, often in aggressive ways. Looking at rebuttals they most often use baseless allegations in the first rebuttals, along with red herrings and threats with lawsuits and lawyers. These rebuttals might cause price rebounds or short squeezes. The problem for the fraudulent target company, if the short report is based on facts, is the report cannot be rebutted with facts.

## 33.8 Follow Up Publications

Often after publication, the short seller might experience inflow of new information from other parties, like whistleblowers and former employees that will contact with new and more enlightened facts on the case. Pandora's box is open and anybody with a grudge against the company might step forward. Here it is important to do the fact checking, ethical and legal assessment before publishing a follow up.

## 33.9 Ethical and Legal Considerations

Have multiple actors verify details. Mistakes in a fraud report can undermine credibility and erode its impact. The target may focus on the short seller's small factual mistake in their rebuttals and skip the twenty other serious issues they cannot dismiss. Again, seek legal guidance before releasing the report, to see if there are any legal problems or sensitive issues that might be a risk, and make sure all the right disclaimers are in place.

## References

Aristotle. (350 BC, 1991). In: On Rhetoric: A Theory of Civic Discourse. (G. A. Kennedy, Trans.). New York, NY: Oxford University Press. (Original work published 350 BC)

Bellovary, A. K., Young, N. A., & Goldenberg, A. (2021). Left- and Right-Leaning News Organizations Use Negative Emotional Content and Elicit User Engagement Similarly. *Affective Science, 2*(4), 391–396, Retrieved September 14, 2024, from https://doi.org/10.1007/s42761-021-00046-w

Block, C. C. (2024). Eurofins Scientific: Optimized for Malfeasance. Muddy Waters Research. Retrieved September 14, 2024, from https://muddywatersresearch.com/wp-content/uploads/2024/06/Eurofins_OptimizedMalfeasance_20240624_sm.pdf

Fang, A., & Ben-Miled, Z. (2017). Does Bad News Spread Faster? 2017 International Conference on Computing, Networking and Communications (ICNC). https://doi.org/10.1109/iccnc.2017.7876232

Hindenburg Research. (2024). Equinix Exposed: Major Accounting Manipulation, Core Business Decay and Selling an AI Pipe Dream as Insiders Cashed Out Hundreds of Millions, Hindenburg Research. Retrieved September 14, 2024, from https://hindenburgresearch.com/equinix/

Scorpion Capital. (2024). *Japan's Most Actively Traded Stock is a Colossal Fraud and Ticking Time Bomb, Reminiscent of Olympus, Toshiba, and Other Infamous Accounting Scandals.* Retrieved September 14, 2024, from https://scorpionreports.s3.us-east-2.amazonaws.com/6920.pdf

# Part VI

## Revisiting AI & ML from a Corporate Fraud Perspective

# 34

# Artificial Intelligence, Machine Learning & Corporate Fraud

## 34.1 Artificial Intelligence (AI)

Artificial Intelligence (AI) are broad scientific and applicable fields, which cover a range of techniques, which purpose is to create somewhat intelligent systems. These systems often mimic cognitive functions associated with human intelligence. These fields e.g. include:

- *Expert Systems,* simulating the decision-making ability of a human expert, as described by Feigenbaum (1980)
- *Genetic & Evolutionary AI Algorithms* that are inspired by the biological processes of evolution, such as inheritance, mutation, selection, and crossover, studied by e.g. Holland (1992)
- *Fuzzy Logic Systems* – As alternative to Boolean integer logic - either No or Yes (0 or 1), Fuzzy Logic systems may reason about information as any of the many open unit interval numbers in between 0 to 1. The closer you get to 1 the more certain. The basis of this field is found in the seminal works of Zadeh (1965)
- *Machine learning,* a branch of artificial intelligence, employs statistical methods to allow machines to enhance their performance on tasks through practice and exposure to data. The phrase Machine Learning was originally coined by Arthur Samuel in Samuel (1959). However, the work is so broad that the field itself cannot be attributed to one person and the aspects of Machine Learning as they are today also are not covered in the referred article.


J. Sørensen, *Shorting Fraud*, https://doi.org/10.1007/978-3-031-81834-9_34

While it is encouraged to experiment with all types of AI in a practical setting, Machine Learning will be the main focus with regards to corporate fraud detection in this primer. This is because machine learning involves feeding data to an algorithm, allowing it to learn patterns and make data-driven decisions. Working with corporate fraud and 60,000 listed companies, there are tons of documented historical data publicly available, which ML models may work with. Furthermore, the amount of data grows each day, becoming increasingly accessible.

## 34.2 Types of Machine Learning Models and Corporate Fraud Detection

Machine learning entails feeding a substantial amount of data to a machine, enabling it to learn from this information and subsequently predict outcomes, identify patterns, or categorize the data.

The investor's interest is how can the Machine Learn to detect Corporate Fraud? There are several ways to categorize Machine Learning covered in a plentitude of foundation books, on the principals and practical ways of Machine Learning, see e.g. Bishop (2006) & Géron (2022). The many ML aspects covered in these books may be used to distill a general strategic overview in two dimensions on how to approach Machine Learning and relate them to corporate fraud detection.

- The first dimension described in Sect. 34.2.1 touches on how the machine learns from the data related to corporate fraud.
- The second dimension in Sect. 34.4.2 looks at the output of what the machine learnt from the data on corporate fraud.

### 34.2.1 ML Learning Methods and Corporate Fraud Detection

The first dimension illustrated in Table 34.1 gives an overview of the learning methods, how they may be used in relation to corporate fraud and some examples of the growing number of ML algorithms which may be used. Notice that multiple algorithms might be used by several learning methods.

Table 34.1 Overview of main ML Learning methods, corporate fraud utilization and algorithms

| Learning method | How the machine learns corporate fraud | Corresponding algorithms |
|---|---|---|
| Supervised Learning | Algorithms are trained on labeled data sets. The machines are given data with an "answer key" telling how the data should be interpreted. This may be used to create models for classification and prediction. In the case of Corporate Fraud, a supervised machine learning model may be trained to spot anomalies in financial statements indicating fraud. The model is trained on historical data of both legitimate and fraudulent financial statements. The machine will then distinguish between fraud and non-fraud on certain patterns or features in the data | Decision Trees, Random Forest, K-Nearest Neighbors (K-NN), Naive Bayes Classifier, Support Vector Machines (SVM), Gradient Boosting Machines (GBM), Neural Networks, Linear Regression, Polynomial Regression, Logistic Regression |

(continued)

**Table 34.1** (continued)

| Learning method | How the machine learns corporate fraud | Corresponding algorithms |
|---|---|---|
| Unsupervised Learning | The algorithms are trained on unlabeled data sets in a more explorative way. The models must uncover patterns on their own without human guidance. It is often used to identify patterns within large, unlabeled data sets. This can e.g. be used in anomalies detection, like outliers that do not conform to the normal trend in the data. This could be sudden and strange fluctuations in expenses on income statements | K-Means Clustering, Hierarchical Clustering, DBSCAN, Principal Component Analysis (PCA), Kernel PCA, Isolation Forest, Autoencoders |

(continued)

**Table 34.1** (continued)

| Learning method | How the machine learns corporate fraud | Corresponding algorithms |
|---|---|---|
| Semi-Supervised Learning | Algorithms are trained on both labeled and unlabeled data sets. First, they are fed a small amount of labeled data—afterwards a much larger quantity of unlabeled data. It is often used when large volumes of labeled data are unavailable. If the investor has successfully investigated and classified a smaller number of companies as fraudulent and non-fraudulent, based on their financial statements. On top of that the investor has a larger number of financial statements the investor does not have labeled that is also taken into consideration in the learning model | Self-training, Co-training, Transductive learning, Multi-view learning. If modified, Decision Trees, Neural Networks, Support Vector Machines |

(continued)

**Table 34.1** (continued)

| Learning method | How the machine learns corporate fraud | Corresponding algorithms |
|---|---|---|
| Reinforcement Learning | This is like teaching a robot that remembers its mistakes and successes. The algorithms learn through a trial-and-error process in specific environments. They are provided with feedback following each outcome, allowing them to optimize actions to achieve particular outcomes. It is used to make algorithms that conduct a sequence of decisions or actions. For example, reinforcement learning can be used in a scenario where the model learns to make decisions, such as approving or declining a financial statement, based on maximizing a reward function | Q-Learning, State-Action-Reward-State-Action (SARSA), Deep Q Network (DQN), Policy Gradients |

### 34.2.2 ML Prediction Methods and Corporate Fraud

In the second dimension the investor looks at the output of the ML model and what it tries to predict. Each of these has its own strengths and weaknesses and may be used as part of a particular workflow setup for the investor. Table 34.2 gives an overview of the types and examples of how they may be used to detect corporate fraud.

## 34.3 Text Screening, Analysis and Fraud Detection with Natural Language Processing (NLP)

Using text information to detect potential corporate fraud is not new. Manually, human analysts are extensively screening textual information to find red flags of fraud. This includes e.g. reading adverse media screening, the management discussion in annual reports and what the CEO says on earnings calls.

As have been discussed prior in the book, text-based ML models might be able to assist finding the inconsistencies or patterns that might indicate corporate fraudulent activities.

With the rise of common usage of language models like Chat GPT, Natural language Processing (NLP) models have become more common.

A subset of NLP is called Natural Language Understanding (NLU), which focuses on the comprehension and interpretation of human language. These NLU models extract meaning, context, and intent of text to get a better understanding of the text.

In contrast to more General Language models like GPT, it is possible to develop specialized language models focusing solely on fraud, to screen vast amounts of textual data to detect risk of fraudulent activity. From a data processing capacity often much faster than the human mind can do.

NLU is concerned with the comprehension and interpretation of human language. In the context of fraud detection, this might involve analyzing text data to identify patterns or anomalies that could indicate fraudulent activity relating to the corporation. This may involve techniques such as sentiment analysis, text classification, and entity recognition.

**Table 34.2** The relationship between types of prediction models and their utilization examples for corporate fraud

| Prediction/Output type | Brief explanation | Corporate fraud example | Algorithm examples |
|---|---|---|---|
| Classification | These models predict discrete outputs | A model that predicts whether a financial statement is fraudulent or not, based on various indicators | Decision Trees, Naive Bayes, Support Vector Machines |
| Regression | These models predict continuous outputs | A model that predicts expenses based on revenue and other factors. Significant deviations from the expected values could indicate manipulated expenses | Linear Regression, Ridge Regression, Lasso Regression |
| Clustering | These models group input data into clusters based on similarity. The output is the cluster to which each input data point belongs | A cluster of companies in the same industry has similar revenue and profit margins<br>Meanwhile, a company within this cluster shows significantly higher profits despite having similar revenue. The outlier is potentially manipulating numbers to inflate its profits | K-Means, Hierarchical Clustering, DBSCAN |

(continued)

**Table 34.2** (continued)

| Prediction/Output type | Brief explanation | Corporate fraud example | Algorithm examples |
|---|---|---|---|
| Dimensionality Reduction | These models reduce the dimensionality of the input data. The output is a set of features that highlight the most essential information in the original data | A model that reduces the number of financial ratios of a company to a smaller set for easier fraud detection. | Principal Component Analysis (PCA), t-SNE, Autoencoders |
| Association Rule Learning | These models discover interesting relations or associations among a set of items. The output is a set of rules that show which items often occur together | A simple financial statement fraud example could be: IF (Net profit margin increases significantly) AND (Cash flow from operations decreases) THEN (Potential revenue manipulation) | Apriori, FP-Growth |
| Anomaly Detection | These models identify unusual or suspicious patterns in the data. The output is a binary label indicating whether each data point is normal or an anomaly | A model that detects anomalous patterns in a company's financial statements that could indicate fraud. Like sudden abnormal surges in line items | Isolation Forest, Local Outlier Factor (LOF), One-Class SVM |

### 34.3.1 Sentiment Analysis

This technique can be particularly useful for investors when analyzing public communications such as press releases, earnings call transcripts, and social media posts from a company. An overly optimistic sentiment in these communications, not supported by the facts in the financial statements could be a red flag. This discrepancy might suggest the need for further investigation into the company.

### 34.3.2 Text Classification

This technique can be utilized to sift through a vast range of external text data, like news articles, analyst reports, and social media statements on companies, with the aim of classifying the text in categories like "financial irregularities," "insider trading", "accounting malpractices", etc.

### 34.3.3 Entity Recognition

This technique involves identifying key pieces of information within a text, such as names of individuals or companies, locations, and monetary figures. As an investor looking for signs of corporate fraud, the investor could use entity recognition to analyze public documents and communications related to a company. For instance, the investor might look for mentions of the company operating in known tax havens, or associations with individuals or entities that have a history of suspicious activities. This could raise red flags.

## 34.4 Practical Application of Machine Learning in Detection of Corporate Fraud

This section will focus on how ML might practically support screening and detecting corporate fraud. In addition, it will detail some practicalities about working with ML models.

### 34.4.1 Learning from Financial Statement Big Data

Financial statement data is important for two reasons. The first reason is that cooking the books is a common type of corporate fraud, where the numbers in the financial statements themselves are tampered with.

The second reason is that, even though the numbers in the financial statements in isolation look fine to the human eye, there might be something else going on under the surface, seen in a broader context that the human mind may not catch.

This can be revealed by ML models that may not only look at the individual company's financial statement in isolation, but potentially all public companies in the universe, for their entire lifespan.

ML has the potential to analyze a single company's financial statement in the context of the financial statements of all the 60,000 publicly listed companies in the world, across geographical regions, company sizes, company age, industries, sectors etc. Analyzing from millions, billions, or trillions of data points in the total universe of publicly listed financial statements available.

### 34.4.2 How to Get Financial Statement Data for Machine Learning Models

In many jurisdictions publicly listed companies' financial statement data is publicly available for free in electronic format.

For example, publicly listed companies in the US are obliged to file annual reports (known as the 10-K) and quarterly reports (10-Q) with the Securities and Exchange Commission through "The Electronic Data Gathering, Analysis, and Retrieval" (EDGAR) system. These filings are placed in a database publicly available to download financial statements for free as far back as 1994.[1] This means that the investor has access to more than 30 years of financial data.

### 34.4.3 The Standardization Problem of Financial Statement Data

Many ML algorithms require standardized financial statement data to properly work. The financial statement data in e.g. EDGAR is far from standardized. The investor will find financial statement data variations between industries, sectors, companies in the same industry or even the exact same company over time. If the investor expands ML models beyond EDGAR and the US, it gets even more complicated with factors like different formats, languages, currencies, etc. Therefore, the investor needs to go through the data preprocessing steps of cleaning, integration, transformation, reduction, and discretization.

#### 34.4.3.1 Data Cleaning

The financial data may include many unimportant or missing parts. To deal with this, data cleaning is conducted. Data Cleaning comprises dealing with

[1] Accessing EDGAR Data. https://www.sec.gov/os/accessing-edgar-data.
Using EDGAR to Research Investments. https://www.sec.gov/filings/edgar-guide.

noisy data, missing data, etc. Financial statement data often contains missing values or errors due to various reasons such as data entry errors, discrepancies in data sources, etc. For example, a company might not report a specific line item in a particular year. In such cases, missing values are filled in using techniques like mean imputation, where the missing value is replaced by the average value of that feature.

#### 34.4.3.2 Data Integration

In integration, several different and often heterogeneous data sources are joined into one common source. If financial data is pulled from multiple sources (e.g., different regulatory databases), there will be inconsistencies. For example, one source might report revenue in millions of Dollars, while another reports in millions of Euros. In this example, there is a need to adjust one of the sources to make the currency units consistent.

#### 34.4.3.3 Data Transformation

The data is transformed or consolidated into formats suitable for usage. Financial ratios such as return on assets (ROA), or debt-to-equity ratio are commonly used in financial analysis. These ratios are derived from the raw financial statement data and may have to be calculated and transformed before the model can interpret them.

#### 34.4.3.4 Data Reduction

Data Reduction tries to present a condensed depiction of the data. Financial statements can contain a large number of line items, but not all may be necessary for a specific analysis. For instance, if the model focuses on costs only, revenue line items could be purged.

#### 34.4.3.5 Data Discretization

This part is done to transform the data in a way that can be easily analyzed. This involves transforming continuous data into discrete bins. For example, instead of using the exact size of the company, the investor might categorize companies into "small cap," "mid cap", or "large cap".

These steps are often time consuming and may utilize a high amount of human intervention and oversight to ensure that the data are not polluted or corrupted.

## 34.4.4 Getting Financial Big Data—Make or Buy

Working with big data sets of both structured financial data like financial statements and unstructured financial data like news articles, it often comes down to a make or buy decision.

If the investor has the resources and manpower, she might collect these big data sets across the globe in raw data format. Then clean, integrate, and transform it herself. However, this may be a big and slow task. The primary advantage is that the investor will have much more insight and control over the big data sets and their quality.

Since financial analytics and data is already an industry the investor might speed up the process by buying big data sets that to some extent have been cleaned, integrated and transformed already. This way the investor may concentrate more on the analytics than preprocessing of data.

### 34.4.4.1 Structured Financial Data

There are many financial data providers supplying this kind of data the investor needs. Big vendors like Moody's, Standard & Poor's, FactSet, Refinitiv or Bloomberg. These data providers can supply the investor with updated bulk data needed in standardized and ready to utilize in ML models. However, even with the biggest data providers, there is always some preprocessing, depending on the models the investor wants to develop. The investor also needs to verify the quality of the data received from any provider. Even the biggest providers may send polluted and corrupt data that may render the investor's models useless.

### 34.4.4.2 Unstructured Data for NLP/NLU Models

With regards to corporate fraud there is a cornucopia of written text data sources, which can be used to build NLU models detecting corporate fraud. In addition to written text data sources, one may also consider the human spoken text in audio and video media. Audio and video transcription tools are available to collect this type of text. Furthermore, data providers also collect transcripts of earnings calls which may e.g. be bought on Amazon Web Services (AWS) Market.

Here is an overview of some of the most common types of text data sources divided into two main categories. Data sources that cover the entire landscape of listed companies from a general perspective and data sources that cover the individual listed company.

- General Data Sources
  - News Media Outlets – especially business media
  - Social Media postings
  - Court Databases litigations
  - Patent and intellectual property rights databases - Patent Applications and trademark databases, etc.
  - Data aggregators of earnings calls
  - Industry Conferences, Events and Exhibitions
  - Market Research firms and company benchmark reports
- Company specific data sources
  - Corporate Websites
  - Press releases and corporate announcements
  - Financial Reports—the management comments, outlook, etc.
  - Earnings calls
  - Interviews of CEOs and top managers
  - Equity Analysts reports and Investment Research
  - Special Features or Documentaries

#### 34.4.4.3 Collection of Unstructured Text Data Sources—The Make or Buy Decision

As with structured financial data, the investor can get text data in two separate ways. The first a DIY approach and the second buy them from data set providers. Both approaches come with some advantages and some disadvantages. Especially when the investor wants to create new models that are not plain vanilla.

#### 34.4.4.4 Data Self-Scraping. Self-Preprocessing and Self-Storage

While much of the above unstructured data could be collected by scraping the internet and the various news sources by yourself, self-scraping is in most cases not recommended. First, there are the questions about intellectual property rights, collecting, storing, and using text data created by other parties for commercial purposes. Secondly, even with small amounts of data it may be a cumbersome task, collecting, preprocessing, and storing the data in data warehouses. However, in some cases DIY scraping and storage might be the only possibility.

#### 34.4.4.5 Financial News and Data Providers

As mentioned in Sect. 34.4.4.1 there are several financial data service providers. As with the fundamental financial data on the listed companies many data service providers also offer financial news aggregation services. Besides the big players there are hundreds of more specialized companies that aggregate financial news and other types of data from the above data categories. In addition, there are free open-source databases around the world with varying quality that might be used as an alternative.

**The Big Players** like Factiva, S&P, Refinitiv, Bloomberg, Dow Jones, Moody's, etc. offer both general bulk datasets and customized data sets which might be used to train NLU models. Below the pros and cons:

- Pros
  - Broad geographical & extensive historic coverage
  - Data standardization, at least with their own data
  - Potential one stop shop
  - Good with off the shelf vanilla data sets
- Cons
  - May be hard for them to deliver highly customized datasets
  - Juggernaut organizations move really slow if it is not plain vanilla and costs might skyrocket
  - Data sets skewed on top markets & top players like NYSE, LSE, Hamburg, Tokyo, etc.
  - Comes with a heavy price tag

**Niche Players** may offer specialized, localized data not captured by the big players. The Pros and Cons:

- Pros
  - Business model may be centered around ML /AI data sets
  - Localized data
  - Also focus below Fortune 500
  - Highly Customized types of data sets, preprocessed
  - More agile to work with
- Cons
  - Narrower focus, might not integrate well with other types of financial data
  - Limited historic coverage to provider's business lifespan
  - The investor does not know about the reliability and validity of the datasets

## 34.5 Machine Learning Caveats and Challenges When Detecting Fraud in the Real World

As opposed to working with ML-Models in an academic setting, where one may make some assumptions and limitations, working with ML in more practical settings poses problems as we already have seen with getting the data. There are many other problems, below are three important, which have been observed working with models detecting fraudulent companies.

### 34.5.1 Calibration of False Positives and False Negatives

Working with 60,000 companies and millions or billions of data points, there are two basic practical problems the investor will need to address as the first thing on the investor's agenda after the investor has a quality dataset to train from.

The first is false positives. A false positive is the ML model telling the investor a legitimate company is fraudulent. The risk is the investor drowns in these false positives of ordinary legitimate companies. In Sect. 3.1, we guesstimated that 6000 to 8000 companies had a level of material fraud. However, if tools in the framework result in 45,000 hits, the investor has a problem.

Either the corporate world is much more depraved than initially estimates from general fraud research suggest. Else, which is more likely, the investor's ML-Model has categorized legit corporations as fraudulent. With 45,000 hits the investor drowns in irrelevant hits. It means the investor needs to rethink or re-calibrate the model or investigate if something is wrong with the data set the investor works on.

The second problem is false negatives. This is when the investor's model misses to find actual fraudulent companies. Luckily, from a corporate fraud perspective, the investor is not a law enforcement agency, or a creditor, but a potential investor with a shorting perspective. So, if the investor misses out on one big fraudulent target it is not a big problem. There are still 6000–8000 other fraudulent targets. Only if the investor systematically misses out on all big targets, there is a problem from a fraud short investment point of view.

Therefore, for the investor, the false positives are a greater problem than false negative, since they mean the investor spent time and money on cases that are not worth anything from a fraud short investment perspective—they are just investigation costs.

### 34.5.2 Not Comprehending the ML Model and Being Able to Create Short Reports

Another problem the investor might encounter is that the model is fantastic in finding fraudulent targets. However, the investor does not understand how it does it. In that case the investor may work blindly. This is a problem if the investor cannot support a short research report with facts. The problem is that the human brain likes problems with simple causality relations. However, sometimes the ML models may give multidimensional answers of fraud that are hard to comprehend and explain in a straightforward way for the human mind.

### 34.5.3 Reality Might Evolve Over Time Rendering the ML Model Obsolete

Due to economic cycles or "fraud-fashion-cycles", new control methods and regulatory standards, the reliability of the ML model might change over time. This means that the investor must dynamically assess and retrain and build new models as the world changes and new data becomes available.

## References

Bishop, C. M. (2006). *Pattern Recognition and Machine Learning*. Springer.

Feigenbaum, E. A. (1980). Expert Systems in the 1980s. Stanford University. Retrieved September 14, 2024, from https://stacks.stanford.edu/file/druid:vf069sz9374/vf069sz9374.pdf

Géron, A. (2022). *Hands-on Machine Learning with Scikit-Learn, Keras, and TensorFlow: Concepts, Tools, and Techniques to Build Intelligent Systems* (3rd ed.). O'Reilly Media.

Holland, J. H. (1992). Genetic Algorithms. *Scientific American Magazine, 267*(1), 66.

Samuel, A. L. (1959). Some Studies in Machine Learning Using the Game of Checkers. *IBM Journal of Research and Development, 3*(3), 210–229. Retrieved September 14, 2024, from http://www.cs.virginia.edu/~evans/greatworks/samuel1959.pdf

Zadeh, L. A. (1965). Fuzzy Sets and Systems. In J. Fox (Ed.), *System Theory (Microwave Research Institute Symposia Series XV* (pp. 29–37). Polytechnic Press.

# Index




J. Sørensen, *Shorting Fraud*, https://doi.org/10.1007/978-3-031-81834-9

MIX
Papier | Fördert gute Waldnutzung
FSC® C083411

Kolibri 360 GmbH
Ferdinand-Jühlke-Straße 7
99095 Erfurt, Deutschland
produktsicherheit@kolibri360.de